The United States Coast Guard
1790-1915

The United States Coast Guard 1790-1915

A DEFINITIVE HISTORY

(With a Postscript: 1915-1950)

BY

Stephen H. Evans

CAPTAIN, U. S. COAST GUARD

1949

THE UNITED STATES NAVAL INSTITUTE

ANNAPOLIS, MARYLAND

First printing, 1949.
Second printing, 1951.

PRINTED IN THE UNITED STATES OF AMERICA

To my brother

ARTHUR BLISS EVANS, JR.

Lieutenant (junior grade)

U. S. Coast Guard Reserve,

lost in action against the enemy

while serving on board

U.S.S. Leopold (DE-319),

North Atlantic Ocean

9 March 1944

Author's Note

SHOULD THE definition suggested herein assist the pubic to a better understanding of the Coast Guard's zone of action and should it serve as an aid to the professional orientation of newcomers to the service, my purpose in presenting it shall have been most amply served.

To the late Admiral Russell R. Waesche, U. S. Coast Guard (Commandant, 1936-1945), I am indebted for advice and encouragement in planning the work and for permission to use official photographs and the source materials contained in official records and files. To avoid a plethora of footnotes, I have cited few of these records specifically; for the most part, they consist of letters dealing with the operations and policies of the Revenue-Cutter, Life-Saving, and Lighthouse Services written by Secretaries of the Treasury, captains of cutters, and other officials in times long past; of ancient log-books; and of administrative notes and records in profusion. Those cited have been identified by the note "*C. G. Archives.*" (Most of these are now stored in the National Archives, in Washington.) Although incomplete, especially for the years prior to 1830, these documents have been invaluable to a reconstruction of the service's general background and as credible sources of much detail. For assistance in sifting quantities thereof, I am indebted to Professor A. A. Lawrence, U. S. Coast Guard Academy.

Other important sources include: pertinent government publications (especially the *Annual Reports, Registers,* and *Regulations* of the above-mentioned services), 1790-1915; newspaper and magazine literature subsequent to 1800; specialized works on shipping, history of marine engineering, naval history, maritime law, *et cetera.* These have been cited specifically only to support direct quotations or when, in a few instances, it has appeared that reader-interest might be so served.

An *Index to Laws* governing the Coast Guard and a *Bibliography,* both contained in Smith and Powell's *The Coast Guard* (The Brookings Institution, Washington, 1929); *Bibliographies* of the Life-Saving, Lighthouse, and Revenue-Cutter Services, contained in *House of Representatives Document #670, 62d Cong., 2 Sess.* (Government Printing Office, Washington, 1912); and a *Bibliography of the Coast Guard* (a mimeographed pamphlet prepared by the Public Information Division, U. S. Coast Guard Headquarters, Washington, 1945) have been valuable study aids.

Political, social, and economic backgrounds throughout have been based on standard works.

STEPHEN H. EVANS
Captain, U.S.C.G.

Washington, D.C.,
1 June 1949.

Preface

The Coast Guard, a part of the Armed Forces of the United States, is the principal federal agency for maritime law enforcement and marine safety.

LIKE MANY another section of the American governmental system, this complex organization sprang from comparatively simple origins. As far back as Washington's first administration, the necessity of empowering the federal government to perform certain basic functions for insuring safe navigation and enforcing national laws afloat appeared obvious, and early Congresses established a number of small federal agencies to carry out specific phases of the work. All of these agencies remained essentially unifunctional except the Revenue-Cutter Service, a military organization of men and ships which by an early date had earned a reputation for expertness in dealing with a notable variety of such assignments. Successive attempts by the federal government to centralize responsibility, to eliminate duplication of effort, and to redirect federal activity towards greater public benefit, resulted eventually in the amalgamation of many of these agencies to form one force, the United States Coast Guard. By 1915 the first merger (combining the Revenue-Cutter and Life-Saving Services) had been effected, and the process of building into the federal structure an integrated agency responsible for all federal functions in the field of maritime law enforcement and marine safety had emerged as a definite governmental trend.

The definitive phase of Coast Guard history, recorded in this volume, thus extends from the time of George Washington to the era of the first World War (*c.* 1790-1915). A *postscript* relates the early period to a developmental phase extending from 1915 to 1949.

Contents

Illustrations

The United States Coast Guard

1790-1915

CHAPTER I

Underway

PRESIDENT WASHINGTON'S inauguration, on April 30, 1789, ushered in a new order: a federal system for establishing justice, insuring domestic tranquility, providing for the common defense, promoting the general welfare, and securing the blessings of liberty to Americans of every generation. The men destined to begin the work of translating these lofty ideals into reality faced no simple task. Political pathfinders, they were beset by the cold necessity of establishing precedents, of determining initial policies, and of cutting the early lines of federal administrative action. Men of drive and foresight were needed for such work, and the young nation was fortunate to boast many talented citizens on whom it could depend. There was, for instance, Thomas Jefferson for Secretary of State; fighting General Henry Knox for War; and Edmund Randolph for the Attorney General's post. To fill the difficult Treasury job, the President nominated his own good friend and Revolutionary comrade, Alexander Hamilton, known in those days as "a lion of Federalism." Next to Washington himself, Hamilton was to become the most influential statesman in the whole administration, for his was the hand fated to draw the pattern of America's early economic growth.

The federal government's first coast guard functions sprang from Hamilton's bold economic plan. In brief review, the latter proposed three basic policies. First, the government's prestige and credit at home and abroad were to be insured by a demonstration of financial stability: charges on the $70,000,000 debt inherited from the Revolution were to be met according to the letter of the bonds, and routine running expenses of the government were to be defrayed from income. One way to provide funds for this fundamental undertaking was by levying a tariff for revenue, and the Revenue Act of 1789 made provision for such a tax.

Second, industrial independence was to be sought to insure the political independence which the Revolution had already won. Even Jefferson, ever hopeful of preserving in the United States a predominantly rural economy, admitted that "manufacturers are as necessary to our independence as to our comfort." But in 1790 the country was woefully weak in industries. Under British rule, American manufactures had been restricted; current theory held that colonies exist only to provide raw materials for the mother country and to serve as outlets for her manufactured goods. During the Revolution, a number of small industries (including munitions plants necessary to defense) had sprung up in the colonies and flourished for a time, but cessation of hostilities brought disaster to many of these wartime enterprises as Britishers, seeking to retain their economic foothold, flooded the country with cheap articles produced under England's advanced industrial system and drove out American goods. In 1791, when Hamilton advocated protectionism in his famous *Report on Manufactures,* American industry was truly in its infancy, and protection was indubitably to the long-range national benefit. After 1792, for many years, the tariff had a protective bias, a factor of extreme importance in the country's industrial development.

Third, the American merchant marine, a mainstay of colonial economy but desperately weakened by losses in the war, was to be given a chance to regain its old importance. By making customs duties discriminatory (that is, lower on goods imported in American ships), this aim was rapidly achieved. Further, discriminatory tonnage tax rates that virtually excluded alien vessels from the coastwise trade likewise were adopted.

Besides working out the fiscal details of the foregoing plan, Hamilton took practical precautions to insure its success. He recognized the fact that uncontrolled competition was not the only hazard to the growth of seaborne commerce. If the public interest demanded that shipping be protected by special dues and tax rates, as he felt sure it did, then there might well be other dangers against which suitable preventive measures could reasonably be taken. In this vein he proposed the establishment of a lighthouse service to protect shipping, in some degree, from the hazards of rocks and shoals.

Here was no less than a proposal that the federal government accept public responsibility for safety at sea, a suggestion with the most far-reaching implications but one which, in the specific case, rested on American precedents of long standing. Lighthouses had, in fact, been maintained in America from the public purse ever since 1716, when the General Court of Massachusetts Bay Colony set up Boston Light. A colonial statute provided that the keeper should set the light "diligently" from sunset to sunrise, fixed his pay at £50 per annum, and decreed a punishment for neglect of duty. Between 1716 and the Revolution, lights had similarly been established at Sandy Hook, Morris Island, the entrance to the Delaware, the mouth of the Savannah, Cape Henry, New London, and a few other coastal points. On August 7, 1789, President Washington approved the Act of Congress which incorporated these aids to navigation into a federal system and launched the national government upon its course of guarding the coast in the interest of safety and security afloat.

This, the ninth Act of Congress, was the first to provide for any public work. Under the Act, all expenses

> in the necessary support, maintenance, and repair of all lighthouses, beacons, buoys, and public piers [previously] erected, placed, or sunk . . . at the entrance of or within any bay, inlet, harbor, or port of the United States, *for rendering the navigation thereof easy and safe*

were to be defrayed out of the federal Treasury.[1] So liberal a gesture soon induced the states to cede their lighthouses to the central government, and thus the Lighthouse Service, first of several coast guard agencies, emerged into public usefulness and esteem.

Administrative control over this establishment in the early days was exercised by the Secretary of the Treasury, either directly or through the Commissioner of Revenue (1792-1802, 1813-1820), the Fifth Auditor (1820-1845, 1848-1852), or the Chief of the Revenue-Marine Bureau (1845-1848). The total number of aids to navigation operated by the federal government under the early system rose from about 45 in 1789 to around 1600 in 1852.

Another practical move developed from Hamilton's realization that the tariff, on which he pinned so much of his hope for the nation's economic future, would not command universal support. Aliens had ample temptation to avoid payment of the customs revenue, and the Secretary evidently suspected that even among American merchants there might be a "fraudulent few" against whose free-trading proclivities it would be well to set "every possible guard."[2] To him it was obvious that smuggling could not be suppressed by paper statutes: *the Treasury needed a strong right arm.* He therefore sought and, on August 4, 1790, obtained from Congress authority to launch a seagoing military force in further support of the national economic policy. This service became the nucleus of the United States Coast Guard.

The organic Act called for "the establishment and support of ten cutters" for the purpose of enforcing customs laws.[3] But Hamilton anticipated an expansion of this small fleet both in size and function, and it was possibly for this reason that he urged Congress to create the professional corps of commissioned officers. (To give the officers military rank, said he, "would attach them to their duty by a nicer sense of honor.") The basic Act authorized a total of 40 officers—a master, first, second, and third mate for each cutter—and created them "officers of the customs" to cloak them with legal powers and immunities requisite

[1] Act of August 7, 1789 (1 Stat. L., 53). (Italics ours.) See also George Weiss, *The Lighthouse Service* (The Brookings Institution, Washington, D.C., 1926); E. S. Clark, "The First Lighthouse in the United States," in *U. S. Naval Institute Proceedings,* April, 1937; and George R. Putnam, *Lighthouses and Lightships of the United States* (Houghton Mifflin Co., Boston and New York, 1933).—First lightship in the U.S.: off Craney Island, Virginia; 1820.

[2] Hamilton, quoted in H. D. Smith, *Early History of the U. S. Revenue-Marine,* ed. Elliott Snow, 1932; 2.

[3] Act of August 4, 1790 (1 Stat. L., 145, 175).

to their principal task. One Hopley Yeaton, of New Hampshire, commissioned on March 21, 1791, stood at the top of the list of masters; his commission was the first issued by President Washington to any officer afloat. Eventually, under a provision of the Act of March 2, 1799, military ranks of "captain" and "lieutenant" were authorized for cutter officers in lieu of the original "master" and "mate."

The first complements and pay scales for the service were established by the 1790 law. Besides one master at $30 a month and three mates at $20, $16, and $14, respectively, each cutter was allowed four mariners at $8 apiece and two boys at $4. These scales were adjusted from time to time by additional legislation.

Careful research fails to reveal whether or not a distinctive uniform was worn by these earliest cutter crews, although it may be assumed that some effort was made at uniformity of dress and that the general style and colors (red and blue) of the Continental Navy set the mode. In any case, individual commanding officers doubtless claimed considerable latitude in the whole matter. By around 1819, however, according to Smith's *Early History of the U. S. Revenue-Marine,* the official "uniform of lieutenants in the Cutter Service consisted of a blue body or swallowtail coat, rolling collar and double breasted. A button on each corner of the collar, and six on each lapel with four in the skirts. Epaulettes worn on either shoulder according to rank. Buttons stamped with the armorial bearings of the United States." Smith is authority also for citation of an 1830 order of the Treasury Department prescribing uniform regulations for officers; captains at this period were required to wear "blue dress coats, rolling collar, nine buttons on each lapel, four on each cuff, four on each pocket flap and four on skirts. All seams of coat to be piped with yellow cord. Two plain gold epaulets. Trousers blue to be worn outside of boots. Vest blue or white with four buttons on each pocket flap. Hat, pattern known as 'Stove pipe,' ornamented on left side with a black cockade with brass buttons in center." Thereafter uniform regulations were issued by the Department from time to time and prescribed styles generally similar to those of the Navy (but with distinctive buttons and insignia) for all cutter personnel.

To distinguish cutters from all other ships, the Act of March 2, 1799 authorized the President to prescribe for them a distinctive pennant and flag. In a letter dated August 1, 1799, to Collectors of Customs, the Secretary published the approved design:

> . . . an ensign and pennant consisting of sixteen perpendicular stripes, alternate red and white, the Union of the Ensign to be the Arms of the United States, in dark Blue on a White field.[4]

[4] In *C. G. Archives.*

Early legislation was less specific, however, in furnishing the cutter force with an official name; for this reason a variety of semi-official designations came into use, both in governmental parlance and in the press. The terms "system of cutters" and "Revenue Service" were commonly employed in the early days. "Revenue-Marine" was popular almost to the end of the 19th century. Congress first referred to the service as a named organization in a law (12 Stat. L., 639) passed in 1863, in which the term "Revenue-Cutter Service" received official sanction. This name was in general use by 1890 or thereabouts and so remained until supplanted by "Coast Guard" in 1915.

The original ten cutters were built and manned by 1791, and in that year anti-smuggling operations commenced in earnest. The work consisted essentially of cruising on the coast, hailing in-bound ships, examining them and certifying their manifests. But it was by no means a humdrum routine, for it was marked by frequent brisk encounters with smuggler crews. The latter—daring, skillful sailors—had no intention of abandoning a lucrative trade at the first frown of a federal government. These men were determined to ignore tariff restrictions until they were sure the government could enforce them, that is, until smuggling risks outweighed smuggling profits. To increase free-traders' hazards, Congress authorized the cutters to fire into vessels that failed to heave-to upon command.[5] And although ten small cutters could not hope to track down, fire into, and seize every smuggler on the Atlantic coast, they could and did achieve Mr. Hamilton's ultimate aim: by presenting a constant threat to every violator, and by making good the threat at every opportunity, they gradually established an effective blockade of the American shore and took the heart out of the smuggling game.

For several years, protection of the customs remained the only statutory duty assigned the service. The work, however, involved an important related activity: the enforcement of navigation laws. Early Congressional enactments regulating navigation were *promotional* in character: they were designed to help build up a native shipping industry by safeguarding it from foreign competition. But the line between customs and navigation laws was not always clear. There was a close alliance, for instance, between navigation laws governing the ownership, documentation, and employment of ships and the whole policy of discriminatory tariffs and tonnage taxes. For this reason enforcement of the navigation laws was vested originally in the Treasury, and the enforcement of certain sections devolved upon revenue-cutter and customs officers as a logical phase of their duty in that Department.[6]

[5] Act of March 2, 1799 (1 Stat. L., 627, 699).
[6] Navigation laws of another type—primarily concerned with the safety of navigation

Since boarding vessels in the enforcement of law always brings service personnel into a delicate relationship with the crews of legitimate ships, Hamilton was at great pains to insure that all contacts with the public be maintained at an impersonal, legal level. In his first letter of *"Regulations,"* he outlined a policy for the conduct of the Revenue-Marine's public relations which proved so successful that it eventually became a traditional part of the spirit of the service. Said he:

> While I recommend in the strongest terms to the respective officers, activity, vigilance, and firmness, I feel no less solicitude that their deportment may be marked with prudence, moderation and good temper. Upon these last qualities, not less than the former, must depend the success, usefulness and consequently *continuance* of the establishment in which they are included. They cannot be insensible that there are some prepossessions against it, that the charge with which they are entrusted is a delicate one, and that it is easy by mismanagement to produce serious and extensive clamour, disgust, and alarm.
>
> They will always keep in mind that their countrymen are freemen, and, as such, are impatient of everything that bears the least mark of domineering spirit. They will, therefore, refrain, with the most guarded circumspection, from whatever has the semblance of haughtiness, rudeness, or insult. If obstacles occur, they will remember that they are under the particular protection of the laws and that they can meet with nothing disagreeable in the execution of their duty which these will not severely reprehend. This reflection, and a regard to the good of the service, will prevent at all times a spirit of irritation or resentment. They will endeavor to overcome difficulties, if any are experienced, by a cool and temperate perseverance in their duty—by address and moderation, rather than by vehemence or violence. The former style of conduct will recommend them to the particular approbation of the President of the United States, while the reverse of it—even a single instance of outrage or intemperate or improper treatment of any person with whom they have anything to do, in the course of their duty,—will meet with his pointed displeasure, and will be attended with correspondent consequences.
>
> The foregoing observations are not dictated by any doubt of the prudence of any of those to whom they are addressed. These have been selected with so careful an attention to character, as to afford the strongest assurance, that their conduct will be that of good officers and good citizens. But, in an affair so delicate and important, it has been judged most advisable to listen to the suggestions of caution rather than of confidence, and to put all concerned on their guard against those sallies to which even good and prudent men are occasionally subject. It is not doubted that the instruction will

—began to find their way into the federal statutes at a later date. This development will be reported in subsequent chapters. See also *Law Enforcement by the U. S. Coast Guard* (a loose-leaf pamphlet published by the Coast Guard *circa* 1937), 22 *et seq.;* Alexander Hamilton's letter of instructions to commanders of revenue-cutters, June 4, 1791, quoted in Smith, *op. cit.,* 8-11; Smith and Powell, *The Coast Guard* (The Brookings Institution, Washington, 1929), 3; *Navigation Laws of the United States, 1935* (a Department of Commerce publication, Government Printing Office, Washington); L. M. Short, *The Bureau of Navigation* (The Brookings Institution, 1923), 1-2; and P. M. Zeis, *American Shipping Policy* (Princeton University Press, 1938), 3.

be received as it ought to be, and will have its due effect. And that all may be apprized of what is expected you will communicate this part of your orders, particularly, to all your officers, and you will inculcate upon your men a correspondent disposition.[7]

Hamilton addressed this charge to hardy Yankee sailors. Most of the officers and seamen who manned the early cutters doubtless had been raised in the colonial merchant fleet. Such men had cruised the seven seas with colonial products, earning reputations for long-headed seamanship that found ready welcome aboard the cutters. Others, probably, had brought into the colonies shiploads of contraband proscribed by the British Navigation Acts; to them, the ways of smugglers were open secrets. Some, of all ranks and rates, had served through the Revolution in privateers or in ships of the state or Continental navies; these men were handy with pistol and cutlass and knew how to lay a gun.

John Foster Williams and Elisha Hinman were two veterans who brought military prestige into the Revenue-Marine's commissioned corps.[8] Captain Williams had seen hard fighting in the Massachusetts State Navy. In his *History of the Navy,* Maclay cites an instance in 1779 when Williams, in command of the 14-gun State cruiser *Hazard,* engaged the 18-gun *Active,* an English privateer. The *Hazard's* guns poured a terrible punishment into the *Active,* cutting her almost to pieces and killing or wounding nearly 40 men—four times the American casualties. At the end of an hour's bombardment, the crippled privateer hauled down her colors, leaving the victory to the men under the pine tree flag.

Rewarded with a more formidable command, the State cruiser *Protector,* 26 guns, 230 men, Williams sallied forth from Nantasket Roads on another commerce-destroying voyage the following spring. On June 9, 1780 he fell in with the English *Admiral Duff,* a heavy privateer carrying thirty-six 12-pounders on the gun deck and a crew of 250 British tars. Against this worthy adversary the *Protector* fought a battle that Paine, in his *Ships and Sailors of Old Salem,* describes as "one of the most heroic and desperate engagements of the Revolution." Williams' ship, employing a ruse of war not uncommon in that day, was sailing under English colors, but the *Admiral Duff* was not deceived. As the two ships bore down upon each other, their boatswains called the crews to quarters. Gun ports slammed open, tackles creaked, gun crews ran out their guns,

[7] Smith, *op. cit.,* 10.

[8] The account of Captain Williams' Revolutionary career is based on R. D. Paine, *The Ships and Sailors of Old Salem* (Lauriat Company, Boston, 1927), and E. S. Maclay, *History of the Navy* (D. Appleton and Company, New York, 1894) Vol. I, Ch. V; Hinman's on Maclay, *op. cit.,* Ch. III-IV; L. F. Middlebrook, *Maritime Connecticut during the American Revolution* (The Essex Institute, Salem, 1925) Vols. I-II, *passim; General Register of the United States Navy,* 1782-1882 (T. H. S. Hamersly, Editor and Publisher, Washington, 1882); and C. C. Hanks, "A Cruise for Gunpowder," in *U. S. Naval Institute Proceedings,* March, 1939.

and seamen hove on sheets and braces, trimming sail—then quiet descended and both crews stood silently awaiting the closing of the battle range. Here and there a gun captain blew impatiently upon his match, held ready to touch off the first blasting salvo. An eye-witness, Luther Little, midshipman in charge of one of the *Protector's* after 12-pound batteries, tells the story of the sanguinary affair which followed the breaking of this tense hush by the flash and roar of the *Protector's* furious attack:

> We steered down across her stern, and hauled up under her lee quarter. . . . The colors changed at the first flash of a gun, and as the thirteen stripes took the place of the English ensign they gave us three cheers and fired a broadside. They partly shot over us, their ship being so much higher than ours, cutting away some of our rigging. The action commenced within pistol shot and now began a regular battle, broadside to broadside. . . .
>
> The action continued about an hour when all the topmen on board the enemy's ship were killed by our marines, who were seventy in number, all Americans. Our marines also killed the man at the wheel, caused the ship to come down upon us, and her cat-head stove in our quarter galley.
>
> We lashed their jib-boom to our main-shrouds, and our marines from the quarterdeck firing into their port holes kept them from charging. We were ordered from our quarters to board, but before we were able the lashings broke. We were ordered back to quarters to charge our guns when, the other ship shooting alongside of us, the yards nearly locked. We gave her a broadside which cut away her mizzen mast and made great havoc among them. We perceived her sinking, at the same time saw that her main topgallant sail was on fire, which ran down the rigging and caught a hogshead of cartridges under the quarterdeck and blew it up. . . . She went down on fire with colours flying.
>
> Our boats were injured by the shots and our carpenters were repairing them in order to pull out and pick up the men of the English that were afloat. They succeeded in getting fifty-five, one-half wounded and scalded. The first lieutenant told me that such was their pride when on the brink of a watery grave, that they fought like demons, preferring death with the rest of their comrades rather than captivity, and that it was with much difficulty that many of them were forced into the boats. Our surgeon amputated limbs from five of the prisoners, and attended them as if they had been of our own crew.
>
> . . . The *Admiral Duff* had two American captains, with their crews, on board as prisoners. These [the captains] were among the fifty-five saved by our boats.
>
> . . . During the battle while Captain Williams was walking the quarterdeck a shot from the enemy took his speaking trumpet from his hand, but he picked it up and with great calmness continued his orders.[9]

With such victories behind him, Williams entered the Revenue-Marine on March 21, 1791. His first job was supervising the construction of the first cutter, the *Massachusetts,* whose commander he became.

[9] Paine, *op. cit.,* 109-10.

Elisha Hinman was a native of Connecticut. He was born in 1734, went to sea at the age of 14, was a captain at 19, and for many years sailed to Europe and the Indies. A shipping man himself, doubtless he bitterly resented every English restraint upon colonial trade. At the outbreak of revolt he left a lucrative business "to devote his whole service to the country," an endeavor in which his efforts never flagged.[10]

Hinman was appointed lieutenant in the Continental Navy in January 1776 and in the brig *Cabot,* 14, sailed with Commodore Esek Hopkins' squadron in the first American venture on the sea: an amphibious expedition against the British naval supply depot in New Providence (Nassau). The raiders took a rich haul of munitions and immediately ran with their loot for New London. They carried away also His Majesty's Collector of Quit-Rents and the Bahaman Governor—prizes of somewhat doubtful value. On the homeward voyage the squadron engaged several men-o'-war, but only at considerable cost to the Americans in life and limb. Hinman was among those wounded in a midnight encounter with H.M.S. *Glasgow,* off Long Island, April 6, 1776; he thus became one of the first casualties in the war at sea.

This distinction apparently reinforced his hatred of the king, and he was soon at sea again, this time commanding *Cabot,* playing havoc with English trade. From late May until October he roamed the northeast coast, capturing seven English ships in seven separate encounters. One prize, the *Clarendon,* brought nearly £11,000. The Captain's share must have eased his recent wound to some extent, at least. By the first of November, the *Cabot* had sent in four more ships and a brig, one of which was a Jamaican mounting 16 guns.

In a rearrangement of the Navy list, October 10, 1776, the Continental Congress confirmed Hinman as a captain and ranked him Number 20 in his grade—two numbers below John Paul Jones, whom Hinman later suceeded in command of the ship *Alfred,* 24.

The *Alfred* under Captain Hinman seized several prizes—including one worth £60,000—and cruised for a while in European waters. She then put into L'Orient, whence in company with the *Raleigh,* 32, she sailed for home sometime in February 1778. Both ships were loaded with valuable military supplies for the Continental forces. Hoping to bag a few more British merchantmen, the little squadron took a southerly course and, on March 9, sighted two strange sail. Not merchantmen but men-o'-war, the *Ceres,* 14, and *Ariadne,* 20, these bore down rapidly upon the heavy-laden *Alfred.* The *Raleigh* was hull-down on the horizon, and Hinman found himself badly out-gunned and forced to fight a forlorn hope while his companion sailed down wind to safety. Finally, for the

[10] Quotation is from the epitaph on Hinman's tomb, Cedar Grove Cemetery, New London, Connecticut.

first and only time in his long life, Hinman was forced to strike his colors. A court-martial, months later, acquitted him with honor, but the captain of the *Raleigh* frigate was dismissed for deserting the *Alfred* in the face of the enemy.

Hinman's captors carried him to England and threw him into Fortune Prison, a pesthole from which, thanks to good luck and the assistance of friends, he soon escaped. For a time he hid in London, where he had the small pleasure of reading handbills offering £500 for his head. Guarding this member carefully, he made his way to France, whence eventually he secured passage home.

He seems to have been fairly athirst for revenge by the time he landed in New London, and in April 1779 he sailed in the privateer sloop *Hancock,* 10, to resume his depredations. Within two months he took the English schooner *Mulberry,* forced the privateer *Bellona* to surrender, helped seize the *Game Cock, Polly, Hunter, Clinton,* and topped off his adventures with an action in which the *Hancock,* accompanied by the *Beaver* privateer, cut off and captured the *Lady Erskine,* 10 guns, from a British fleet of over 20 sail.

In another New London privateer, the ship *Deane,* 30 guns, 210 men, Captain Hinman continued his harassment of British commerce from June 1780 until June 1781, when he transferred to the privateer *Marquis de Lafayette,* a 16-gun brigantine. Apparently he finished out the war aboard this vessel, cruising to the West Indies, Virginia, and Holland in search of British booty and capturing at least one privateer, the British brig *Dispatch.*

The Peace of Paris made an end to the Captain's epic blows for Freedom, and the warrior returned to private life. It is said that in 1794 President Adams offered him command of a new frigate, to be called the *Constitution,* but that Hinman declined on account of advancing age. Perhaps he was only tired of distant cruising. Whatever his whole reason for declining the naval post, he was willing and hearty enough in 1798 to accept command of the cutter *Alert,* stationed in his own New London port.

Diligent search of Coast Guard archives reveals little concerning the old patriot's career in the Revenue-Marine. In fact, unfortunately, almost all trace of the men who sailed the cutters of the 18th century has disappeared from service files. But if Williams and Hinman are fair samples, the Coast Guard may well be proud of its early personnel.

A full record of the Hamiltonian cutters, too, passed long ago from memory and file, but enough remains to give a general idea of what these ships were like. The Secretary's orders to collectors of customs concerning construction of the vessels apparently were not accompanied by detailed plans. Collectors in the vicinity of projected cutters' cruising grounds were directed to secure bids locally, and, aside from limitations on cost and general dimensions, the customs men apparently were left to shop around. Doubtless it was American shipbuilding experience, not the Department's specification, that dictated the original fleet's design.

By 1790, American experience and practice had developed a sharp-model "Virginia-built" schooner, later known as the "pilot-boat" or "Baltimore clipper" type. Colonial shipbuilders, faced with demands for light, fast, easily-managed, seaworthy vessels, handy in beating in and out of harbors and through winding river channels, had produced in the Virginia-built schooner a truly indigenous build and rig. H. I. Chapelle, an authority on American sailing ships, states:

> By 1790, if not earlier, the schooner was the national rig of both the United States and Canada. . . . Though it seems definitely established that the type first developed in southern waters, it spread northward at an early date. The lack of definite information regarding the early evolution of the sharp-model schooner makes any attempt to trace this matter mere speculation. It is reasonably certain, however, that the sharp schooner did not at once become a distinct type, and also that there was no "first" sharp schooner. The process of evolution was gradual, and before the model was fully developed its construction had spread along the whole coast, from Maine to the Carolinas, wherever a fast schooner was wanted.[11]

These vessels had proved their sailing qualities as traders, pilot-boats, smugglers, slavers, and pirates. They could take almost any weather and out-sail almost anything afloat. They could slide easily through tortuous channels and skim across shoal waters. They cost comparatively little to build, and they required few hands to sail them. In the work of safeguarding the revenue, these schooners promised both economy and effective operation. To the Secretary and his collectors they must have seemed the logical—the ideal—answer to the problem of what a cutter really ought to be. Although records of the first class of cutters are incomplete, it is known definitely that most of them were two-masted schooners, doubtless laid to the general Virginia-built plan though differing somewhat among themselves in details and dimensions.

With regard to the latter, the dimensions of the *Massachusetts* are fairly representative. She was built at Newburyport, Massachusetts, in 1791, by Searle and Tyler, under Captain Williams' watchful eye. Smith quotes a description by Benjamin Lincoln, Collector of Customs at Boston:

> She has one deck, two masts. Her length is 50 feet above her upper deck. Her depth [of hold] is 7 feet 8 inches, breadth 17 feet 8 inches. She measures 70 43/95 tons. She is a square-stern schooner, has quarter badges,

[11] H. I. Chapelle, *The History of American Sailing Ships* (W. W. Norton and Company, New York, 1935); 221-2. See also Chapelle, *The Baltimore Clipper* (The Marine Research Society, Salem, publication No. 22, 1930), for a study of the origin and development of this type of vessel.

and an Indian's head for figure-head. She has a long quarter deck and a deep waist.

She probably measured about 40 feet on the keel, carried three or four light swivel guns, and, in the fashion of the day, had a foretopsail schooner rig.

Characteristic of the Baltimore clipper as expressed in the early cutters were the sharp lines of bow and stern; the shallow draft and pronounced drag and deadrise; the graceful sheer and very low freeboard; the raking masts; long, light bowsprit and jibboom; light spars; and high pile of canvas. While these clipper characteristics were not always found in vessels purchased from private owners or hired for the service, they were consistently built into every recognizable *class* especially laid down for the Revenue-Marine throughout the sailing era. And beyond that, for many a day, the ghost of the clipper-cutters hovered near the men who drew the Coast Guard's hull designs.

The first class of cutters included the *Massachusetts* (1791), *Scammel, Vigilant, Active, Virginia, General Greene, South Carolina, Diligence, Pickering,* and *Argus.* Besides performing their normal mission, these little ships for several years constituted the United States' only fighting force afloat. Obviously, they were too light to pinch-hit for a navy very long, yet, notwithstanding their small size, for a little while they stood as America's first line of defense against an Old World power.

Peace lasted until the late 1790's, but during that decade American relations with France went from bad to worse. French officials insulted and sometimes refused to receive U. S. diplomats; French ships despoiled American commerce; French captains maltreated Yankee seamen to the point of torture. Presidents Washington and John Adams both urged Congress to act in the national defense, but rearmament was sluggish in getting underway. At last, late in the century, Congress increased the complements of cutters from ten men to "not exceeding 30 marines and seamen." This Act, entitled, somewhat ironically, "An Act providing a Naval Armament," empowered the President to "cause the said revenue cutters to be employed to defend the seacoast and to repel any hostility to their vessels and commerce, within their jurisdiction, having due regard to the duty of said cutters in the protection of the revenue."[12] What an assignment for such microscopic men-o'-war!

But depredations on commerce eventually forced Congress to create a navy. Several frigates were built in 1798, and the Navy Department was organized the same year. On March 2, 1799 Congress stated the general rule that until 1915 was to govern relations between the Revenue-Marine

[12] Act of July 1, 1797 (1 Stat. L., 621). On the imbroglio with France, see esp. G. W. Allen, *Our Naval War with France* (Houghton, Mifflin, Co., Boston and New York, 1909).

and the new Department: at the President's discretion, the cutters were to cooperate with the Navy, during which time they were to be under the direction of that Department's Secretary.[13]

Belated efforts at providing adequate defense, however, soon proved that navies cannot spring up overnight. Conditions for seaborne commerce out of Boston became so hazardous that a committee of leading merchants, determined to lend a hand in safeguarding their own interests, drew up plans for a new revenue-brig to be built for their home town. Oliver Wolcott, Secretary of the Treasury, realized that larger, heavier-armed cutters could help the Navy meet the emergency. He told the Boston committee to go ahead with their plans, but, he added, it "ought to be recollected that Congress are providing a naval force for the defense of Commerce, and that a principal—though not a sole—object of the Cutter establishment is the protection of the Revenue."[14]

Thus, by an early date, the military role of the service had been established, but at the same time the fundamental difference between the Navy and the cutter branch had definitely been recognized. Clearly, the former had been created solely for military operations and the latter primarily for the enforcement of maritime law. It was obvious, therefore, that the cutters' availability as naval reinforcements in time of war was—however valuable—a secondary, collateral design.

The Bostonians commenced their cutter and named her the *Pickering*. She was built at Newburyport, while her sister ship, the *Eagle,* was laid down at Philadelphia. Five cutters of the same size were constructed for the government at various other places. This second class, totaling seven units, was built (so Chapelle thinks) after a plan by Josiah Fox. They replaced most of Hamilton's original fleet, and several bore their predecessors' names. (Handing cutter names down from earlier to later units eventually became common practice.) Fox's cutters were of the Baltimore clipper type, but were considerably larger than Hamilton's original ten. The increased size was intended to accommodate more and heavier guns and larger crews. Rigged as fore-and-main topsail schooners, the vessels displayed splendid maneuvering qualities. (The *Pickering* and *Eagle* sometimes are referred to in various documents as brigs, brigantines, and jackass brigs.) As a class, they were 58 feet on the keel, with a 20-foot beam and a 9-foot depth of hold; 187 tons. The *Pickering* carried 90 men and 14 light guns; the others, 50 to 70 men and 10 to 14 guns. This group included the new *Pickering,* a new *Scammel, Diligence,* and *Massachusetts,* and the *Eagle, Governor Gilman,* and the *Governor Jay*. A new *Virginia* (a 50-footer), a new *South Carolina* (possibly a 58-footer), and the second

[13] Act of March 2, 1799 (1 Stat. L., 627, 699).

[14] *Naval Documents Related to the Quasi-War Between the U.S. and France,* Captain Dudley W. Knox, U.S.N., ed. (Washington, 1935); Vol. I, 56.

General Greene (a 98-ton sloop, 10 guns), were built about the same time. Four or five additional cutters were acquired by purchase, and a schooner, the *Bon Pere,* captured by the *Eagle* from the French in 1799, was also added to the cutter fleet.

In the early part of 1798, several of the *Pickering* group were still under construction. Collectors and naval agents in various ports wrote letter after letter to Philadelphia (then the national capital) explaining the delay in rearmament and asking for more money. The question of control over the *Pickering* remained unsettled until July 5, when the Secretary of the Navy wrote Wolcott suggesting that the Treasury direct the construction of all cutters and that "when They are ready for a cruise you then turn Them over to my Department."[15]

The *Pickering* class and the *General Greene* were so transferred during 1798; others remained on revenue duty, "defending the seacoast" as well as they were able. On July 11, the *Pickering,* Captain Chapman, was ordered to join Commodore John Barry's squadron, consisting of the *United States,* flag; *Delaware,* Captain Stephen Decatur, Sr.; and *Herald,* Captain Sever, in a cruise "from Cape Cod to The West Indies, 3 or 4 degrees to windward of Barbadoes . . . Through The West Indies." About a week later, Captain John W. Leonard, commanding *Governor Jay,* and Captain George Price, commanding *General Greene,* were ordered to proceed to sea with their cutters and "join the ship *Ganges,* Captain Dale, U.S.N., and cruise under his command from Long Island to Cape Henry." And in August, the *Virginia,* under Captain Francis Bright, with three other cutters accompanied Captain Samuel Nicholson's newly finished *Constitution* on a sweep along the coast south from the Virginia capes.[16]

These were the first instances of the Revenue-Marine's cooperation with naval units—the first entries in a joint log of wartime service. During ensuing operations, the cutters, besides cruising with Navy squadrons against privateers along the Atlantic coast and in the West Indies, performed convoy and dispatch details. For the latter they were especially well-adapted. They served thus until the summer of 1799, when all were returned to the Treasury except the *Pickering, Eagle,* and *Scammel;* these, retained with the Navy, were added to squadrons under famous commodores—Tingey, Truxton, and Decatur, Sr.—and cruised with them in the West Indies against French privateers. The *Eagle* and the *Pickering* made particularly good records both while operating in company with naval vessels and as lone raiders. For a while the *Pickering* was com-

[15] *Nav. Doc., op. cit.,* Vol. I, 167.

[16] *Record of Movements, Vessels of U.S.C.G.,* a mimeographed compilation in two volumes prepared by Coast Guard Headquarters, Washington, *circa* 1935; Vol. I, 86, 92; *Columbian Centinel,* issues for August 11 and September 1, 1798.

manded by the Navy's gallant Edward Preble, who began in her his rise to fame. An action typical of their work was reported in the *Columbian Centinel* for June 22, 1799; this account credited the *Eagle* with recapturing the ship *Nancy* and the brig *Mehitable* from the French privateer *Revenge* in a very brisk engagement. Captain H. G. Campbell of the *Eagle* was commissioned a master commandant in the Navy and in 1800 was made a full captain, to the great loss of the Revenue-Marine. Altogether, the *Eagle* seized five armed vessels and assisted in the capture of four others, out of a total of 90 taken during the punitive enterprises.

Peace with the French was ratified on February 3, 1801. It left the Revenue-Marine with 17 vessels, many experienced officers and men, and a creditable record of accomplishment in peace and war under Federalist administration.

CHAPTER II

Cutters and Cutlasses

JEFFERSON'S administration started with a promise of economy, and Albert Gallatin, the new Secretary of the Treasury, lost no time in reducing the cutter establishment to its pre-war tonnage. As early as July 1801 he was asking advice from collectors on the subject of whether or not smaller cutters could protect the revenue as adequately as the fleet Wolcott had sponsored. General opinion was in the affirmative, apparently, for most of Wolcott's cutters were either relinquished permanently to the Navy or sold. The *Massachusetts* went at public auction, and, except for her captain and oldest first lieutenant, her crew was discharged. The Collector at Boston was authorized to employ a barge until a replacement cutter could be built; the latter was to have a crew of only six and was to be not more than 45 tons burden. The first tendency of the administration, then, was to pare pay-rolls and to build small, cheap cutters reminiscent of the original fleet.

But early cries of economy notwithstanding, the Jeffersonians soon expanded the Revenue-Marine. To handle the war-scare of their day they instituted an embargo; the President hoped to bring about a peaceful settlement of the problems of impressment and neutral trade by denying Europe access to American products. This stringent embargo, ruinous to American commerce, was replaced by a Non-Intercourse Act prohibiting trade only with Great Britain and France and their possessions. Time proved the whole policy of "peaceable coercion" a failure: it did not bring England to terms; in a single year, 1807-08, exports dropped from $108,000,000 to $22,000,000, imports from $138,000,000 to $57,000,000; during the embargo, 55,000 seamen and 100,000 mechanics (estimated) were thrown out of work, ships lost $12,500,000 in net earnings, and the customs revenue fell from $16,000,000 per year to almost zero. But for awhile, isolationism drew considerable support.

To enforce commerce restrictions on more than 800,000 tons of American shipping registered for foreign trade, the governments of Mr. Jefferson and his successor needed more cutters and more men; accordingly, on July 6, 1809, Congress authorized twelve new vessels. Smith reports that they carried from 6 to 10 light guns, 15 to 30 men, and averaged 125 tons each. After enforcing the disastrous restrictions, these cutters helped, in a modest way, to reassert the freedom of the seas; upon them fell a share of the naval burden in the War of 1812.

Alexander Hamilton
Patriot and Statesman
Secretary of the Treasury, 1789-95
(From a portrait by C. L. Ransom, in the Office of the Secretary of the Treasury. Official C.G. photo.)

First Lighthouse in America

Boston Light, on Little Brewster Island

(From a mezzotint engraved at Boston *c.* 1729 by William Burgis. Official C.G. photo of a copy in Headquarters, U. S. Coast Guard.)

First Revenue-Cutter in America
The *Massachusetts,* 1791-96
(From a painting by Hunter Wood, in Headquarters, U. S. Coast Guard.)

The Cutter *Eagle* Engaging the *Revenge* in the Quasi-War with France, 1799
(From a painting by an unknown artist. Official C.G. photo.)

Cutter (*rt.*) and English Brig, War of 1812 Period
(From a painting by an unknown artist. Official C.G. photo.)

Most memorable of these ships was a new (1809) *Eagle,* made famous not by her successful operations (which, incidentally, were creditable enough) but by the manner of her defeat. This cutter had been built for the New Haven station and was commanded by Captain Frederick Lee. Her initial duty, in the words of Secretary Gallatin, was to "prevent the escape of vessels"—another way of saying that she was to enforce restrictions on commerce. After the War of 1812 broke out, the *Eagle's* activities took a more exciting and more popular turn: she patroled in the Sound against raiders, convoyed merchantmen to New York, and captured a number of valuable prizes.[1]

On one late afternoon in October 1814, this cutter ran out of New Haven to assist an American merchantmen, the *Susan* of New Haven, reported to have been captured by an enemy sloop. The *Susan* was not sighted during the evening, but in the misty dawn the cutter found herself closing both with the captor and with the British 18-gun brig *Dispatch.* Against the sloop's one 18- and two 4-pounders and the brig's 32-pound cannon, the *Eagle* could match only four 4's, a pair of 2's, and musketry. Hopelessly outclassed and prevented from running, the *Eagle* drove ashore near Negros Head, Long Island. There her crew and 40 volunteers who had sailed in her from New Haven staged a gallant though futile defense. They stripped the cutter of her guns and dragged them up a high bluff, and from nine o'clock in the morning until two in the afternoon a fierce cannonading ensued. The *Dispatch* alone fired 300 rounds. The cutter's flag, twice shot away, was twice replaced by a sailor from the hill "amid the cheers of his undaunted comrades and a whole broadside from the enemy." It is said that the cutter crew, after expending all their own shot, tore up the log book for wadding and returned the enemy's small shot that lodged in the hill. By their gunfire and musketry the Americans managed to prevent the capture of their ship, but the latter was dismasted and "greatly injured."[2]

After sporadic attacks during the night, the British on the following morning sailed away. Captain Lee got the *Eagle* afloat and hoped to return to New Haven, but before the crippled cutter could reach safety the enemy surprised and captured her. Probably the British used her to annoy further the good people of the Sound country. But Captain Lee and his crew, with their little ship and their pop-guns, had written a brave page.

Alfred Mahan, in his *Sea Power in Its Relations to the War of 1812,*

[1] *Rec. Movt.,* Vol. I, 113-6.

[2] The account of the *Eagle's* defense is based on eye-witness reports and news items contained in the *New York Evening Post,* June 17 and October 12, 14, 18, 1814. See also *Rec. Movt.,* Vol. I, 114-6; and Smith, *op. cit.,* 28-9.

comments on the great number of English merchantmen captured during the war. Although the cutters were so small and lightly armed that they could not successfully engage all comers, they were, nevertheless, responsible for a fair share of these seizures and also for valuable work in safeguarding American shipping from predatory privateers. Credit must go to a revenue-cutter, in fact, for the first capture of an English merchantman in the War: late in June 1812 the *Jefferson,* Captain William Ham, seized and carried into Norfolk a British brig. The cutter *Surveyor* fittingly celebrated the Fourth of July and the opening of hostilities with the capture of a "valuable British ship from Jamaica." Notice of a number of such seizures appeared from time to time in the press and doubtless exerted a heartening effect on Americans, to whom dispatches telling of the enemy's capture of American ships in American waters were entirely too familiar.[3]

Captain George Brooks, in the cutter *Madison,* showed a splendid initiative and vigor in the work of retaliation. As recorded by the *Columbian Centinel* (August 8-12, 1812), he reported from Charleston Roads on July 17, 1812, that six Jamaican merchantmen were on the coast and that he would "be on their track next day." The following week he redeemed his promise by bringing in "the fine British brig *Shamrock,* 6 guns and 16 men."

But the British were in U.S. waters in force, and the *Eagle* was not the only cutter to be overtaken by heavy odds. The *Madison* was lost to the enemy in 1812, and the *Surveyor* was captured one rainy night the following year, as she lay anchored in the York River. Manned by only 15 men, she was attacked by a boarding party of 50 Englishmen in boats from His Majesty's frigate *Narcissus,* Lieutenant John Crerie, R.N. The boarders approached with muffled oars, from such an angle that Captain Samuel Travis, in the *Surveyor,* was unable to bring his guns to bear. He therefore gave his men two muskets each and bade them hold their fire until command. No sign or sound went up from the *Surveyor* to show that the attackers had been observed until the Englishmen were within pistol range; then with a whoop the cutter men cut loose their muskets and stood by to repel boarders. They had little time to wait, it seems, for "with the rattling volley came the cheers of the attacking party, who dashed alongside despite the leaden missiles, and a desperate hand-to-hand conflict ensued on the deck of the *Surveyor.* Although outnumbered and surrounded by the enemy, the crew did not flinch, contesting the deck with stubborn courage in response to ringing appeals from Captain Travis, who did not surrender his vessel until further resistance would have resulted in useless and wanton shedding of blood."

[3] *E.g.: New York Evening Post,* June 29, 1812; *Nile's Register,* July 4, 1812. See also E. S. Maclay, *A History of American Privateers* (D. Appleton Company, 1891; 226).

In this brief and bloody struggle, five cutter men were wounded; seven British were wounded and three killed.[4]

The following day, Crerie returned Travis' sword with a note whose sentiment impresses one as much with Crerie's gallantry as with Travis' own:

H.M.S. *Narcissus*
June 13, 1813.

Sir:

Your gallant and desperate attempt to defend your vessel against more than double your number excited such admiration on the part of your opponents as I have seldom witnessed, and induced me to return you the sword you had so ably used, in testimony of mine.

Our poor fellows have severely suffered, occasioned chiefly, if not solely, by the precaution you had taken to prevent surprise. In short, I am at a loss which to admire most—the previous arrangement on board the *Surveyor,* or the determined manner in which the deck was disputed inch by inch.

You have my most sincere wishes for the immediate parole and speedy exchange of yourself and brave crew.

I am, Sir, with much respect,

Your most obedient servant,
John Crerie.[5]

A few months after this incident, and almost as though to avenge it, Captain John Cahoone in the cutter *Vigilant* forced a troublesome British armed sloop to strike. This vessel, the privateer *Dart,* had operated for some time in Long Island Sound; by seizing 20 or 30 American vessels she had marked herself as a first-rank public enemy. Her one mistake was to appear off Newport Harbor, October 4, 1813, with a freshly captured ship and brig: she was reported in Newport, and Captain Cahoone took 20 Navy volunteers abroad the *Vigilant* and "immediately made sail" to engage the enemy. Coming up with the sloop, Cahoone gave her a broadside, then "laid aboard and carried her by boarding." The *Dart's* six 9-pound carronades and six swivels far outgunned Cahoone's light ordnance and in a prolonged gun duel probably could have blown the cutter out of the water; the matter was decided by the *Vigilant's* speed and the readiness of her captain and crew to sail down the muzzles of the British cannon.[6]

Military services performed by cutter personnel opened the way early in 1814 for placing Revenue-Marine battle casualties upon Navy pension

[4] Smith, *op. cit.,* 27.
[5] *Rec. Movt.,* Vol. I, 117.
[6] Quotations are from a dispatch addressed to Commodore John Rogers, U. S. frigate *President,* by Captain Jos. Nicholson, naval commander in Newport; reported in *Rec. Movt.,* Vol. I, 120. See also *New York Evening Post,* October 8, 1813.

rolls. This was the first and for almost a century remained the only provision made for the retirement of disabled cutter men.[7]

Ten or eleven cutters disappeared from the list during the war and represented losses both from military action and normal deterioration; the end of hostilities in 1815 saw the need for new construction.

Detailed drawings showing some of the sailing cutters built from about 1815 on are in existence. They disclose increased dimensions, in later models, up to about a hundred feet on the waterline, but few radical changes catch the eye. A subtle process of change was at work, however, gradually producing refinements in form (such as the underwater lines or the cut of a sail) and in fittings (such as the general abandonment of the tiller for the wheel, which seems to have taken place in the 'thirties). These small changes were in the direction of increased sailing and seagoing qualities and were cumulative in their effect; towards the end of the day of sail they gave to cutters a remarkable degree of efficiency and artistic perfection.

In 1815, William Doughty drew plans for an extreme type of Baltimore clipper which he laid down in three sizes: 31, 51, and 80 tons. These were usually rigged as fore-topsail schooners with the addition of a square lower foresail, or "course." The plans show fine lines, the usual drag, a square stern, raking masts, and other "Virginia-built" characteristics. A light rail took the place of bulwarks. The 51-tonners were 56.7 feet long, 17 feet broad with a six foot depth of hold. The armament of the several models varied. According to Chapelle, "some [had] 12 or 18-pounder carronades, or long 9's, 12's, or 18's. In addition, the larger boats sometimes carried one long 4 or 6; cutters' guns were usually made of brass. The plans all called for the pivot-gun amidships, which if not always the sole gun was always the heaviest."

The *Alabama* and *Louisiana* were laid to the 51-ton plan. They were built during the summer of 1819 at a cost of about $4,500 each, fully equipped, and were stationed on the Gulf of Mexico. In frequent adventures against pirates and slavers who haunted southern waters at the time the two diminutive cruisers soon sailed and fought their way to national fame. In its issue for October 20, 1819, the *New York Evening Post* carried an eye-witness report of their first encounter with a pirate ship—the *Bravo,* commanded by the freebooter Lefarge and owned by the notorious Lafitte. The Brethren of the Coast sailed under a "Patriot" flag with a commission signed by one Humbert, self-styled Lieutenant-General and Governor of the Province of Texas.

The *Post's* story is quoted below (the writer was abroad the *Alabama*):

[7] Act of April 18, 1814.

On the 31st of August we discovered three strange sails ahead. The wind being very light, we immediately set all sails and wet them down. We got our sweeps out and made every exertion to come up with them. At 2 p.m. they separated, one standing for us. At quarter past two, Captain Loomis [commanding *Louisiana*] fired a shot ahead of the nearest, and made a signal for us to board her. We did so, and found her full of people who had been robbed of everything by the Pirates before we hove in sight. We put them on board the *Alabama* then pulled away hard on our sweeps to come up with the other vessel. The Pirate bore down on us; at half past two he hoisted the Patriot flag. Captain Loomis, being nearest him, hailed and ordered him to haul down his flag, when he immediately poured into Captain Loomis's vessel a volley of musketry which was promptly returned and with interest. This continued for a few minutes, when we brought our large guns to bear upon him and gave him a broadside which made all the Pirates run below. We immediately boarded at the same time, in the boats of both cutters. We found on the Pirate a crew of 18 men, besides officers and 12 prisoners; most of the latter were black. We found that two men had been killed on board of her during the action. She was called the *Bravo*. Mr. Jordan, the 1st officer of our cutter, took possession of the other vessel, which proved to be a prize to the Pirates. She was a Spanish schooner, laden with flour, and when she was taken had on a number of passengers, both ladies and gentlemen, who were treated by the Pirates in a most shameful manner. They were robbed of everything, even to the clothes on their backs, and when the ladies begged for something to cover them, the Pirates drew their swords on them, using the most brutal language.

The *Louisiana's* first officer and three of her men were wounded in the exchange of musketry. The action took place somewhere to the north of the Tortugas, whence the cutters took their prizes into Bayou St. Jean and committed the pirates to prison to await trial.

This affair was only a prelude to the work of suppressing buccaneers—a work, incidentally, in which the American and British navies also took a hand, in amicable cooperation. An intensive search of Coast Guard archives has produced no trace of the *Louisiana's* and *Alabama's* logs, but numerous references to the cutters' campaign have been found in the newspapers of the day. The Savannah *Republican,* for instance, on May 23, 1820, carried a story of their raid on Breton Island, a pirate operating base and stronghold. Here seamen from the cutters landed in force and burned buildings, woods, and everything in sight. Another report stated that the two ships then bore away "to the Westward to break up the haunts of Pirates in that direction." Destruction of strongholds and bases marked the beginning of the pirates' end.

In another issue, August 29, 1820, the Savannah paper printed an extract from a letter written by Captain Loomis to a "gentleman in New York":

I arrived here in Belize on the 17th [July] after a short cruise of 20 days. I have succeeded in taking four more Pirates, which I have now in confinement on board the *Louisiana*. I have about $4,000 worth of dry goods which they have robbed and which they were endeavoring to smuggle into the United States. They had some negroes which had landed but have been followed and taken. I captured these fellows 250 miles to westward of this river.

Still carrying on the same sort of work in 1822, the *Alabama* on March 25 made three captures for violations of the Slave Trade Acts. A little later, according to the *New York Evening Post* for November 18, 1822, the *Louisiana* returned to Pensacola from a cruise on the coasts of Florida and Cuba; during this adventure she captured five piratical vessels of between 80 and 100 tons each. Two of these she burned, and three she

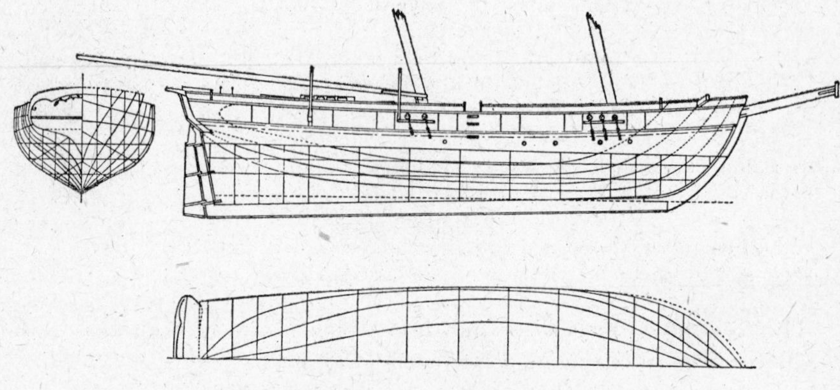

Lines of Humphreys' *Morris*, 1830
(From U.S.N. C.&R. Files.)

sent into New Orleans as prize. Piracy was becoming a distinctly hazardous occupation. In time, probable loss began to outweigh probable gain, and the buccaneers vanished from the Caribbean and the Gulf. The achievement marked a new degree of safety on the sea.

Cutters in Doughty's 1815 design were supplemented by a few shallower draft schooners also designed by him. The several Doughty models were standard cutter types until the 'thirties, when plans for new and larger vessels were drawn by Samuel Humphreys, a famous constructor in the Navy. The new vessels were to be somewhat larger than Doughty's, so as to afford accommodations for more men and longer cruises. The improvement was accomplished admirably by the architect, who managed it without any material increase in draft and who gave his cutters finer lines than any class had had so far. Humphreys' cutters were fore-topsail schooners of 73 feet 4 inches between perpendiculars, 20 feet 6 inches extreme beam, 7 feet 4 inches depth of hold, 112 tons. They cost about

$11,000 apiece. They had various armaments, but generally carried six 12-pounder carronades or 6-pounder long guns.

About seventeen of this class were built during the 'thirties; their roster included *Morris, McLane, Campbell, Taney, Ingham, Woodbury, Hamilton, Wolcott, Jackson, Dexter, Crawford, Gallatin*—names which have appeared and reappeared in the cutter fleet for generations. Both the drawings and the service records of these splendid vessels bear witness to magnificent sailing prowess. Some of the cutters attained reputations which came close to investing them with living personalities. A Boston journalist reporting to the *Army and Navy Chronicle and Scientific Repository* for April 25, 1844, could refer to one in words like these:

> The U. S. Revenue Cutter *Hamilton* is now on the marine railway, undergoing repairs and having new copper put on her bottom. Those who have admired the beauty of the cutter while at anchor will now have an excellent opportunity of viewing her model throughout. Underwater, it will be seen, she is as clean as a dolphin and equally beautiful. No wonder she sails swiftly or that her gallant captain [Josiah Sturgis] is so proud of her.

The following tribute from Chapelle, who more than any other, possibly, has preserved both the facts and the spirit of the age of sailing vessels, must be quoted as a last salute to the memory of an able ship:

> Like her sisters, the *Hamilton* was a very fine sailer and was used as the supreme test of any schooner claiming a reputation for speed. In races with opium smugglers, fast pilot-boats, fishermen, coasters, and yachts, few vessels passed her either on or off the wind.[8]

These longer, faster cutters were Humphreys' answer to new problems confronting the Revenue-Marine: Indian war, transport duty, winter cruising. Indian unrest in Florida during the late 'thirties was a legacy of Andrew Jackson's punitive expedition against the Seminoles back in 1818. White men in the southern frontier country saw trouble brewing when a new generation of Seminoles refused to move to lands in the west. A letter from the Collector at St. Marks to the Collector at New Orleans demanding protection illustrated the current fear of the red men:

> Dear Sir:
>
> I wrote you (officially) a few days since asking you to send the Revenue Cutter under your charge to this port to assist in the protection of it. I must now be pardoned for *urging* it privately. We are in the midst of an Indian war. The Seminoles are fighting their last fight. They intend to die before they will remove and intend to kill and destroy all that come in their way. They have declared themselves and are acting up to it. They have killed many defenseless white persons and burned every habitation they have approached and we are hourly expecting their arrival 2000 strong in this part

[8] Chapelle, *op. cit.*, 205.

of the territory. In this state of things I consider my office wholly unprotected and there is much in it that would be desirable to save, besides which I would like a place to retreat to with my better half if such a measure would become necessary for the preservation of life. I hope you will give the cutter immediate dispatch, well manned, armed, and provisioned. Please let me hear immediately from you. . . .

Jesse Willis[9]

James Breedlove, Collector at New Orleans, replied in a couple of weeks that he was sending the cutter *Dallas* at once. This vessel furnished protection to St. Marks and Tampa during the first four months of 1836. Her recall was the signal for the long-feared attack upon St. Marks. To the relief of this village the *Jackson,* Captain Hunter, carried a gun, two officers, and 32 men.

All in all, ten cutters took part in the Seminole War. "Their prompt and ready cooperation with the Army . . . called forth the highest commendations from the commanding generals."[10] Their light draft permitted them to do work no frigate could have accomplished in the shallows off the Florida west coast. Some carried guns and supplies, others transported soldiers and marines, to strategic points. From time to time, landing parties of revenue-cutter men went to the relief of beleaguered settlements or trailed redskins through sand-burrs and palmettoes into the Everglades. By 1840 the Florida white man's cabin, crop, and scalp had been made secure. In appreciation for their part in bringing the Great White Father's law into the land, it is said, the cutter men were assigned a quarter section homestead each.

[9] File of Collectors' Letters, 1836; in *C. G. Archives.*

[10] Captain Webb, U.S.N., Commanding U.S.S. *Vandalia,* to Commodore A. J. Dallas, U.S.N., April 12, 1836; quoted in *Rec. Movt.,* Vol. I, 81.

CHAPTER III

Towards Consolidation

THE NUMBER of cutters in commission during the Revenue-Marine's first half-century ranged from ten to twenty at a time; three or four officers and perhaps twenty men were an average ship's company. Yet, small as it was, this service turned in a record of notable achievement, compounded of every element vital to the growth of a truly great tradition. The accomplishment seems little less than remarkable in view of the fact that the Revenue-Marine's early administrative system lacked many essentials of a strong, coordinated organization.

Although in theory the Secretary administered revenue-cutters through collectors of customs, he actually exercised only a nominal control. Individual collectors enjoyed wide latitude in running the cutters assigned to their respective districts. For practical purposes, each unit was a separate entity, an adjunct to a local customhouse, and it is probable that few citizens in this period ever thought of the cutters as forming collectively a unitary agency. Under these conditions, little uniformity of operating policy or of personnel management could be expected, and the resultant handicap to joint operations between cutters of adjacent districts must have been substantial.

The degree of supervision exercised over the captains depended largely on personal relationships between captains and semi-autonomous collectors. Thus it was possible for some captains to be semi-autonomous, too, and for methods of procurement, accounting, and enlisting and discharging crews to vary widely among different cutters. Lack of adequate supervision by a central authority made adherence to main-line administrative policies a matter of merest chance.

Another chronic weakness of the early system lay in the fact that officers' promotions often were based more on politics than on seniority or merit. Floods of letters of recommendation from business men and politicians necessarily accompanied every request for appointment or promotion in commissioned grades. Since they were habitually written in superlatives, these recommendations were of questionable value in guiding the selection of the best men for the jobs—they were, in fact, little more than guides to political expediency. An officer generally remained on his original ship and station as long as his political luck held out; thus some became veritable fixtures in the localities where they were known. Luckless ones, on the other hand, had no security; many a commission, subject in those days to revocation by the President on recommendation of the Secretary, was forfeited to the political bossism of local collectors. Personal preferment paved the only safe road to success. The fact that many officers in the early period made distinguished records speaks more for those officers as individuals than it does for the grab-bag personnel policies then in vogue. Obviously, such policies insured neither the government nor the individual officer against political racketeering.

Over a long period, many officers fulminated and fought for the elimination of administrative evils. They won no medals in these campaigns, but they earned reputations as spearheads of a drive for service betterment. Outstanding were Captains Fraser, Shepard, Henriques, and Shoemaker, each of whom will be mentioned later on. But, although they might protest against unfavorable conditions, revenue-cutter men could do very little towards reform without support from the Department. Occasionally a Secretary of the Treasury championed their cause. One of the first was Louis McLane, Secretary in 1832.

Soon after taking office, McLane launched an investigation of service personnel. The desirability of a retreat from local control in appointments and promotions immediately came to light, and McLane—too good a Jacksonian to slam the door on patronage altogether—at least made a bow to the merit system when he laid down the following policy:

> With a view to greater efficiency in the cutter service in future, vacancies will be filled by promotion from among the officers in that service, when that shall be found preferable to other appointments, having regards to fitness as well as seniority.[1]

McLane found, also, that as a result of slow promotion and scarcity of ships in the Navy between 1825 and 1832, a number of naval officers had been commissioned in the Revenue-Marine. Some apparently were none too happy in their new jobs. As a token of dissatisfaction with duty on cutters, they retained their naval uniforms, and their lack of enthusiasm was reflected in their work. While it could be said that both naval and revenue-cutter officers were trained seamen raised under similar professional codes, it was fairly obvious that differences in outlook and experience (stemming, no doubt, from basic differences in the statutory functions of their respective corps) separated them into two distinct professional groups. Confident that "experience had shown the employment of officers of the Navy in the revenue-cutter service liable to objection," McLane formulated a new policy: the two corps were to be untangled and kept separate in the future. Accordingly, commissions held in the Revenue-Marine by naval officers were revoked on April 30, 1832. (A

[1] Circular letters to officers, January 17, 1832. In *C. G. Archives.*

dozen or so officers resigned from the Navy to retain their Revenue-Marine commissions.) This policy's immediate effect was to clear the service of all officers except those whose primary professional interest, loyalty, and pride lay in the Revenue-Marine. It led, in time, to vital consequences.

As early as McLane's day, the service watched over a wide variety of national interests afloat. Revenue-cutters enforced customs and navigation laws; anti-wrecking, plundering, piracy, and slave trade acts; quarantine regulations; neutrality laws; and one of the first federal conservation statutes, the Timber Reserve Act, a measure prohibiting export of the Florida liveoak lumber needed in building stout hulls for U.S. men-o'-war. In addition, cutters often gave assistance to vessels in distress, and the captains acted as inspectors of lighthouses and buoys whenever this work "did not interfere with the duties prescribed by law." By the 1830's, therefore, the service was an agency for enforcing law; for preventing loss of life, property, and freedom; and for reinforcing the Navy in time of war.[2]

New technical developments soon expanded its activities still further. Steamboats already were whistling on the river bends, and a few steamers were laying down their smudge upon the ocean. But steam was a dangerous shipmate, unpredictable and undisciplined; frequently amuck, it left blasted boilers and bodies in its wake. In 1832, 14% of all the steamers in operation were destroyed by explosions; a thousand or more people perished with them. Hazards so acute cried for control, and Congress finally (1838) enacted the first navigation law for the "better securing of the lives . . . on board vessels propelled in whole or in part by steam." This Act launched an enduring national policy of regulating private enterprise in the interest of safety afloat. It provided for the inspection of steamboat hulls and boilers, for the employment of skillful engineers to stand steaming watches, and for the equipment of steamers with certain safety appliances such as lifeboats, fire pumps, and hose.[3]

Federal port agents, empowered to make necessary inspections and to issue certificates to masters whose steamboats complied with all requirements, were necessary to the administration of the new law, and a Steam-

[2] Quotation from *Regulations*, U. S. Revenue-Marine, 1834; 11. Early enactments: *Wrecking*, March 3, 1825 (R.S. 5358); *Plundering*, March 3, 1825 (R.S. 5361); *Piracy*, March 3, 1819 (3 Stat. L., 510); *Slave Trade*, May 10, 1800 (2 Stat. L., 70); *Quarantine*, February 25, 1799 (1 Stat. L., 619); *Neutrality*, April 20, 1818 (3 Stat. L., 447, 449); *Timber Reserve*, February 23, 1822 (3 Stat. L., 651).

[3] Act of July 7, 1838 (5 Stat. L., 304). On later extensions of steamboat inspection legislation, see L. M. Short, *Steamboat-Inspection Service* (Institute for Governmental Research Publication No. 8), (D. Appleton and Co., New York and London, 1922); 1-27. See also Lieutenant Holmes F. Crouch, U.S.C.G., "Merchant Marine Inspection: A Major Function of the Coast Guard," in *U. S. Naval Institute Proceedings*, July, 1948.

boat-Inspection Service began taking shape to meet the need. From 1838 to 1852, U. S. district judges were authorized to appoint inspectors at ports of entry within their districts. In the latter year, the system was reorganized (under nine "supervising inspectors" who were authorized to appoint "local inspectors" in their respective districts) and tied into the Treasury Department. From a purely logical standpoint, the agency might well have been set up as an integral part of the Revenue-Marine: the steamboat laws were marine safety measures and cutters already were engaged with numerous duties in the same general category. But in 1838, two factors prevented integration. First, the Revenue-Marine had no shore offices from which to carry out inspections and grant inspection certificates, essentials of the steamboat work, and, second, there were no engineers in the service at that time. In fact, few marine engineers—except river men like Captain Henry Shreve, the celebrated pioneer western steamboat builder—were to be found in the United States in those days. It was fairly obvious, therefore, that it would be just as easy and just as cheap to set up and maintain a special steamboat-inspection unit as to give the Revenue-Marine the job. (This hardly applied in later years, after the Coast Guard had acquired an extensive shore establishment and had developed a group of experienced and well-qualified engineering officers of its own.) Further, little evidence of any consistent tendency toward rationalization of governmental agencies during the period comes to hand; governmental functions were still relatively simple, and, in all probability, "rationalization" and "integration" were words seldom if ever heard. These reasons undoubtedly account, in part, at least, for the organization of the Steamboat-Inspection Service as a separate agency.

Neverthlesss, an important share in the burden imposed by the new legislation did fall on the Revenue-Marine, for administrative policy delegated to the cutters the responsibility of seeing to it that no vessels were operated without complying with "all requirements regarding matters covered by the steamboat-inspection laws."[4] A similar enforcement authority was given to the Customs Service. While steamships were scarce in coastal waters, this duty was fairly light, but it grew heavier as the number of steamers increased. Normally, it involved examination of inspection certificates, check-up of required safety apparatus, and related details, as incidents of routine coastal boarding operations. In this respect, the cutters formed a field enforcement agency for the new phase of federal effort to insure safety at sea.

Thus, with fair consistency, the scope of service operations coincided with the full range of maritime safety and law enforcement duties given

[4] Short, *Steamboat Inspection Service, op. cit.*, 64.

to federal authorities by the early Congresses. But it is apparent that chance and administrative expediency traced the early line of service development. There was no well-defined "philosophy of coast-guarding" to act as a rational guide to service evolution in the 1830's, and none, in fact, emerged for many years.

Secretary McLane's reorganization contributed more to the eventual emergence of such a concept than did any other single factor. McLane differentiated Revenue-Marine officers as a distinct seagoing class. He distinguished between naval officers, to whom war and preparation for war must always be primary concerns, and revenue-cutter officers, whose attention focussed closely on maritime safety and law. In time, and in consonance with federal law and practice, cutter men came to look upon the latter as the special province of their profession; quite as vital, constant contact with shipping gave them invaluable experience and insight into general maritime problems. The combination of these factors enabled Revenue-Marine officers to create a distinctive tradition, to work out distinctive techniques, and to develop distinctive professional interests and ideals of public service. In this gradual process, cutter officers were transformed into a corps of seagoing experts in maritime affairs—men ready by training, inclination, and experience to tackle any maritime assignment that Congress or the President might give them. As a corollary, a rational definition of the service's precise position in the federal government eventually took form.

Outstanding among pre-Civil War officers whose careers exerted a favorable influence upon these currents was Alexander V. Fraser, the Revenue-Marine's first military commandant. Fraser was an honest, canny Scot. As a youngster he attended the Mathematical, Nautical, and Commercial School at 231 Water Street, New York City. His instructor, one M. Nash, writing a recommendation for him in 1826, certified that he had attained a "very accurate and complete knowledge of Navigation and Nautical Astronomy as well as a distinguished reputation as a practitioner, especially in finding the Longitude by Lunar Observations and the use of a Chronometer."[5] A little later, as mate and then master of a merchantman, Fraser sailed in the East India trade. This was the toughest finishing school a young seaman could select—it offered first-hand courses in hurricanes, Horse Latitudes, and Sulu pirates, and it turned out master mariners who "took no back-wind from anyone," so confident were they of their professional superiority.[6]

With such qualifications to offer, Fraser in 1832 applied to Andrew

[5] This and many other details concerning Fraser's career are from Fraser's Personnel File, in *C. G. Archives.*

[6] Quotation from S. E. Morison, *Maritime History of Massachusetts* (Houghton Mifflin, 1921); 285.

Jackson for a commission in the Revenue-Marine. The President appointed him second lieutenant, and Fraser immediately reported on board the *Alert,* Captain W. A. Howard, commanding. The *Alert* and several others cutters were in Charleston, South Carolina, at the time, engaged in upholding the authority of "King Andrew's" federal government against the nullificationists. It became Fraser's duty to board sugar ships from Havana and compel them to anchor under the guns of the cutter and Castle Pinckney and to discharge their sugar, which was stored in the fort until the consignees paid the import tax.

By the next year, Fraser had his foot upon the ladder of promotion. He secured letters from Captain Howard, who wanted him in his ship, and from former Secretary Dallas, as well as from the heads of certain firms like C. Price & Morgan, and Hollingshead, Platt & Co., of Philadelphia. The record of Fraser's efforts to advance in the service illustrated the necessity of securing one's own promotion in that day by means of political pressure, in the absence of an effective merit system. In 1835 he was still trying to obtain advancement to first lieutenant, this time by sending in long commendatory letters signed by leading members of Democratic Clubs of the City and County of New York. No success came of his efforts, and so, having received an excellent commercial offer, Fraser took a furlough from March 26, 1836 to March 12, 1838. He spent this two-year period in command of the ship *Himmaleh* on a voyage to Japan, China, and the Malayan Archipelago. On his return to New York, he wrote the following letter to Secretary Woodbury:

March 8, 1838

Sir:

I have to report my arrival at this port after a long and tedious passage from China. I am informed of my promotion and hope I may deserve it. The *Alert* being without a First Lieutenant, and being certain that Captain Bicker would wish me with him, I would request that should it meet with the views of the Department I might be appointed to that vessel. . . .

Your Obt Servt
Alex V. Fraser
U. S. Rev. Cutter Service

This request was granted, and Fraser went abroad the *Alert* just in time to help inaugurate winter cruising, a new and adventurous cutter duty which Congress had written into the statutes during his stay abroad. The law called for an intensification of the Revenue-Marine's traditional work of assisting vessels in distress, a work performed prior to 1832 only as a customary obligation of the sea. In 1832, Secretary McLane had ordered several cutters to cruise along the coast for the purpose of giving seaborne commerce special protection during the winter season. This experiment in search and rescue operations was such a success that Congress legalized the activity by the Act of December 22, 1837, authorizing the President

> to cause any suitable number of public vessels, adapted to the purpose, to cruise upon the coast, in the severe portion of the season, when the public service will allow of it, and to afford such aid to distressed navigators as their circumstances and necessities may require.[7]

Legislation along these lines seems amply justified. From about 1830 to 1855, when the clipper fleet was flourishing, American merchant tonnage steadily increased. Towards the end of this period of shipping prosperity, the great bulk of American trade was being carried in American bottoms. During the 'thirties, more and more packets, coasting schooners, whalers, clippers—windjammers of all descriptions—beat in and out of U.S. ports. Trade was good, and quick trips made quick profits. The Age of Speed was streaking in. Possibly American sailing ships were too successful in meeting the new emphasis that profits put on Time; certainly the clippers' astounding speed-runs acted as deterrents to general replacement of sail by steam until well after England had taken the lead in steamship operation. "Square-riggers on schedule" was the watchword of U.S. shipping in the 'thirties and 'forties. Bonuses went to those tough skippers, buckoes, and iron men who could pile on canvas and break records on their runs despite doldrums, hell, or hurricanes. Such a man was Joseph C. Delano, for instance, who in 1830 drove the *Columbia* of New Bedford home from London in 16 days.[8]

Racing "b'guess and b'God" through the North Atlantic's wintry snows and blows, this multitude of sailing ships encountered fearful risks—risks that in a later day of mechanized fleets and electronically-aided navigation would be little more than spectres of the past. About ninety sea-going American vessels were totally wrecked each year, and the coasts of Long Island, Cape Cod, and Jersey became symbols of destruction. To meet the voyaging public's demand, a life-preserver was invented in the 'thirties; shipping companies offered the commodity to passengers who could afford to buy. Joseph Francis began marketing his lifeboat in 1837, and a group of volunteers manned a lifeboat at Rockaway that same year. Congress, therefore, was abreast of the times when it authorized the special protection, and, since 1837, assistance to life and property in distress has been one of the service's most important and most widely acclaimed activities. A long series of thrillers on the story of the Coast Guard might be written around the rescues made under this and subsequent authorities. In the flowery words of a civilian chief of the Revenue-Marine Bureau:

[7] 5 Stat. L., 208.

[8] R. G. Albion, *Square-Riggers on Schedule* (Princeton University Press, 1938); 162-3 and *passim.*

Those aware of the privations and perils incident to ordinary coasting in the winter season, will not regard the discharge of these duties as pastime, nor suppose these triumphs over storm and wave are achieved without hazard. Conquests that "wrest from the greedy sea its prey" are rarely easily won, and often demand a heroism as great as was ever displayed on the field of battle.[9]

In such work Alex Fraser was given his big chance. He spent three years in the *Alert,* apparently assuming command when Captain Nicholas Bicker felt too ill, old, or infirm to go to sea, and he carried out the winter cruising program diligently. When the time came for him to seek promotion to a captaincy, he was able to produce a record of much valuable assistance performed on the New York station. New York's marine insurance men indorsed him for a captaincy and at the same time declared their hope

that the government will furnish you [Fraser] with a proper vessel for cruising on our coast during our cold and blustery season, for besides the saving of property to the Country and revenue of the Government and relief to suffering seamen, they know not a school better calculated to make bold and hardy seamen, a class admitted to be useful and necessary in peace and in War.[10]

After marshalling many high-powered recommendations, Fraser was promoted in 1842 and given command of the *Ewing,* built only the year before at Baltimore.

(The Captain Bicker mentioned above, a veteran of the Revolution, was one of the oldest captains in the service. He finally became so decrepit that he confused his orders badly and was forced out. [There were no pensions for aged personnel at the time.] The old gentleman died on July 15, 1843. Fraser was Chief of the Revenue-Marine Bureau by then, and he sent a circular letter to every ship in the service ordering flags half-masted and thirteen guns fired in memory of his old commanding officer.)

Frasers' step up occurred while the Revenue-Cutter Service was under fire from Congress. Actuated by one of its periodic efforts at economy, the Committee on Commerce wrote a report in 1840 attacking not only the cutters, but also the Coast Survey and the Lighthouse Establishment. The Committee was understandably indignant at finding that the cutters were supported not by Congress, through regular appropriations, but by the Secretary, "out of the Revenue before it goes into the Treasury." The Secretary

[9] S. I. Kimball, *Annual Report of the Revenue Marine* (Govt. Printing Office, Washington, 1872).
[10] In *C. G. Archives.*

> appropriates and pays, without the sanction of Congress, and even without its knowledge. . . . [The service] costs the country whatever he shall direct. The country knows nothing of the expenditures. . . .[11]

Further, inquiring into the collectors' use and abuse of authority, the Committee was displeased to find that "the crews, ships, and boats are subject to their orders, for pleasure, interest, or public service." Finally, the Committee pointed out that while the expenses of the service had risen from $164,000 to $222,000 between 1830 and 1840, the revenue collected had decreased from $22,000,000 to $13,500,000 in the same period. The Committee was hardly fair in its use of figures, however, for it failed to mention that tonnage and certain other duties had been repealed or lowered after 1830, or that 1837-40 saw a serious business depression, or that the cutters, besides protecting the customs, had engaged during the period of the report in many maritime safety duties (including winter cruising) and had helped fight the Seminole Indian War. The Committee recommended replacing cutters with small sloops, but took no effective action towards removing serious evils of administration.

However, economy-minded Congressmen remained on the war-path. Early in 1843 they made another attack, this time suggesting abolition of the whole system and assignment of naval units to revenue duty. Against this, however, the Committee on Commerce stood firm, resolving that

> to substitute officers and vessels of the Navy for the performance of the duties now discharged by means of the revenue cutters, and which are peculiar to such a service . . . is not demanded by reason of any defects in the existing system, nor any principle of true economy, nor any advantage it possesses over the present arrangement. So far from this, the committee are satisfied that sound policy requires that the revenue service and the naval service should be kept distinct. . . .[12]

This resolution, of course, was a strong reenforcement to the policy laid down previously by Secretary McLane. The Revenue-Cutter Service was sound enough in principle, that is, it was an essential and distinct federal agency, but no one could long defend its obvious administrative faults. Congressional criticism had a constructive effect. It awakened the Treasury Department to the service's need for administrative renovation. To the new Secretary, John C. Spencer, this meant setting up a stronger and more intelligent central authority in Washington; he determined to bring an experienced captain to the capital and put him in charge of a Revenue-Marine Bureau, in the Treasury. Spencer selected Alex Fraser as the logical man and offered him the job. Fraser's Scotch blood betrayed itself in his reply, for he said he would like the position

[11] Smith,, *op. cit.*, 47-8.
[12] *Report* of the Committee on Commerce, February 19, 1843. Copy in *C. G. Archives.*

very much *if* it carried an increase in salary and suitable allowance for living quarters and a servant.

Such preliminaries out of the way, Spencer wrote Fraser a formal offer and outlined the duties of the new post, as follows:

April 12, 1843.

Sir:

It has occurred to me that the interests of the Government and the advantage of all concerned would be much promoted by placing this branch of the public business in charge of an officer familiar with its details and qualified by practical knowledge to judge of the wants and necessities of the service. Confiding in your intelligence and disposition faithfully to serve the public in the premises, I have therefore detailed you for duty in the Department and now assign to you under the supervision of the Secretary of the Treasury, the charge of the business referred to. Generally your duties will consist in the supervision of all matters appertaining to the Revenue-Service requiring the interposition of the Department. Your duties are comprehended under the following heads, viz:

1st. The charge and investigation of all estimates for the Revenue Service and the administrative examination of all accounts for disbursements made by Collectors for the Revenue Vessels previous to their being sent to the Auditor for settlement.

2nd. The construction and equipment of new vessels and the repair or other disposition of the old ones.

3rd. The charge of all applications for appointments in the Service, the transmission of commissions, the assignment of officers to their stations, disposition of the vessels, force to be employed in them, and the arrangement for their cruising.

4th. The care, preservation and superintendence of all public property placed on board the Cutters and deposited on shore.

5th. The investigation of all charges for neglect of duty or other misconduct and the preparation under the direction of the head of the Department of all letters touching these details.

Suitable accommodations will be provided for you in the Department and a subordinate officer to be selected by yourself will be detailed to assist you in case it should become necessary.[13]

Here were the essentials for a centralized, unitary organization, with basic functions of command vested in a service officer. Responsible members of the commissioned corps had long awaited just this opportunity, and Fraser did not disappoint them. As soon as he had seated himself at his new desk and ordered Second Lieutenant George Hayes to Washington as his assistant, he proceeded to institute changes long overdue in the Revenue-Marine. On January 9, 1844 he submitted the service's first annual report, a long and inclusive document which summarized the situation as the first Commandant saw it and outlined the changes he had

[13] Misc. Letters, Vol. for 1843. In *C. G. Archives.*

made or hoped to make. On forwarding the report to Congress, Spencer declared that Fraser already had established

> order and system. Economy in expenditures and efficiency in service have been greatly promoted. The officers and men feel that the service has been elevated, and a corresponding zeal in the discharge of their duty has been strikingly exhibited.[14]

Regarding ships, Fraser's report explained a radical break with the past: the construction of iron steamers. Fraser inherited this innovation from the previous Treasury regime: as far back as 1840, the House of Representatives had instructed its Committee on Naval Affairs to inquire into the expediency of employing armed steamers in the Revenue Service, and Spencer's predecessor had introduced the new construction policy in 1842, but no new cutters had been launched when Fraser arrived in Washington. In 1842, such a building program was extremely daring. But Fraser supported the plan. He enumerated the advantages of iron as compared with wood in ship construction. He cited the famous English experiment with the iron-hulled *Aaron Manby*. He mentioned the costliness of repairs and replacements occasioned by dry rot in wooden vessels. Particularly on southern stations, borers and rot ruined wooden ships in short order—sometimes in less than six years. He compared known costs for iron cutters, and he rightly concluded that, in the long run, iron had the edge in economy. Further, he cited the increasing use of steam propulsion and its many advantages over sail. As an example, he mentioned that smugglers in steamers often got away from sailing cutters by running the tortuous inside passages along the coast, where wind ships could only make headway slowly. For several years there had been talk of building steam revenue vessels; to Fraser they became positive necessities in the brightening dawn of a new technology. In January 1844 he was able to report that steam cutter construction was six months underway.

[14] *Report,* January 9, 1844, in file of Secretary's Letters, 1844. In *C. G. Archives.* Published as *H.R. Doc. No. 45, 28 Cong., 1 sess.*

CHAPTER IV

Smoke on the Horizon

THE PASSAGE of the Revenue-Marine from the age of wood and wind to that of smoke and slice-bars was a rough one, full of all the early disappointments and discouragements that characterized the same transition in the Navy and the merchant marine. Since it marks a picturesque phase in service history and contrasts sharply with later technological times, its story is worth being told here in some detail.

Though Fraser approved the iron steamer policy, his advice and that of most of his officers was disregarded in the important matter of design. Fraser sponsored the radical change from sail to steam only because he knew that steamships daily were proving their worth. Side-wheelers had given a fairly consistent performance up to date. For a generation—punctuated, it is true, by frequent boiler explosions—side-wheelers had run the inland waterways, and for more than a decade they had been making money at sea. Though experience in steamship propulsion was limited, that which did exist was founded predominantly on side-wheel operation. But the decade of the 'forties was a period of high adventure in engineering. One episode dealt with the attack on the problem of underwater propulsion. Many adventurers thought up, sketched, and patented dubious methods; these they urged ship-owners, the Navy, and the Revenue-Marine to try out, on a royalty basis. Naturally, Fraser did not feel justified in spending federal money on mere dreams. He was fully aware that underwater propulsion (as contrasted with side-wheel) promised two major gains. First, it should reduce resistance to the passage of a ship through the water and, second, it should reduce danger to the propelling apparatus from gunshot. But the Captain felt responsible not for making the Revenue-Marine into an engineering laboratory but for providing the nation with reliable revenue-cutters. To him, as he looked over the engineering field, it appeared that all forms of propulsion except side-wheel were still in the world of fantasy. Fraser and most of his officers recommended side-wheel models for the new construction.

But powers over which the good Scot exerted no control accepted designs noteworthy for their abandonment of this principle. Two models were adopted, one offered by John Ericsson and one by a Lieutenant W. H. Hunter of the Navy. Both models, using steam as an auxiliary to sail, employed underwater methods of propulsion. The latter, of course, necessitated radical departures from the usual side-wheel practice in such important matters as shaft connections, engine speeds, and boiler pressures. In its own way, each model contributed to progress in marine engineering. The perspective of a hundred years makes choice of Ericsson's design, at least, seem somewhat less ill-advised than that choice appeared to Fraser. But the Captain had ample reason for maintaining that neither model had as yet proved satisfactory for active duty, and, whatever the degree of bias he may have brought to his view, the fact remains that disregard of his advice saddled the service with steamers whose failure

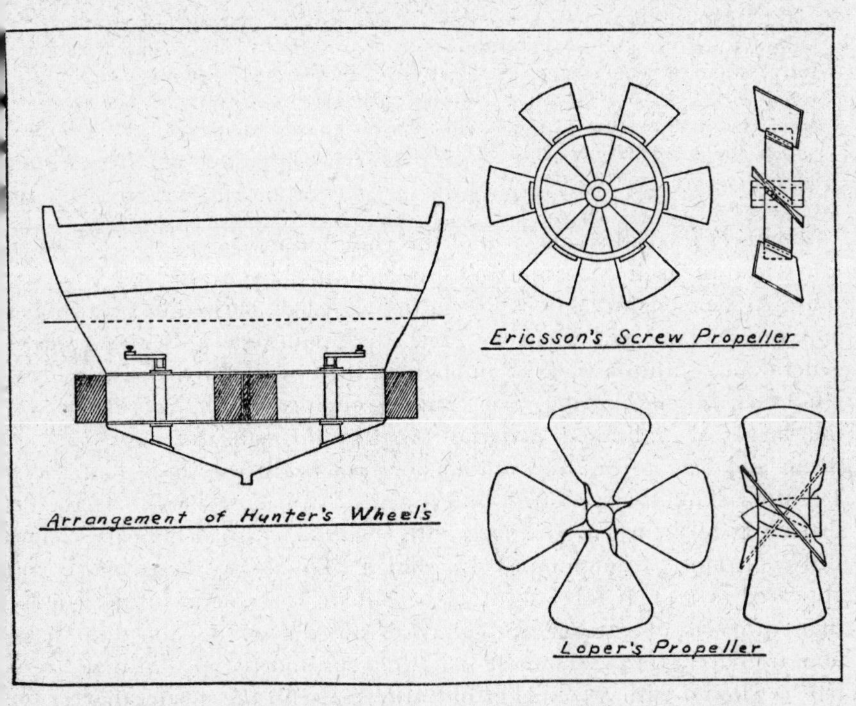

Hunter's Wheels and Ericsson's and Loper's Propellers
(From Bennett, *Steam Navy of the United States.*)

was so phenomenal that it delayed the profitable employment of steam in cutters for the next ten years.

As to the waste of public funds and the loss in efficiency in the Revenue-Marine's day-to-day operations which this failure incurred, Fraser had no illusions, and he could accept no long-range recompenses predicated on engineering progress. Forced in 1846 to defend the service and himself against the fiasco, he damned both models and their several proponents with a fine show of impartiality. Said he:

> Reposing confidence in the judgment and professional knowledge of those by whose advice the Honorable Secretary was governed, the vessels were commenced in the summer of 1843. . . . The projectors were allowed to

> carry their plans into execution without interference or restraint. . . . [The] service . . . has been made the unwilling vehicle through which every experimentalist in steam or naval architecture sought to introduce, at the public expense, plans which had either been denounced at their inception or abandoned after trial by practical men. . . . Remonstrance was made by those who were best qualified to judge, but . . . the contracts had been entered into; and I venture the assertion that there was not one of those who contracted to execute the work who did not from the first anticipate a failure. . . .
>
> I have been thus prolix on this subject for the purpose of placing it before Congress in its true and proper character. . . . In so doing, I am fully aware of what I am to expect from those whose interests are interfered with. . . . *But I have two points of duty to perform:* the first to the government, the other to the service of which I am a member; and *both of which shall be performed to the utmost of my ability, irrespective of all consequences.*[1]

Whatever the full inside story of this choice of models might have been, the selection itself was influenced at least in part by the spirit of the times. Marine engineering in the 'forties was characterized by great hopes and great plans and often by great disappointments. If there was a general and enthusiastic faith in engines, there was nonetheless a general ignorance of engineering, even among engineers. The world was on the brink of unlimited material progress through the harnessing of steam and iron to produce untold horsepower. In the three-quarters of a century since Watt, solid technical gains had been achieved. Here and there a factory turned its wheels with steam, a railroad bore its Puffing Billy, a mine steam-pumped its sludge. To almost everyone, steam appeared as a great force ready to be put to work for men. No wonder that enthusiasm for steam ran high. Everyone was talking and thinking—none too accurately—about the new colossus and its possibilities. Newspapers glowed with accounts of inventions, and in the 'forties devices for the use of steam in ships multiplied apace. Ericsson's and Hunter's were only two of many.

Enthusiasm for steam ran high—but as yet there was no great or solid body of related knowledge to outline standards. Much basic investigation was in progress. Following Count Rumford, who around 1800 had suggested that heat was a mode of molecular motion, Carnot in 1824 had contributed important concepts on the relation of absolute temperatures to efficiency, but these long escaped attention. Joule in 1843 published his first determination of the mechanical equivalent of heat. The next year, the year the new cutters were launched, the Chevalier de Pambour published his *Théorie de la Machine à Vapeur,* held by

[1] *Revenue Marine Service Annual Report, 1846;* published as *H.R. Doc. No. 17, 29 Cong., 2 Sess.* (Ritchie and Hiess, print.) (Italics ours).

Thurston to have been "the first logical theory of the steam-engine." Sir William Thompson, Hirn, Clausius, and the great Rankine did not make their most important contributions to the theory of heat engines until nearly ten years later.[2]

Thus, in the early 'forties, although people knew that workable engines had been tinkered together, and although "professors" catered with popularly-priced lectures to the public demand for knowledge of the wonders of steam, the fact is that organized knowledge on the subject was very scarce. Of inventions, both of new gadgets for steam engines and of new ways of putting steam engines to work, there was a swelling stream. Adventurers and cranks elbowed practical experimenters for the limelight. Every crackpot with a cylinder and a boiler hitched together could style himself "inventor," talk fast, and hope to make a million. And in that day there were few men qualified to say just who was and who was not a *bona fide* engineer. Because the field was ripe for quackery, charlatans threw off the trappings of medicine men and astrologists and wriggled into the ranks of engineers. Grete de Francesco, in his authoritative work *"The Power of the Charlatan,"* offers the following *exposé*:

> When sciences are in that critical stage when they seem to hold out unlimited opportunities to whet the desires of the masses, the charlatan always steps in. He now turned to mechanics, as it began to broaden out into technology . . . the alchemy of the new generation. . . . The excited imagination of Americans, playing with the future of science, was accordingly to be exploited by quacks in the nineteenth century. . . .[3]

Almost anybody's guess as to the value of an invention was as good as another's. Tested standards (whereby the performance either of the Ericsson propeller, of the Hunter wheel, or of the engine-and-boiler combinations used to drive them, might have been forecast or compared) did not exist.

Even if Ericsson and Hunter had dreamed dreams of perfect power plants, innumerable obstacles tending towards failure lay between plans and accomplishment in 1843. In 1790, Hamilton's ten cutters had been built to fairly generally accepted standards. Constructed by different men at different places to no single detailed plan, nevertheless they had fallen into a fairly definite class. Designers of the iron steamers of 1843 had few established standards to guide them. Lack of tested experience in building with iron and powering with steam made *every* new ship in that day something of an engineering adventure, a job for a pioneer.

[2] R. H. Thurston, *A History of the Growth of the Steam Engine* (D. Appleton & Co., New York, 1902), 456.

[3] *The Power of the Charlatan* (Yale Univ. Press, New Haven, 1939), 229 *et. seq.* For a typical "professor's" lecture notice, see Washington (D.C.) *National Intelligencer* for January 25, 1843.

Some technical problems which arose must have discouraged even the most optimistic and ingenious of those engineers-*sans*-handbooks.[4]

Not until about 1850, for one thing, were American machine-shops and machinists equipped and able to turn out precise work in the new medium, iron. Most of the necessary tools were available—the lathe for some time had been adapted to working iron, and Nasmyth had produced the steam hammer in 1839. By that date, the machinist had a fairly full kit of metal-working tools. But it takes a generation or two at the very least for men to assimilate such radical changes in techniques as those attending the transition from wood to iron as the world's dominant material. In 1843, American machinists were on the threshold of a new era but they still placed their main dependence on manual forging-and-filing to produce the ultimate in precision.

By 1843, a beginning had been made towards standardization of screws, bolts, parts, and scantlings, but standardization as it existed a century later was an ideal scarcely appreciated or even forecast. Lack of tested standards for scantlings allowed each new design in iron to run the risk either of being too weak or too massive. In 1843, designers were forced to rely more on "judgment," as they called it, than on experimentally derived knowledge of the proper size and shape for structural parts, both in hulls and in power plants. When they made their structures too light, disaster followed; when they made them too heavy, they increased weight, draft, and initial cost, reduced speed and buoyancy, and ran up the cost per mile of operation. The usual tendency was to err in this direction.

On a broader front, the relation of power and form to speed and resistance of ships, small knowledge existed. The beautifully curved hull forms of sailing vessels like the *Joe Lane* ("queen of sailing cutters," described in a later chapter) were evolved by experience. The wind ship constructor sometimes described the product of his art in mathematical terms and preserved the record as a reminder when building similar vessels, but, in general, as he cut the lines of each new ship he was more an artist than an engineer. He brought a touch, rather than a reasoned exactitude, to his work. With the advent of the costly and unfamiliar iron steamship, however, precise mathematical relations between power, form, and speed of vessels were needed if each new ship were not to be

[4] On early marine engineering, see esp. S. C. Gilfillan, *Inventing the Ship* (Follett Publishing Co., Chicago, 1935); George W. Dyson, "Charles H. Haswell and the Steam Navy," in *U. S. Naval Institute Proceedings,* February, 1939; Charles H. Cramp, in *North American Review,* April, 1894; Rear Admiral H. G. Bowen, *"100 Years of Steam in the U. S. Navy"* (a Newcomen Address; New York, 1937); W. C. Church, *Life of John Ericsson* (Scribner's, New York, 1911); F. M. Bennett, *The Steam Navy of the United States* (Nicholson Press, Pittsburgh, Pa., 1896).

either identical with some prototype or else a pure experiment. If the former, progress would be impeded; if the latter, costs might be alarmingly high. Efforts had been made to determine these relations prior to 1843, but not until 1856, by his famous experiments, did William Froude make possible the mathematical comparison of ships and the investigation of ship performance by towing models in a tank. "Judgment" and rule o' thumb were the best guides Ericsson and Hunter had as they laid the keels of the first steam cutters.

When it came to the selection and lay-out of machinery they may well have prayed for guidance divine. Essentially Watt-type, single-cylinder, low-pressure, slow-moving engines had to be fitted aboard each particular ship to best probable advantage. The bulky engines of 1843 had nearly as heavy mechanical losses as the engines of Watt's day. Huge pistons, imperfectly fitted and extremely heavy moving parts, multitudes of cranks, levers, cogs, and bearings through which power was transmitted—all these added up to immense dissipations of energy. Horizontal or oscillating cylinders took great quantities of grease—but the tallows and vegetable oils available were far below the standards of later lubricants. At high temperatures the early lubricants broke down into fatty acids and attacked the engine parts. If the plant employed a surface condenser, some of the excess lubricant carried over to the boilers, where it coated the heating surfaces with a non-conducting film and the acids ate away the boiler structure. Low pressure operation gave some protection to the lubricant but reduced plant efficiency. Jet condensation permitted operation at somewhat higher pressures, but this was an even more wasteful process, for all the exhaust heat units were spurted overboard with the condensate and lost. In addition, craftsmanship for producing iron or steel boilers thoroughly reliable at high pressures was lacking, as was steel in suitable quantities and shapes. Low pressures, heavy mechanical and thermal losses, discouragingly low plant efficiencies, and high fuel consumption, therefore, characterized most steam plants of the time.

Other difficulties faced designers in the choice of accessories and auxiliaries. Numerous patented products, many of unproved worth, were available. For instance, there were several types of "cut-off" on the market. Intuition, perforce, rather than accurate performance data, was often the guide to selection. In 1843, the designer had to make his pet accessories fit his plant and his plant fit his ship as best he could. And often the result was something of a jig-saw puzzle. Probably both luck and genius were determining factors in the choices involved. Thus Fulton in his designs used, misused, and failed to use many good ideas put forth by other men. Here lay the beginning and often the end of reputations involved in inventing the steamship. Applied mechanics, metallurgy, and many other sciences brought certainty to the designer's "judgment" in the century after 1843 and reduced the gambling spirit that once unavoidably characterized the profession.

A great deal of this spirit must have entered into the award of contracts for the first steam cutters. Mixed with the skullduggery that Fraser implied there was certainly ignorance and beyond doubt a large measure of buoyant enthusiasm for every wild promise of engineers. But the Ericsson and Hunter models were not as completely untried as Fraser's bitter comments might lead one to believe. The great innovation of each model was its peculiar device for underwater propulsion. Each inventor had seen his own propeller drive ships before he contracted for the cutters. Each had a number of enthusiastic and reputedly practical men among his supporters. John Ericsson, designer of the *Legare* and *Jefferson,* will be introduced first.

While residing in England about 1836, Ericsson, a Swedish engineer, had installed a screw-propeller on a small tug which attained a speed of 10 knots on its trial trip. Faced with the apathy and ironclad conservatism of the British Admiralty towards his achievement, he came a few years later to the United States, at the insistence of Captain John F. Stockton, U.S.N. In 1842, Ericsson constructed the U.S.S. *Princeton* and equipped her with an Ericsson screw—the first screw-propelled warship the world had seen. This vessel logged 14 knots on her trials, carrying 11 pounds of steam. She signalized a rather rapid acceptance of the screw. Six steamers were fitted with Ericcson screws in 1841, 9 in 1842, and nearly 30 in 1843.

Obviously, many people had faith in Ericsson's designs, and their faith, as records indicate, was by no means based on failures. Ericsson was changing the course of marine engineering. He was known in his day as a great designer, a great engineer. His word carried authority in engineering matters. His *Princeton* had made 14 knots. Though his cutters, the *Legare* and *Jefferson,* must be classified as experiments, they certainly were not the "wretched" experiments Fraser later dubbed them as he damned the whole Ericsson-Hunter program. Ericsson's achievements, his reputation, and his undoubted ability gave considerable justification to acceptance of his model.

Bennett, in his history, *The Steam Navy of the United States,* describes the Ericsson screw as follows:

> It was composed of a cast brass hub with six arms, the latter being surrounded by a copper band or drum, on which six brass blades were riveted. . . . Both arms and blades were of true helicoidal twist.

This was neither the first nor the last screw design; John Stevens, for instance, in 1804 had designed a simple screw that worked. Ericsson's was merely a complicated version of the screw-propeller idea. In the development of the modern screw, Gilfillan's *Inventing the Ship* records frequent reversions towards the simplicity of the Stevens model. Experience proved this a profitable trend; Bennett, for example, cites experiments on the *Princeton* in 1845 that showed the "common" screw (probably a simple Stevens-like 4-blade type without Ericsson's drum) to be around 11 percent more efficient than Ericsson's propeller. While the latter as installed on the *Legare* certainly was off the path of simplicity, it worked fairly well and filled in some of the unknown territory between the crude experiments of 1804 and the precisely balanced, accurately gauged, high-speed screws of a later day.

Though only fragmentary official records of the *Legare* remain and though no pictures have been discovered, some idea of the vessel can be formed from the following news item found in the *Army and Navy Chronicle and Scientific Repository* for October 19, 1843:

IRON SHIPS FOR GOVERNMENT SERVICE

We visited yesterday, one of the vessels now being built of iron in this city [New York], for the United States Revenue Service. The vessel is clinker built; length 140 feet [on deck], depth 10½, width of beam 24½, 330 tons measurement, and to be fitted with Ericsson's propellers of about 3½ feet in length. She is now in a very favorable condition for exhibiting the mode of construction, and the strength and character of the work. Her ribs are of wrought iron 4½ inches by ¾ inch, placed at a distance from 18 to 20 inches apart; the sheet iron, which is attached to the outside of these ribs and forms the shell of the vessel, ⅜ths of an inch thick, the end joints of which about flush, and are connected by a lap piece passing over the joint on the inside 4½ inch wide and ⅜ths thick; seams overlap 2 inches; the rivets are ¾ of an inch diameter, and are hammered firmly to their places while in a heated state; there being portable forges for that purpose. The sheeting is punched and the holes countersunk with the greatest exactness by a machine. The shell is fastened to the ribs by iron knees firmly bolted to both. The whole arrangement presents the appearance of great strength, and is calculated to produce the fullest confidence in the security of this character of vessels. The model of the vessel to our eye is not only perfect, but beautiful. Ships of iron have many advantages over those of wood, and we look with interest to these first efforts at their introduction into our navy [sic], but with the fullest confidence in the result.—*N.Y. Courier*.

Another item in the *Chronicle's* issue for April 18, 1844, reports the launching:

LAUNCH OF AN IRON REVENUE CUTTER

An iron ship, for the Revenue Service of the United States, was launched from H. R. Dunham & Company's Iron Works, at the foot of 33rd St. N. R., New York, on the 6th instant, at eleven a.m. She is 360 tons burthen, 140 feet long, and is pronounced by judges to be one of the best models of naval architecture ever seen.

The journalist who reported on the lines of the new iron steamer (the *Jefferson* was similar in design) conceivably was influenced by the fact that "during the construction of the *Legare* her model was approved of by several of the most eminent ship builders and Captains in this City." Intuition rather than tested experience necessarily was the basis of such approval. No doubt the Ericsson model was seaworthy enough under steam alone. "The officers who have served on board the *Legare* [were] . . . loud in their praise of her sea-going qualities and Captain Fraser himself [said] . . . the *Jefferson* . . . in a sea-way performs admirably."[5] The *Legare* ended her days as a lightship at Pass Mary Ann, which duty in itself was something of a test of seaworthiness. But Ericsson was a *steam*-ship builder; his last thought was of sails, although the service needed them on its first steamers both for economy and range. The *Legare* was a poor sailer—not quite as bad as Hunter's monstrosities, perhaps, but like them too narrow of beam "to sustain her under a press of canvas. [Her dimensions] . . . *for sailing vessels* be ridiculed by naval architects."[6]

As to the *Legare's* power plant, little factual information exists. It is known that her horizontal engine had a cylinder 36 inches in diameter and a 32 inch stroke. Thirty-eight pounds of steam cut off at about half stroke gave 38 r.p.m., producing 9.04 miles per hour at a cost of 630 pounds of coal. This pressure was considered quite high at the time; the Navy carried only around 10 pounds. A Stevens cut-off was used. Ericsson was limited to jet condensation originally, but in 1847 he was permitted to install an "independent action" surface condenser of original design, from which he obtained an improved vacuum and higher plant efficiency resulting in a saving of almost 10% in fuel. He was also limited in the size of his cylinders. (These restrictions were placed in order to form a basis of comparison with Hunter's vessels.) Forced draft with closed fire-room was used; the blower was belt-driven from a small blower engine.[7]

On one exploit, at least, the *Legare* could lay claim to an important measure of success. This was her race with the British side-wheel steamer *Great Western*. The latter was already famous. The first steam vessel built for regular transatlantic service, she had had a record of successful crossings since April 1838. Her performance of 9 knots under sail and paddle-wheel was well-established. The race between the *Great Western* and *Legare* was a race between side-paddles and propeller, between past and future, between acknowledged achievement and "wretched" experiment. The *Legare* won. Ericsson notices:

[5] Ericsson letter dated February 13, 1846. In *C. G. Archives*.
[6] Fraser, quoted in Smith, *op. cit.*, 60. (Italics ours.)
[7] Articles of Agreement (Ericsson contract), April 22, 1843; Articles of Agreement (Ericsson contract), May 7, 1847. In *C. G. Archives*.

> her run with the steam ship *Great Western* from New York to Sandy Hook—a distance of 18 miles—on the 20th July 1844. On this occasion the *Legare* had all her sails furled while the *Great Western,* the wind being fair, had her principal sails set. In leaving the Battery the *Legare* allowed the *Great Western* to get half a mile ahead—she then made chase, overtook and passed her competitor and arrived at Sandy Hook under bare poles in 1 hour and 27 minutes from the time of leaving the Battery; taking the lead of the *Great Western* by nearly a mile! On making this trial run the *Legare* was bound for the South and equipped for sea, with full complement of coal on board. . . . To my knowledge there is no sea-going paddle wheel steamer of the dimensions and immersed cross-section of the *Legare* that has ever attained a greater speed than that vessel during her trial run with the *Great Western*—nor is there a single steam frigate in the British Navy at this moment capable of making such a speed with war equipment and a full complement of coal on board.[8]

Certainly not the last word in propulsion, the *Legare's* propeller by its victory over the *Great Western's* paddles did help demonstrate the possibility of ultimate success with an underwater method.

Despite all this, the *Legare* was definitely a failure as a revenue-cutter. As a sailer she could not carry canvas, and as a steamer she was quite unreliable. The latter fault lay in the fact that propeller drive required higher engine speeds and consequently higher pressures than the side-wheel installations on which marine engineering experience was based and to which the materials of the day were adapted. While sea-going side-wheelers turned at only about 20 r.p.m. and carried possibly 15 pounds of steam, the *Legare* turned up 40-50 r.p.m. and carried around 40 pounds. This slight difference was revolutionary in 1844. Packing that was tight at 15 pounds pressure blew out at 40. Bearings that ran fairly cool at 20 r.p.m. would fry eggs at 50. Lubricants broke down more quickly at the higher speeds and temperatures. Boilers scaled up, foamed, and primed at 40 pounds while they steamed fairly satisfactorily at only 15 or so. What was more, plant lay-out experience was all with side-wheel installations; despite Ericsson's genius he undoubtedly made numerous bad guesses in his over-all design. Finally, operating engineers experienced in handling such a revolutionary power plant were few and far between; the *Legare's* black gang learned exclusively on the job. Obviously, far greater skill and more attentive watch-standing were required by the quick-moving engine of the *Legare* than by some long-stroked, slow-moving side-wheeler. And efficient watch-standers cannot be produced in a flash. The *Legare* was fortunate to last out several years of troubled service. A burnt-out boiler was her final agony before decommissioning eased her pain.

Very little of credit can be said of the four cutters designed by Lieu-

[8] Ericsson letter, *op. cit.*

tenant Hunter, although it must be mentioned that Hunter had fairly influential support and considerable backing from well-known engineers who pinned great hopes on his horizontal wheels. The ill-starred *Spencer, Bibb, McLane,* and *Dallas* were his productions. But whereas Ericsson had had considerable success with his propeller before he installed it on a cutter, Hunter's experimental U.S.S. *Union* (built for the Navy) had produced more enthusiasm than its trials justified. In the fabulous 'forties, reports of steam trials sometimes took on a lyric quality:

> There was something very mysterious about the appearance of this vessel [the *Union*] as, without any outward show of her locomotive power, she silently glided away from the wharf, leaving a wake so placid that an egg-shell might have ridden upon it in safety. . . . You could hardly realize that the vessel is in motion or the engine at work. So free are we from all the disagreeable jarring and noises of ordinary steamers, that any old lady accustomed to the sound of her coffee-mill might cross the ATLANTIC with us without endangerment of her nerves.[9]

> [The *Union's*] movement was beautiful, and so unlike the ordinary motion of steamers that we could scarcely believe we were steaming. Her motion was like that of a well-broken horse, that raises you not from the saddle. She really moved along like a thing of life, and almost as consciously graceful as a belle of the Avenue.[10]

Captain W. A. Howard of the Revenue-Marine, detailed to observe the performance of the *Union* on a run from Norfolk to Boston, reported the speed under canvas alone as equal to that of "any pilot boat" and the steaming qualities "incomparable."

But all these beautiful flights of hope, superlative, and simile could not help the Hunter model. Bennett, a tougher-minded critic than those quoted above, reports that the *Union* "was unable to develop a better average than 5 knots . . . with a favorable wind she made on some occasions 9 or 10." Captain Howard alone among Revenue-Marine officers favored Hunter's design; Fraser's *Annual Report* for 1846 classified Howard's advocacy as "hasty and ill-advised." Hunter's "submerged wheels" were no more than horizontal paddle wheels fitted in trunks in the vessel's hull so that the paddle-tips projected beyond the skin of the ship. The lower end of each wheel-shaft fitted in a bearing, or step, and the other end formed a crank to which an engine gave motion. When the wheel revolved, the paddle-tips one after another cleared the skin of the ship and pushed the vessel along. Obviously, much power was lost in sloshing the water around in the trunks; Bennett estimates the

[9] Washington (D.C.) *National Intelligencer,* January 17, 1843.

[10] Naval Constructor Francis Grice, quoted in *National Intelligencer,* February 23, 1843.

loss at 50 to 70%. Although possibly the *Union* could make 9 knots for short distances with her boilers panting, she could not equal even the *Legare's* performance under steam. Nor could Hunter's cutters, the *Spencer, Bibb, McLane,* and *Dallas.* These suffered from high shaft speeds even more than the *Legare* did, and their trunk cavities made them cranky under sail. In retrospect, it appears that the *Legare* was a far better ship than any that Hunter built, and that entirely objective, scientific critiques of the *Union* under sustained power and varying conditions would have exposed many faults and discouraged completely all thought of purchasing submerged-wheelers.

Remaining evidence on the performance of Hunter's cutters underlines the mid-century's lack of experience and materials for handling high pressures and engine speeds. For instance, the *Spencer's* top of 50 r.p.m. would send her rolling down the Narrows at 6-28/157 miles an hour, but at this speed, Fraser said, the "rabbit's metal" melted in the journal. (The *Legare* made 8-92/110 miles an hour on the same run.) The *Spencer* was supposed to carry upwards of 100 pounds of steam (about double the *Legare's* pressure), but, as might have been expected, the boiler foamed, primed, and salted up so viciously that it was seldom forced above 40 or 50 pounds. Further, the throttle stuck at pressures over 50. And although the *Legare* could make 9 knots on about 630 pounds of coal per hour, the *Spencer* in 43 hours of steaming at various speeds averaged half a ton per hour. With temperatures in summer ranging above 125°F on the floor-plates, the coal-passers must have sweated nearly ton for ton with the fuel supplied.

The following contract signed with the West Point Foundry Association on July 25, 1843, describes the *Spencer's* plant:

> Two Horizontal High Pressure Engines, cylinders 24 inches diameter, 3 feet stroke, fitted on cast iron frames and attached to two submerged propellers on the plan known as *Hunter's,* of ten feet diameter and 3 feet wide, paddle of wheel 12 inches deep, the Engines to be connected to one wrought iron Boiler 23 feet long and 8 feet diameter of shell, to contain not less than 1400 feet of fire surface, and calculated for Anthracite or Bituminous Coal. Smoke pipe not to extend more than 15 feet above deck, and a fan, driven by a separate engine, to be used in place of natural draft. The whole of said Machinery to be fitted in its place, and put in operation on board said Revenue Vessel for the sum of sixteen thousand dollars ($16,000) to include cast iron floor for Engine and fire room, and such oil tanks, tools, and appendages as may be required for the Engines and Boilers.[11]

Captain Fraser commanded the *Spencer* on her trial cruise in September 1844, and Chief Engineer William W. Wood nursed her mill along. To his Steam Journal, Chief Wood confided his tribulations:

[11] In *C. G. Archives.*

> Fired up, in the harbor of New York, and weighed anchor. Started the engines at 11:30 a.m., arrived at the lightship at 4 h. 9m. p.m. Altogether steaming 3 h. and 37 m.; coal consumed including 900 lbs. used in raising steam, 5 tons 800 lbs.; Pressure of steam on the boiler from 75 to 80 lbs. per inch; each engine averaging (cutting off at 1/3 stroke) from 53 to 54 revolutions; blowers were worked from 350 to 400 revolutions; boilers foaming so as to render it impossible to work full stroke or cut off at ½ stroke. Found no difficulty in keeping steam at the above pressure, but could not steam any longer without cleaning out the furnaces, and the arches of the boiler having settled deemed it prudent not to carry more than 55 or 60 lbs. per inch on the boiler until stay bolts were put in to secure them. Thermometer in the engine room averaging 112°F.
>
> Cleaned out the furnaces and started from lightship under steam and canvas. One engine only woıking without any effect [sic]; the starboard engine being closely shut off, the rabbit's metal having melted out of the brasses of main-shaft pillow block. Detained one hour with belt of blowing engine. . . . Average pressure, 45 lbs. average revolutions, 40.
>
> [Later] Engines in order, fired up. Pressure 60 lbs. The blow off pipe leading from the safety valve blown into the engine room, the valve having stuck up, and it being impossible to go below and shut it. The belt of the blowing engine being burned up, was delayed until evening. . . .
>
> [Later] Fired up. Started engines with 12 lbs. pressure. After putting on a new gum-elastic belt on blowing engine, worked up steam to 45 lbs., the square inch. Took in sail. Revolutions of engines 45, boilers foaming so as to destroy much of the working effect in the engines.
>
> Some alterations are essentially necessary, as well as some repairs, arising from such parts being so constructed as to wear and give way after a few hours working of the engines.

Similar difficulties were experienced with the other submerged-wheelers. In the Mexican War the *McLane* distinguished herself as a crank ship: while maintaining the blockade of Tabasco she was forced to lie for several months "moored in the river near Frontera and unable from defects in machinery to have escaped had an attack been made."[12]

Attempts were made to salvage something of the Government's investment in these ships. The *Bibb, Dallas,* and *McLane* were altered to side-wheels. The engines were not re-located, but their motion was re-directed through cog-wheel gearing. The patchwork job done on the *McLane,* declared Fraser, "was the greatest failure and blunder of the whole fleet, having neither speed, stability, or capacity for carrying fuel." The *Spencer* was altered to use a propeller invented by a Captain Loper. Thus rigged, she was the first twin-screw iron steamer ever used in government service. However, none of these forlorn hopes was successful, chiefly because of the many new mechanical difficulties each introduced. Both types of alteration required complicated cogs and gears to accom-

[12] *Annual Report, Revenue-Marine Service, 1848;* published as *H.R. Ex. Doc. No. 30, 30 Cong., 1 Sess.*

DEFENDING THE *Eagle* IN THE WAR OF *1812*

(From a mural by Aldis B. Browne, II, in Satterlee Hall, U. S. Coast Guard Academy.)

ATTACKING A *Seminole Indian* STRONGHOLD

(From a mural by Aldis B. Browne, II, in Satterlee Hall, U. S. Coast Guard Academy.)

Model of Doughty's 80-ton Cutter *Dallas,* 1815
(Courtesy of The Mariners' Museum, Newport News, Va.)

Cover-sheet, *"The Cutter Hamilton Quick-Step"*
(Published *c.* 1845, in Boston, by Oliver Ditson.)

Salvageable
(From a L.-S.S. lantern slide, *c.* 1880.)

Life-car in Operation
(From a L.-S.S. lantern slide, *c.* 1880.)

U.S. Revenue-Cutter *Forward*

(Engraved on stone by J. Childs and printed by F. Kuhl, of Philadelphia, *c.* 1850.)

Sidewheel Cutter Overhauling Smuggler

(From a painting by an unknown artist, in Satterlee Hall, U. S. Coast Guard Academy.)

modate Hunter's engines to the new drives. The result was compound failure.

A total of eight cutters was constructed under the first iron steamer program; two, the *Polk* and *Walker* (thus far not mentioned), were side-wheelers. Fraser might have hoped these two would be satisfactory, but they were cheap jobs and their iron construction departed from American builders' experience. The *Polk's* hull was improperly fastened, and she leaked so copiously as to endanger the vessel. Her machinery was much too heavy for her size. The *Walker* was unloaded on the Coast Survey as soon as possible; later, she was run down and sunk off Barnegat.

The six hundred twenty thousand dollars spent on these experiments seemed to Fraser more than trifling, particularly since he was saddled with a blame not his own and was forced to accept temporary defeat of a project close to his heart. However, a longer view might well be taken: the money was spent for experience sorely needed in the United States and in the world at that time, a critical period in the transition from sail to steam. It is to be regretted only that the experimentation was performed on so wide a scale; one iron ship for each type of drive would have been a more reasonable beginning. Even so, the lessons learned were surely worth the price.

For one thing, the dramatic failure of these steamers crystallized the policy (first laid down by Captain Fraser) of building into cutters only engineering methods thoroughly tested and backed by accurate performance data. Never again was the service made to accept a whole fleet built on wishful thinking. Although the cutter branch chalked up numerous "firsts" in engineering subsequent to 1844 (among them the world's first synchronous turbo-electric drive [*Tampa,* 1923], first sea-going turbo-electric central power plant [*Ponchartrain,* 1928], and first bridge-controlled, entirely automatic, turbo-electric synchronous drive [*Owasco,* 1945]), these ventures were based on exhaustive preliminary research and on a far more mature brand of engineering than existed in Fraser's day. The *Legare* and *Spencer,* smudging their way across their last horizon, symbolized the necessity of supplementing speculation with tested knowledge as the basis for engineering progress.

The cost of the first steam cutters paid for a little of this knowledge. It paid for lessons in laying out machinery for propeller drive, for experience in designing iron ships, for information concerning high pressures and engine speeds, and for practice in handling relatively quick-moving machinery. These ships helped prove the necessity of compromise in features of hull design for vessels combining sail and steam. In addition, the program introduced iron hulls, surface condensers, and twin screws into the American services.

Finally, the *Legare* and *Jefferson's* tiny measure of success—and particularly the rather dramatic race between the *Legare* and *Great Western*—gave a basis of substantial accomplishment to encourage and guide future development of underwater propulsion. Even Fraser, contending that the Ericsson-Hunter designs were worthless as revenue-cutters, was forced to express his astonishment that such small wheels could propel large vessels rapidly and to admit his conviction that the principle of underwater propulsion had merit.

Few of these recompenses for the failure of the steam cutter program recommended themselves, however, to the good Captain. Convinced that the program had been sabotaged by ill-advised experimenting, Fraser preferred a return to sail rather than further traffic with inventions. But he continued steadfastly to recommend side-wheel cutters. After the Mexican War, the eight iron steamers wheezed and clanked their way speedily into limbo. Congress made replacements with sailing cutters tried and true; for ten years or more, the Revenue Service remained in sail. Then the side-wheel *Harriet Lane* came off the ways and vindicated the Scot's judgment. But his eventful career brought him other satisfactions before that day arrived.

CHAPTER V

High Tide—

ALTHOUGH he was the target for considerable censure as a result of the steamer trouble, Captain Fraser retained his post as Chief of the Revenue-Marine Bureau for several years. Even for awhile after 1844, when Secretary Spencer left the Treasury, the Captain managed to keep enough political support to insure continuance of his policies. But while Spencer was in office, Fraser had all the encouragement and backing any Commandant might need.

Together, he and the Secretary formed a splendid team. Both were men of vision, and, in a day when sectional loyalties were strong, both thought primarily in *national* terms. It was Spencer, for instance, who had invented Fraser's job of Chief of the centralized Bureau. Spencer admitted that the work of directing the cutters had been perplexing to him and had forced him to bring in a maritime expert to carry on the detailed administration. He had been able

> to appreciate the advantages . . . which must flow from the establishment of a Bureau in the Treasury Department, with a chief practically and professionally acquainted with the Revenue Service and possessed of the varied information in relation to our coast, our harbors, and their waters, our coasting trade and foreign commerce.[1]

The two men worked together to give the service a strong centralized administration, to extend its operations within the zone outlined by Congress, to improve its equipment, and to insure competency in its personnel. With such support, Fraser was able to operate the Revenue-Marine as a truly national coast guard, very similar in general pattern to the Coast Guard which in time actually did emerge.

The basis of the Spencer-Fraser reorganization was laid in the *Regulations* they issued in 1843. The *Regulations* of 1834 had been loosely drawn and inadequately enforced. The new ones revised and amplified the old in the light of experience and, in addition, placed restrictions on the collectors' authority and installed a system of reporting and accounting to Washington by the cutter captains. What was more, disrupting old practice, Fraser intended to enforce the new rules uniformly throughout the service.

In this he met resistance both from collectors and from a few officers set in older ways. Notable among the latter was Winslow Foster. This

[1] Letter, Spencer to Fraser, May 6, 1844. In *C. G. Archives.*

salty old sun-downer had gotten his first command as far back as 1821, when Washington exerted no control through regulations or bureau staffs. Foster had a long record of faithful service and a sound reputation as a hell-or-high-water sailorman. But he was not accustomed to looking in a book to find out how to run a ship, and he had an antipathy to bureaucratic control. The fact that Fraser was his junior in point of service made him no less restive when called upon to follow policies and detailed orders issued by the Bureau Chief. He never could—or never would—accommodate himself to the new demands.

Foster represented an era which was passing—an era of wooden ships, of decentralization, and of arbitrary power on the quarterdeck. His officers were men of a new age—age of iron, of integration, and of authority legally bestowed and exercised. While Foster could rant that

> the regulations of the Service are a miserable compilation framed by a set of fawning pimps at Washington such as Fraser, Howard, and others, to tickle the ears of John C. Spencer,[2]

his officers and many another within the service welcomed Fraser's *Regulations* and policy of enforcement. They felt that these measures were required by the public interest and that they added a new dignity and responsibility to all concerned.

A major item on the Spencer-Fraser agenda was their determined approach to a merit system of promotion; the new deal provided for promotion by examination before a board of officers. Further, original appointments were to be made henceforth only in the grade of third lieutenant. The new system was in operation at least by July 25, 1843.

Against the Spoils System, however, Fraser could make little headway. Some officers achieved advancement by passing professional examinations, but others continued to hew to the party line and to meet preferment or disappointment according to the political group in power.

But though Fraser could not prevent he could curtail political manipulation of the service. By using to the fullest possible extent his authority over promotions and expenditures he definitely reduced the influence of collectors and local politicians. Further, he aimed a blow at localism generally: he inaugurated the periodic transfer of officers to new stations in order that they might "acquire a perfect acquaintance with the whole" coast—and incidentally be cut loose from local politics.

As a corollary to the steamer program, Captain Fraser had the satisfaction of seeing Congress establish in 1845 the engineer corps he had requested in his first *Annual Report*. The engineers who had been employed for the steamers were now given recognition in the law. By

[2] Foster Trial, 1846, III, 6 of summation. In *C. G. Archives*.

and with the advice of the Senate, the President was authorized to appoint one chief engineer for each steamer in the service; the Secretary was empowered to appoint assistant engineers in the same number. Chief engineers were to receive the pay and allowances of first lieutenants of the line, and assistants were to get the same as third lieutenants of the line.[3] The first regularly appointed chief engineers were: W. W. Luke, P. H. Bonham, James Wright, Charles French, and Thomas Farron.

The same Act insured the professional competency of the line by providing that

> No person . . . be appointed to the office of Captain, first, second, and third lieutenants of any revenue cutter, who does not adduce competent proof of proficiency and skill in seamanship and navigation.

Not content with revitalizing the commissioned corps, the Spencer-Fraser regime took action to improve the welfare and morale of the enlisted force. A liberal, humanitarian spirit was growing in the world of Fraser's day and was demanding changes in the conditions of labor both at sea and on the shore. Fraser himself, liberal and humanitarian to the core, had little patience with the brutality and oppression that passed for a seagoing personnel policy at the time. In his new *Regulations* he hacked at the roots of existing wrongs. In one article, specifying "nor is any slave ever to be entered for the service," he cut the tap of an old, pernicious practice of shipping officers' slaves as personal attendants and paying their masters for their services; in another, he cracked down on flogging and other brutalities. These reforms tended to raise cutter men's self-esteem and pointed the way toward development of scientific methods of personnel management later on. Finally, not forgetting the material welfare and contentment of the men, Captain Fraser in his first annual report advocated that the petty officers' pay be raised to $30 a month from the $20 allowed under the schedule of 1799—an increase amply justified by the rise in living costs.

Captain Fraser seemed almost mindful of the shape of things to come when he arranged the (temporary) amalgamation of the Revenue-Marine and Lighthouse Establishment. Upon his arrival in Washington, he found the lighthouses under the control of the Fifth Auditor of the Treasury. Fraser rightly classed lighthouse administration as a job for maritime experts; he saw logic as well as practical advantage in unifying the two services. Less than a month after he became Chief of the Revenue-Marine he prevailed on Spencer to issue a general order (May 10, 1843) directing commanding officers of cutters to examine lighthouses and other aids to navigation. This work had been performed by cutters, from time to time, in the past. By stepping-up such inspection duty and

[3] Act of March 3, 1845 (5 Stat. L., 794).

by performing it regularly Fraser was able to demonstrate to George M. Bibb, Spencer's successor, the advantage of unifying the two services still further. On February 19, 1845, Bibb in effect ordered the transfer of the Lighthouse Establishment to the Revenue-Marine by directing that all communications regarding lighthouses be addressed thenceforth to the Chief of the Revenue-Marine Bureau.[4] Under the Bureau's direction, collectors of customs were to have superintendence of the lights in their respective districts just as they did of the cutters. Revenue-Marine officers were to continue as inspectors.

A sidelight on the performance of this new duty remains in the succinct report of Captain Andrew Mathew, commanding Revenue-Schooner *Ewing,* to Charles F. Lester, Superintendent of Lighthouses for New London District. Captain Mathew declared that on examining the lights at Mystic and Stonington he had found "the whole kept clean, the keepers correct"—hard-won praise, no doubt, from a Yankee skipper.

Spencer and Fraser acknowledged the enforcement of navigation laws as being a legitimate cutter activity. Their *Regulations* provided that

> the officers commanding revenue vessels will also examine the papers of coasting vessels, when practicable, to ascertain that they are correct and in force . . .

Acquaintance with the laws "it is their province to execute" was particularly recommended to all officers.

Although there is no reason to credit Fraser with having planned to build a system of shore life-saving stations into his Revenue-Marine, the fact remains that when the Bureau took over the lighthouses it did get a semblance of such a system. Lighthouse keepers in out-of-the-way places had long acted as volunteer life-savers. Congress had heard on good authority that

> it frequently happens that the keeper can render assistance to those that are shipwrecked or to vessels in distress.[5]

An Act in 1847 made "the first appropriation . . . for rendering assistance to the shipwrecked from the shore"; the Act placed $5000.00 at the disposal of the Secretary of the Treasury

> for furnishing the lighthouses on the Atlantic coast with means of rendering assistance to shipwrecked mariners.

But the Secretary did not turn these funds over to Fraser; had he done so, conceivably, Fraser and the lighthouse men might have established a systematized life-saving arm then and there.[6]

[4] Letters of the Secretary of the Treasury, Vol. for 1845; V, 33. In *C. G. Archives.*
[5] *Blunt's Coast Pilot,* quoted in *25 Cong., 2 sess., S. doc. 138.*
[6] Act of March 3, 1847 (9 Stat. L., 175, 176). This money was subsequently used to provide life-saving equipment for the Massachusetts Humane Society.

This opportunity the Captain lost because the letter of the law was not observed; he lost a similar opportunity because the letter of another was deficient. The Act of August 14, 1848, which Representative W. A. Newall steered through Congress, provided merely for the purchase of life-saving equipment (for New Jersey); no provision was made for its upkeep or use. It was to be left on the Jersey beach in the hope that it would be used by volunteers; its preservation was left to chance. Thus, although the Act stipulated that the funds appropriated ($10,000.00) should be expended by an officer of the Revenue-Marine, Captain Fraser as Chief of the Bureau had no authority and no money to work the new equipment into his administrative system.

While Mr. Newall's well-intentioned effort was giving the life-saving branch a false start, it did stimulate interest in life-saving apparatus and led to basic developmental work within that field. Captain Douglass Ottinger was designated by the Bureau to spend the appropriated funds, and he drew upon the New York Board of Underwriters for assistance in selecting suitable appliances. There were few items in those days from which to choose; the original outfits acquired under the Newall Act included only surfboats, corrugated iron life-cars, mortars (for shooting lines from shore to stranded ships), blue flares, and odds and ends of ship-chandlery.

Only the life-cars were unique. Ottinger knew that rescues through the surf by boat required experienced crews, men who had practiced together as a team, and he doubted that volunteers could always make up in willingness what they lacked in trained precision. Further, Atlantic storms could sometimes thwart the efforts even of a seasoned crew to put to sea. What was needed under any circumstance was an easy, fool-proof, all-weather appliance for bringing the survivors of wrecks quickly to the shore. The life-car was designed to meet this need. It was a cigar-shaped, water-tight, metal boat built to be hauled back and forth on a line between a wreck and a shore rescue party. This simple contraption, something of a cross between a porpoise and a submarine when underway in a surf, had many practical defects; it was replaced eventually by the breeches-buoy, an apparatus which proved especially useful in working to wrecks up to 300 yards or so offshore. But the life-car, historically one of the first appliances for the primary purpose of rescuing shipwrecked mariners, was such a simple gadget that it could be handled by a crew of rawest volunteers: it was definitely the answer to Ottinger's immediate problem. An *Annual Report* of the Life-Saving Service declares that it "demonstrated its merits on its first trial by rescuing over two hundred persons" from the wreck of the immigrant-ship *Ayrshire*.

To house these meager outfits, Ottinger built small boathouses at selected sites on the Jersey shore. These were the first federal life-saving stations; Station #1 was located on Spermacetti Cove, near Sandy Hook. Since no paid station crews were authorized, none were provided, and "Captain Ottinger, as any careful man would have done under the circumstances, left the key of each boathouse with someone, probably as suitable a man as he could find who would accept it, and left also with him a printed card of instructions as to the manner of using the articles."[7]

Like Ottinger, many officers were eager to support Fraser's policy of increasing the effectiveness of federal aid to shipping; Secretary Spencer himself commented upon the service's response to intelligent leadership in Washington. Obviously, without such support from most of the officers at sea, Fraser's administrative reforms would have had little practical effect. A mainstay was Josiah Sturgis, previously mentioned, the captain of Boston's beloved *Hamilton*. During this period Captain Sturgis became a by-word for zealous humanitarian work and assistance to shipping up and down the New England coast. Newspaper accounts, pamphlets, and "an original piece of music, entitled *Sturgis's Quick Step*", all testify to the popularity, gallantry, and skill of this fine old-time skipper. He kept a crack ship and an efficient, well-disciplined, contented crew. Said one enthusiastic pamphleteer:

> [he had] on board men who have sailed with him for many years. . . . Let it always be remembered by the despots who manufacture discipline with colts and cats that . . . flogging is unknown on board [the *Hamilton*], yet a better regulated crew or a neater vessel cannot be found upon the bosom of the ocean.[8]

The Captain's gallantry extended in spectacular fashion to the ladies of his wide acquaintance. According to his biographer, he had a penchant for inviting them on board and firing salutes in their honor, "his band, all the while, playing Hail Columbia happy land"—a practice which, to the untold loss of succeeding generations of officers, was never hallowed in the *Regulations*.

But Sturgis could afford to indulge in a few unauthorized salutes; his reputation rested on a peerless professional record. Here is a typical newspaper report of the sort which gradually transformed the skipper of the *Hamilton* into a legendary figure along his native shore:

> The services rendered by the U. S. cutter *Hamilton*, Captain Sturgis, during the past winter, have been the means of saving many lives and a vast amount of property. Having a perfect knowledge of the coast and experience of the dangers incident to shipping by a change of wind or a storm, Captain Sturgis always kept the cutter in a position where her services could be

[7] S. I. Kimball, quoted in *Senate Doc. No. 270, 55 Cong., 2 Sess.;* 14 see also Ottinger's Personnel File, in *C. G. Archives*.

[8] ——, *Brief Sketch of the Character and Services of Captain Josiah Sturgis, of the United States Revenue Service* (W. White and H. P. Lewis, Boston, 1844), a pamphlet, in Coast Guard Academy Library.

rendered most efficient in assisting vessels in distress. We hazard but little in asserting that he has rendered assistance to more than 100 vessels during the past winter. . . .

[*Examples:*]

On the 10th (February) the schooner *Seadrift,* of Duxbury, ashore on George's Island, was tendered assistance.

On the 11th, assisted the brig *New England,* of Boston, to come to anchor and furl sails, the crew having been disabled by the severity of the weather—and the next day got her underway and left men on board to work her up to Boston.

On the 21st, the ship *Hamilton* [not the cutter], of Boston, was discovered aground on Nix's Mate. Captain Sturgis brought the cutter to with both anchors, at a convenient distance ahead of the ship, had hawsers passed from the ship and secured to the cutter, and with the united efforts of both crews, after long and arduous exertions, hove her off into deep water, and assisted her to make sail. . . .

. . . only a few of the cases. . . . During a cruise of seventy days along the coast . . .

and so on and on, building tradition for the Coast Guard.[9]

During most of Fraser's duty in Washington the United States was at war. The Captain doubtless found some of his reforms set aside or delayed by the war effort and by the swelling currents of sectional dissension which that particular war evoked. And as Chief of the Bureau, Fraser must have amassed a great deal of war work of his own: dispatch of a sizeable cutter squadron to the scene of hostilities left plenty of slack to be taken out of the service's normal operations. Stations and cruising grounds had to be reassigned among the few remaining units, and increased supervision of operations was required. But if the war tended to interfere with the full flowering of the Captain's plans for improving the Revenue-Marine, it did give the cutters another opportunity to take their places alongside the Army, Navy, and Marines.

This time, at the dictate of "manifest destiny," the drums rolled for a war of agricultural imperialism. In the early 'twenties Stephen Austin had entered Texas and had dreamed there a great dream. After him flowed a stream of southerners looking for land and more land to grow more and more cotton; soon they too saw Austin's vision. Independent by 1836, the Lone Star Republic sought and obtained annexation to the United States in 1845. Tension between northern Whigs, abolitionists, and southern Democrats mounted dangerously with the admission of the new slave state, and south of the new border Mexican resentment ran high. The next year, U.S.-Mexican relations broke into a conflict which was immediately labelled by Lincoln as "unnecessarily and unconstitutionally commenced by the President" and by the plain-spoken Captain Winslow Foster as having been brought on by the "action of Congress

[9] *Ibid.,* quoting Boston *Morning Post.*

in receiving the people of Texas into the Confederacy." But despite sectional cleavage, the United States had a war to fight.

The theatre of naval operations reached from New Orleans to the Campeche Gulf. The northern part of the area was not unknown to the armed forces. Already, in the late 'thirties, cutters and naval units had sailed there, protecting American shipping from Mexican privateers. In 1838, for instance, Captain Farnifold Green, U.S.R.-M., commanding *Woodbury,* had heard that an American steamer, the *Columbia,* Velasco for New Orleans, had been fired into with "round shot and grape" by a Mexican force somewhere along the Texas coast. He asked permission "to proceed with the *Woodbury* in that direction to offer protection to our merchant vessels." He was directed to cruise between Chandeleur Island and the Sabine and to render to "any vessel sailing under our flag and unlawfully attacked by an armed force" such aid as was in his power.[10]

Later, from the middle of June 1845 until war came on, Captain Winslow Foster in the *Woodbury* made numerous cruises along the coast from the Mississippi Passes as far as Corpus Christi, carrying dispatches and making reconnaissances for General Zachary Taylor, commanding the Army of Occupation. In March 1846, Foster assisted with getting the General's transports to sea and safely convoyed them from Aransas Bay to Brazos de Santiago—a matter in which the General "relied fully upon [Foster's] long experience in nautical matters and knowledge of the coast." The maneuver executed, Foster was addressed as follows:

> Headquarters, Army of Occupation.
> 26 March, 1846.
>
> Sir:
>
> I am directed by the Commanding General to say, that having executed the service which he required of you, he desires that you will proceed to your proper station. . . . He takes this occasion to express his thanks for the handsome manner in which you have extended your assistance and that of your vessel to the operations of the Army, and to offer you his best wishes for your health and happiness.
>
> W. W. Bliss,
> Assistant Adjutant General[11]

It was this movement of troops into the disputed territory between the Nueces and the Rio Grande that touched off the Mexican War.

On May 19, 1846, six days after the United States' declaration, Secretary Walker ordered Captain John A. Webster to form a cutter squadron for the joint purpose of safeguarding the revenue along the coast from

[10] *Rec. Movt.,* Vol. I; *passim.*
[11] *Ibid.*

the Rio Grande to the Mississippi Passes and of helping in the prosecution of the war. For the accomplishment of the latter, Webster was to place his force at the disposition of the Commanding General and was also to cooperate with the Navy so far as practicable.

As a young man, Captain Webster had served in the Navy. He entered the Revenue-Marine as a captain in 1819. The Secretary appointed him to his important new command because of "ability, intelligence, and zeal . . . and above all in consideration of the gallantry [he had] displayed during the late war." His work in command of the Gulf Squadron confirmed the Secretary's judgment. When he returned home in December 1846, ill with fever, he turned over his duties to Captain Foster. Upon recovery, Webster served until 1865, when he was retired on full duty pay by a special order of the Department, a reward for exceptional service.

Eleven cutters sailed from their stations under sealed orders about the first of June. When they reached certain specified latitudes, the captains broke the seals in the presence of their officers and found themselves directed to a rendezvous at New Orleans. Two steamers were forced to turn back because of machinery-troubles, but the three which reached New Orleans were the heaviest-armed vessels in the service. These continually experienced difficulties with their engines. The sailing cutters were lighter-armed, but their shallow draft and reliability made them especially useful for varied inshore duties and for working across the river bars. The steamers *McLane* and *Bibb* each carried four 32-pounders and one or two 18-pound pivots. The *Legare* carried one long 18-pounder and several lighter pieces. The schooners *Woodbury, Ewing, Van Buren* and *Wolcott* carried from four to six 12-pounders, the schooner *Forward* mounted four 9's, and the *Morris* bristled with six little 6's. On August ninth, Webster hoisted his broad pennant on the *Ewing* and thus became the first squadron commodore recorded in the annals of the Revenue-Marine.

Besides carrying out "legitimate duties, by keeping a watchful eye over the interests of the Revenue,"[12] Commodore Webster's squadron assisted the Army in a great many ways; it performed scout, convoy, towing, and blockade duty, transported troops and supplies, carried mail and dispatches, and even put down a mutiny of troops on the ship *Middlesex* (July 26, 1846). It is said that the *Ewing* and *Legare* landed a thousand rifles at Point Isabel just in time for General Taylor to use them in the battles of Monterey and Buena Vista.

In addition to their principal work, with the Army, units of the squadron cooperated with the Navy throughout the war and with the

[12] Letter, Secretary R. J. Walker to Captain John A. Webster, May 19, 1846, in *C. G. Archives.*

Navy took part in several actions. In at least one they had a major part—the first expedition to the Tabasco. For the purpose of bringing this river under American control and of thus preventing war supplies from reaching the enemy from the Yucatan, Commodore M. C. Perry, U.S.N., sailed from Anton Lizardo on October 16, 1846. He commanded as motley a naval force as had ever been assembled. He flew his flag from the U. S. S. *Mississippi;* also in that vessel was a detachment of 200 officers, seamen, and Marines, under Captain French Forest. The *McLane* (6 guns), Captain W. A. Howard, the *Forward* (6), Captain H. B. Nones, the naval steamer *Vixen* (3), and the naval schooners *Nonata* (1) and *Bonita* (1), made up the flotilla.

By October 23, this force reached the Tabasco River. Perry anchored the *Mississippi* outside, since she was much too deep to cross the shallow bar, and the underpowered *McLane* stuck fast attempting to cross in. The *Forward's* light ordnance thus became the Commodore's main artillery support. Undaunted, Perry transferred his flag to the *Vixen* and Captain Forest's troops to barges, and the expedition crossed the bar. Inside the river mouth lay the undefended commercial town of Frontera. The town and all vessels in port, including two steamers which fired up and attempted to escape, were seized without recourse to gun-fire. One steamer, the *Petrita,* was commandeered as a transport for Forest's men, and soon as she and the *Vixen* could take the schooners in tow, the expedition continued on upstream.

The raiders sighted Fort Acceahappa, commanding the most difficult pass in the river, on the morning of the 25th. Whether the novelty of the situation or the glint of the *Forward's* brasses in the morning sun or the sudden arrival of 200 Marines before placid Acceahappa was the decisive factor is not known, but the Commodore reported that "on our approach the men employed in preparing the guns for service fled and we passed unmolested."[13]

Having spiked the guns of the fort, Perry continued on to Tabasco. Here Captain Forest landed with his Marines and a detachment of revenue-cutter men from the *Forward* under Lieutenants John M. McGowan and W. F. Rogers. Musketry was encountered, but apparently the defenders possessed no cannon. Under the circumstances, a few rounds of grape from the *Vixen* and *Forward* sufficed to secure the town's capitulation. The next day the flotilla commenced to withdraw downstream, having accomplished its mission, cleared the river of enemy commerce, and taken in all 10 prizes. Before all the ships had cleared, however, one of the prizes, under Lieutenant Parker, U.S.N., ran ashore before the town. Exploiting what they must have deemed a happy chance, the

[13] Report of Commodore M. C. Perry to Commodore Conner, quoted in *Rec. Movt.* I, 102.

Mexicans broke their truce, opened up with musket-fire on Parker, and killed or wounded several of his men. The *Forward,* closing to cover Parker's efforts to stand clear, logged the ensuing action:

> The enemy opened fire on the *Forward* with musketry. We opened with grape and round from three of our guns—9 pounders with pivot gun—with terrible effect for 20 minutes. . . . a heavy fire of musketry was pouring upon us. At 11:30 Lieutenant Parker with the prize came alongside and made fast, we all this time keeping up a heavy fire upon the town with one of our guns. At 12 we ceased firing by order of Commodore Perry.

Punishment inflicted, the flotilla passed downstream. At Frontera, Perry detailed the *Forward* and *McLane* (the latter having lightened ship and crossed the bar) to maintain a blockade of the river and port; he then returned with his ships and prizes to Vera Cruz. In reporting to Commodore Conner he wrote:

> It is certainly a gratifying task to make known to you . . . the excellent conduct of the officers and men who served under my command in the late expedition to Tabasco. The enterprise and spirit displayed by them on every occasion gave sufficient evidence that in scenes more sanguinary they would do full honor to the corps. I am gratified to bear witness also to the valuable services of the Revenue Schooner *Forward,* in command of Captain Nones, and to the skill and gallantry of her officers and men.[14]

The war was officially ended by the Treaty of Guadalupe Hidalgo on February 2, 1848. In Washington, a little later, Fraser prepared for transfer, his tour of duty done. Behind him he left an orderly administrative system, a national coast guard, and a record of achievement in the public service. He left also a capital boiling with sectional distrust. It was no place for a nationalist to be.

[14] *Ibid.*

CHAPTER VI

—and Low

If the Fraser regime represented a high tide in the affairs of the pre-Civil War Revenue-Marine, the dozen succeeding years in many ways marked a low. Fraser's successor as Chief of the Bureau, Captain Richard Evans, U.S.R.-M., remained in office only until 1849. With Evans' transfer, the Revenue-Marine Bureau disappeared from the federal scene, and Fraser's carefully organized system soon fell apart. In that year, the office of Commissioner of Customs was created by statute, and the Secretary entrusted the administration of the cutter service to the new Commissioner. This official, however, confined his attention almost entirely to his fiscal duties, and most of the administrative functions previously exercised by Fraser slipped back into the hands of the collectors, who thus regained a good deal of their old authority over operations and personnel. Administration of the lighthouse branch returned to the Fifth Auditor.

Several factors account for the gradual recession of the service's fortunes during the period 1848-1860. First, most of the Spencer-Fraser reforms had been effected by *administrative,* rather than by *legislative,* means. Not anchored in the Statutes, Fraser's system was subject to every current and ripple which stirred the troubled waters at Washington. Second, the strongest currents in Washington at the time were those of sectionalism, distinctly disruptive forces. Third, the Treasury no longer had at the head of the Revenue-Marine "a chief, practically and professionally acquainted with the Revenue Service," a maritime expert, such as Spencer had installed. The first two of these factors combined to make decentralization of authority almost inevitable; the third led to neglect of the service and to a waste of its potentialities.

Fraser's administration, with its close supervision and high standards, made the confusion of this later period seem twice confounded. Morale experienced a swift decline. No particular system now governed appointments or promotions, except the necessity for securing recommendations from politically powerful persons. In order to make use of the officers politically, a "Doomsday Book" was started in 1852. Every officer was required to give, in detail, his complete service and political history. Insecurity of tenure dogged the commissioned corps. Discipline relaxed, and cruising regulations were little regarded. Further, expenditures of public property were no longer properly accounted for. Customhouse officials seemed wed to the notion that excursions and junketings aboard the cutters were privileges attached to their offices. A premium was placed on speed when excursion parties were aboard, and costs were considerable for "supplies"—an item which the Department allowed to cover both food and the repair of furniture and other public property. Among the politicians of his home port, a commanding officer was rated as good as the *cuisine* he furnished. On such accounts, certain gentlemen of the press stigmatized the whole service as a "pleasure fleet."[1] With the Revenue-Marine thus bogged in a rotten political morass, there was little that individual officers even as conscientious as Captains John Faunce, Josiah Sturgis, John McGowan, or James H. Merryman could do to raise the general tone.

The disintegration of the Revenue-Marine Bureau led almost at once to multiplication of administrative agencies, with attendant duplication of effort and offices. Probably the most important reason why the Lighthouse and Life-Saving Establishments slipped away from the Revenue-Marine was the fact that no Revenue-Marine officer remained in the Department to oppose the change and to point out the advantages of continued and closer unification. Suffice it to say, the separatist action was ill-advised and delayed rationalization of federal maritime safety agencies for nearly a century.

By the Act of August 31, 1852 (10 Stat. L., 110, 119), Congress established a new administrative device for the lighthouse branch. This Act centralized administrative authority in a Lighthouse Board, composed of scientists and Army and Navy officers, under the general supervision of the Secretary of the Treasury. The celebrated Professor Joseph Henry, of the Smithsonian Institution; Admiral George Dewey and Rear Admiral Robley D. ("Fighting Bob") Evans, of the Navy; Raphael Semmes, later Rear Admiral, Confederate States Navy; and Major General George G. Meade, U.S.A., commander of federal forces at Gettysburg; were at one time or another members of the Board. Although this form of organization eventually showed serious defects and weaknesses, the Lighthouse Service under its direction extended the American system of aids to navigation from about 1600 in 1852 to nearly 12,000 in 1910 (of the latter, nearly 4000 were lighted aids).

In 1854, an Act "for the better *preservation of life and property from vessels shipwrecked on the coasts of the United States*" authorized the Secretary of the Treasury to establish new stations on the coasts of Long Island and New Jersey, to appoint paid keepers ($200 per annum) at each, to repair existing stations or to change their locations, and to appoint a superintendent of stations for Long Island and one for New Jersey. All were to be under the control of the Secretary.[2] This Act

[1] *Annual Report of the Chief of the Revenue-Marine* (Washington, 1872).

[2] Act of December 14, 1854 (10 Stat. L., 597). (Italics ours). A number of Acts similar to the Newall Act (*supra,* Chapter V) had been passed prior to the 1854 statute.

remedied many of the defects of the Newall Act and set up an administrative system for the stations. Had the system been controlled from a central bureau in Washington by a man like Fraser, it would have had considerable chance for success. As it was, lack of expert administration led to grief:

> The new appointees put the stations and equipment in serviceable condition, and for a period the benefit of the step . . . was manifest. . . . After a while, however, owing to the lack of any regulations for the government of the officers, and the failure to hold them for a proper accountability either as to the care of the property entrusted to their charge or as to the discharge of their duties, their administration became lax. . . . This defective and unorganized condition continued, interrupted by spasmodic temporary improvement succeeding some distressing calamity, until 1871, when the organization of the [Life-Saving] service was undertaken by the Department with the aid of Congress.[3]

Thus, in brief, by 1854 the Revenue-Marine was once more merely a "system of cutters," essentially under sectional, rather than national, control.

Notwithstanding, the full record of the service in the dark days preceding war between the states was not entirely barren of accomplishment. Only about fifteen cutters remained on the rolls *circa* 1855, but their logbooks show that they performed a considerable amount of routine cutter work—of work in connection with revenue duty, the anti-slave trade campaign, winter cruising, and sundry other details dealing with maritime law enforcement and safety. In addition, a few instances of notable achievement appear and add their color to an otherwise rather dullish page.

One such instance was the extension of Revenue-Marine operations to the Pacific. Following acquisition of Oregon by treaty with Great Britain in 1846 and of California by the Mexican cession of 1848, the revenue laws had been extended to the new territories and the latter had been included within a newly-erected customs district. To this district the revenue brig *Lawrence,* built in 1848 in Washington, D.C., was assigned. Fraser, learning that his transfer from Washington was assured, requested assignment to the new cutter, and on November 1, 1848 he was given the command. His cruise in the *Lawrence* around the Horn to San Francisco and his subsequent duty in that port during the Gold Rush, opened a new chapter in the history of the Revenue-Marine and gave Fraser ample opportunity to demonstrate high standards of public service.

But first, a description of the *Lawrence,* a cutter built upon the same model as the *Joseph Lane.* Splendid sailers though Humphrey's *Morris,*

[3] S. I. Kimball, quoted in Smith and Powell, *op. cit.,* 27.

Hamilton, and their sisters had been, they failed to mark the utmost of perfection in sailing cutters; this distinction was reserved for the *Joe Lane* class. The *Joe Lane* herself was the Revenue-Marine's Queen of Sail. She was the last graceful gesture of a passing age to the onward sweep of time and technics. Built around 1850 in Portsmouth, Virginia, by Graves and Fereba and christened *Campbell,* she was re-named *Joseph Lane* in '55. Her lines are on file at Headquarters.[4] At first glance they show features common to Baltimore clippers; close inspection and comparison with the lines of Doughty's and Humphrey's cutters, however, show refinements in a thousand details. The finer bow and stern, the slightly increased flair, the more graceful turn of the fore-foot, the

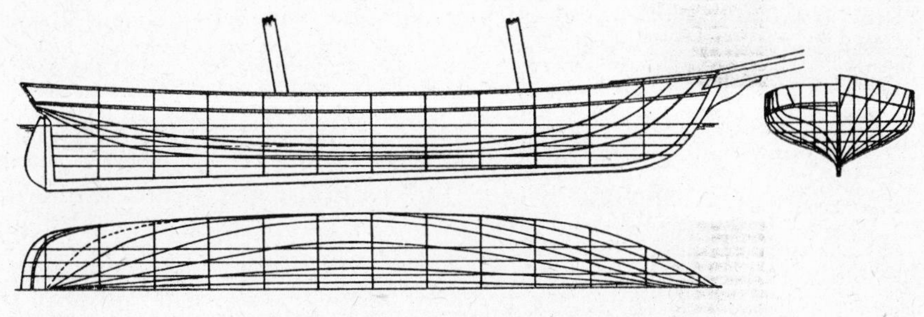

Lines of the *Joseph Lane, c.* 1850
(In C. G. Archives.)

more symmetrical and smoother-curving waterlines, the delicately-rounded stern, the rich carving in the bow, and the poised eagle figure-head: these made of her a work of art. The *Joe Lane's* masts had slightly less rake than her predecessors', she had a sharper deadrise, and her accommodations were more conveniently arranged. She had a very low freeboard. Her principal dimensions were: 100 feet 4 inches on the load waterline; 23 feet extreme beam; 22 feet 6½ inches moulded beam; 8 feet 8 inches moulded depth; draft, 6 feet 9 inches forward, 9 feet 7½ inches aft, at 153.3 tons displacement. She was rigged as a fore-topsail schooner, carrying in addition to her fore-and-aft foresail a course (lower square foresail) and two fore-topsails. Full of years, she was sold out of the service in '69.

The brig-rigged *Lawrence* and a number of other cutters were built late in the 'forties to this plan, and apparently most sailing cutters that followed were influenced by the same design. No further classes of sailing cutters were built after 1866; together the *Joe Lane* class in cutters and the *Rainbow* and *Flying Cloud* and *Lightning* in merchant-

[4] U.S.C.G. C.&R. 38-45, 39-45 (Plans 130-131). In *C. G. Archives.*

men brought a brave finale to America's compositions in wood-and-sail.

Captain Fraser sailed in the *Lawrence* from Washington on November 18, 1848. His orders directed him to place himself under the collector of customs for the new district, to operate on the Oregon coast until Californian commerce developed, and then to operate also out of San Francisco. In addition to securing the revenue, Fraser was ordered to relieve distressed merchant vessels and to make scientific investigations of the harbors he visited. Moreover, since the Coast Survey had just been directed to begin work on the West Coast, Fraser was given specific instructions to aid Coast Survey officers to the utmost of his ability. Finally, he was allowed $12,000 with which to defray the expenses of the voyage to the new station and to pay the officers and men until a disbursing office could be set up by civil authorities ashore.—Little did anyone foresee the events of '49!

Scarcely had the *Lawrence* cleared the Washington wharf than Fraser's personnel troubles commenced. Since the cruise was such a long one, the *Lawrence* had been authorized a larger complement of officers than was generally carried by cutters of the period; a first lieutenant, two second lieutenants, and two third lieutenants were allowed. But most of these were inexperienced. While Fraser was a "shellback" twenty-six times over, three of his politically-appointed lieutenants had had no sea experience, nor had they ever been aboard a square-rigger until they reported on the *Lawrence*. Fraser could not trust them with the deck and was compelled to stand their watches himself.

The surgeon was another problem. Although this young man, a Dr. Overstreet, appeared to know his business, he knew neither the sea nor seamen. The *Lawrence* crew imposed upon his gullibility, and there ensued an epidemic of altogether spurious sickness. Fraser told the executive officer, Lieutenant J. Chaddock, he would rather pay Overstreet a hundred dollars to be out of the vessel than fifty to remain in it. Overstreet overheard the remark and demanded to be put ashore in Rio—without claiming, be it said, the hundred dollar prize. Fraser explained that his remark was founded on the belief that seamen take advantage of an inexperienced surgeon, and that he had made the same remark to Chaddock long before he had met Overstreet. If pressed, however, he continued, he might add that in general he would "prefer one violin as a preservative of health among seamen to two Dispensaries."[5]

But Fraser's problems did not end in the wardroom. The boatswain, James Walker, was making his first voyage in a cutter. He was an old whaling ship man, and he tried to introduce whaler methods of handling

[5] Letter, Fraser to Secretary Walker, March 18, 1849. In *C. G. Archives.*

the crew. Chaddock reported him to Fraser, and Walker tendered his own resignation. Finally, drunk and disorderly, he was put ashore in Valparaiso. Another petty officer, the carpenter, Benjamin Brown, left the ship in Rio because of chronic seasickness on the passage south. Thus, long before the cutter arrived on its new station, the surgeon and two petty officers had taken their departures.

The voyage from Washington to Rio required sixty-one days. Captain Fraser reported a succession of squalls, heavy thunder, vivid lightning, and torrential rain. During twenty-seven days the sails were saturated with rain; vegetation came forth about the ship as though by magic. Some of the iron-work that had been installed at Washington—bands on bowsprits, bobstays, cranes, and chain slings of the lower yards—gave way in the heavy weather. On January 19, 1849 Fraser reported that he had arrived at Rio, but that he could not put out immediately for the voyage around the Horn because of the necessity for repairs. He estimated a delay of ten days.

But he did not reckon on the lack of facilities in non-industrial Brazil. Writing ten days later, he mourned the slowness with which the work proceeded. A Scot and a Presbyterian, he was angered by the exorbitance of Brazilian prices and irked by what struck him as Latin indolence and by the "frequent recurrence of Holy days in a Catholic country."[6] From his letters it appears that the only pleasant personal relationship he enjoyed in Rio was with Commodore Storer of the Navy, who, with a naval store keeper, had established there a fitting-out station for naval vessels on their way to the Californian coast during the late war. Too dour to appreciate the romance of the Brazilian scene, Fraser could accept gratefully the material assistance and friendship of these two efficient men.

Finally—not ten days, but two full months after he dropped anchor at Rio—Fraser set out for the Horn. Voyaging in the most boisterous months of the year in that part of the world, he was three months in rounding South America to Valparaiso, Chile. In a letter of June 20th from Valparaiso he remarked that thirty-seven days had been spent in the vicinity of Cape Horn, between the parallel of the Cape and 59° South and the meridians of Cape St. John and Cape Pillar. It had been necessary to mind the weather with particular care during this part of the voyage, so as to preserve the heavy battery and the four boats which the *Lawrence* carried on deck, and the going had been slow.

In Valparaiso the *Lawrence* found a vanguard of Forty-Niners rushing by sea-route to the California "diggings." At this point Fraser realized

[6] Fraser to Walker, February 6, 1849, from Rio. In *C. G. Archives.*

that an unprecedented search for gold was in progress and was taking an unprecedented number of vessels into Californian waters; his new station would be a busy one indeed. All sorts of ships, some of foreign and some of American registry, were in Valparaiso loaded with freight and passengers for the land of promise. Fraser reported finding American vessels, coastwise for California, loaded with foreign produce and manufactures regardless of the law. Some merchants and shipmasters, anxious to conform if possible, asked the consul at Valparaiso for advice on the laws involved. This official had no adequate information on the subject and welcomed Fraser to the city. The Captain advised as to the letter of the statutes and offered inquiring traders citations from Gordon's weighty *Digest,* but it was obvious to all that the laws had not been composed in anticipation of a gold rush.

While Fraser had been thus engaged the *Lawrence* had been reconditioned and the crew refreshed. On July 19 the cutter was towed out of the harbor by four whale boats, and a course was laid for the Sandwich Islands. Briefly to encompass the remainder of the cruise, be it said that the *Lawrence* reached the islands in September and arrived at San Francisco on October 31st, almost a year out of Washington.

Throughout this historic voyage, Fraser ran the *Lawrence* like a school-ship. He took in hand his raw lieutenants and tried to make competent officers of them. His letters indicate that he gave the young men every opportunity and encouragement to acquaint themselves with the methods and tools of their profession. He explained to them, for instance, that his orders required him to examine unknown harbors and that he therefore needed at least two officers who could assist him in the use of surveying instruments. He asserted the importance of legal knowledge, especially on the *Lawrence's* new station. There was a small library on the *Lawrence,* and Fraser demanded a fair amount of study from the youngsters and reported the progress of each to Washington.

So keenly did Fraser feel the necessity of this training that in mid-Pacific, en route from Valparaiso to the Sandwich Islands, he sat in his cabin and composed a memorable order outlining his views on the training of third lieutenants and the main points in his philosophy of public service. Time has made it necessary to extend his training program, but to his view of public service there is little to be added. To Captain Fraser, public offices existed not to provide pomp or pay for individuals but to insure the performance of work required by the public interests. Here are his own words, as entered in the journal of the *Lawrence,* July 25, 1849:

> The act of the 4th of March, 1799, and all subsequent enactments upon the same subject, contemplated by the language the establishment and maintenance of the Revenue Service, not for the creation of additional officers or for the purpose of augmenting the expenditures of the government,

but to provide an additional guard against infringement of the Revenue Laws, which could not be afforded by officers of the Customs on shore. Nor is its military character given to the service by any of the acts, further than necessary for protection in enforcement of the Revenue Laws—except where by the direction of the President the Revenue Vessels shall be called upon to cooperate with those of the Navy, and for the suppression of the slave trade and piracy.

Efficiency in the officers demands three requisites: a knowledge of Navigation and Seamanship as well as an intimate acquaintance with those laws the observance of which he is bound by his oath of office as well as in consideration of the compensation he receives to enforce.

For the purpose of affording to every officer an opportunity to acquire the necessary information, the grade of Third Lieutenant was created; and the term of service in that grade was deemed sufficient with proper application to prepare for future usefulness.

Every information which is requested on any of these subjects has been and will be cheerfully afforded by the Commander, and for further information a Digest of the Revenue Laws is now placed in the Ward Room.[7]

But for most men who arrived in California in 1849 there was little appeal in public service. Private enterprise was blossoming under showers of gold. And as soon as the *Lawrence* anchored, the executive officer and next in rank left to accept private positions ashore at salaries three or four times that of Captain Fraser. For a while, the only officer aboard to whom Fraser could entrust the ship's affairs or boarding duties was Second Lieutenant Pierce. Fraser never referred to his third lieutenants as officers; he regarded them simply as cadets. Short-handed in the wildest port in the United States, the *Lawrence* must have been hard put to meet the demands placed upon her. That she was a stabilizing influence in the midst of anarchy in the Bay region and that she thus contributed to the maritime development of the Port of San Francisco is manifest in a letter to Fraser written about the time of his transfer East:

Collector's Office,
San Francisco,
November 21, 1850.

. . . Few men have had more difficult or responsible duties to perform. . . . When it is to be remembered that you have been in a harbour where from five to six hundred vessels were riding at anchor, in the midst of great excitement, with crews insubordinate and lawless, without the aid of civil tribunals or civil process, and when day and night you have been called upon to render assistance and to aid masters of vessels in suppressing mutiny and violence, surely it becomes me to bear willing testimony to the necessity of your presence and your promptness in the discharge of your onerous duties. To me your services have been invaluable. . . . May you have a safe and prosperous cruize. . . .

J. Collier,
Collector[8]

[7] In *C. G. Archives.*
[8] *Ibid.*

The Captain was a direct and honest man who saw that ordinary laws and contracts needed enforcement in time of gold rush or out. Acting without the wide grant of law enforcement authority later carried by Coast Guard officers, he was fortunate indeed to live through his California experiences and to return to New York by 1852.

Other cutters followed the *Lawrence* into the Pacific and likewise helped to establish U.S. sovereignty in the maritime provinces of the West. A typical instance of pioneer-day cutter activity in the backwaters of the region made news in the Washington, D.C., *National Intelligencer* for January 3, 1856:

THE INDIAN WAR IN OREGON

> Upon the arrival of the United States revenue-cutter *Jefferson Davis* at the port of Steilacoom, Washington Territory, October 18, Captain Pease learned that the Indians were dissatisfied with the treaties recently made with them by Governor Stevens and threatened to carry on a war of extermination against the whites; and, in consequence of these rumors, at the request of the commanding officer of Fort Steilacoom, remained at this port until affairs assumed a more favorable aspect, for the purpose of assisting in its defense and of affording a safe retreat for the women and children. . . .

The successful reintroduction of steam cutters into the Revenue-Marine was another bright spot in the history of the service just prior to the Civil War. Unfortunately, however, the steamer policy again seemed to be a nemesis to Captain Fraser. In supporting New York shipping interests in a request to have a new steam cutter built for their thriving port, Fraser opposed an Assistant Secretary of the Treasury, and this official's hostility proved fatal to the Captain's long career: by an arbitrary abuse of power, the administration in 1856 revoked his commission summarily. Both indefensible and stupid, this action resulted wholly from personal animosity and cost the government one of the most far-sighted and loyal men who ever sailed in the Revenue-Marine. Fraser rankled under the injustice but made no strong bid to clear his record until the outbreak of the Civil War, when he immediately applied for reinstatement and return to duty. The case dragged on and finally in 1863 was referred to a board composed of Captains Nones, Faunce, and Chaddock, whose strong recommendation in favor of reinstatment won Abraham Lincoln's magnanimous support: the President on July 1 signed a new commission for Fraser as a captain. By this late date, however, personal matters had intervened and forced Fraser regretfully to decline the reappointment.

But back in 1856, although his stand cost him his commission, Fraser won his immediate objective: he got the Revenue-Marine under steam once more. He pressed the New Yorkers' request on his friends in Congress, and Congress (which because of the first steamer fiasco had revoked the Secretary's power to build cutters on his own authority out of customs receipts) in 1857 appropriated funds for the side-wheel cutter *Harriet Lane.*

A board of naval constructors borrowed from the Navy Department selected for the new vessel a design submitted by William H. Webb, of New York. The board and Mr. Webb then settled down to revising the latter's specifications so as to produce the best possible job for the money available ($150,000).

The men who planned the *Harriet Lane* were among the outstanding figures in naval architecture and marine engineering in their day. The

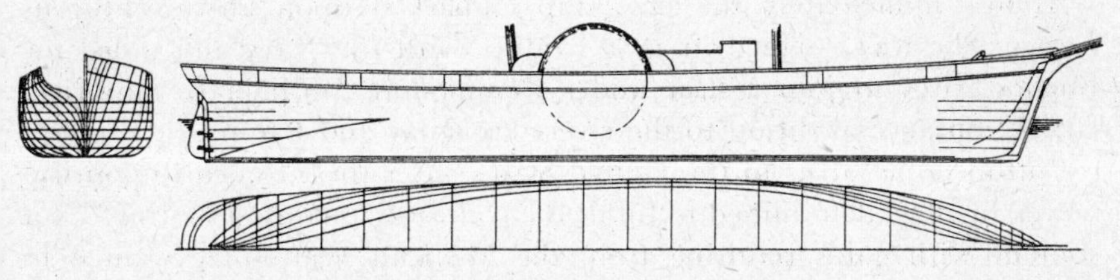

Lines of the *Harriet Lane,* 1857
(Courtesy of The Webb Institute.)

board included Charles W. Copeland, Henry Hunt, Samuel M. Pook, and Francis Grice. The name of William Webb has been commemorated in the Webb Institute of Naval Architecture, New York. That these men planned the *Harriet Lane* with skill is evidenced by the little steamer's record. That they planned towards engineering progress is demonstrated by the refinements they built into her hull and engine. That they planned with an eye to the past and with a sense of their own limitations is shown by the absence of radical features from the whole design.

Built of wood, the *Harriet Lane's* hull was worked into the characteristically fast lines of sailing cutters. She was 180 feet long, 30 feet in beam, 12½ feet in depth, 10 feet in draft, 674 13/95 tons, and carried auxiliary sail. Her side-wheels revolved at 20 r.p.m., her boiler pressure was only about 25 pounds, and she had good speed (around 12 knots). She used jet condensation. Since her plant was well within the experience of those who designed and ran her, she missed many of the faults and miseries of the *Spencer* and *Legare.* Further, she was heiress to the rapid advance in materials and in machine shop practice witnessed by the years from '43 to '57. Marine engineering was somewhat less a matter of guesswork than it had been in the previous decade. Finally, before the *Harriet Lane* went out of service, petroleum (marketed by Drake in Pennsylvania in 1859) had come to displace the inefficient lubricants of the *Spencer's* day—a development which may well have borne upon the success of the *Harriet Lane's* career.

The new cutter's performance jusified Fraser's radical policy of building steamers for the service and must have given the old skipper a great deal of satisfaction to the end of his days. She justified also the pride of her first commanding officer, Captain John Faunce, who concluded his report of her trials with these words:

> And I am happy to say that the *Harriet Lane* is a noble vessel. Mr. Webb, her builder, has spared no pains in fitting her out for the service she is intended for, and I have no doubt she will be able to perform the duties required of her.[9]

Almost immediately the new ship embarked upon an adventurous voyage. She was assigned in 1858 to duty with the Navy and sailed for Buenos Aires to join a fleet under Commodore William B. Shubrick, U.S.N., on an expedition to the rivers Paraguay and Parana.

Cotton imperialists in the United States, after their return to political power in 1853, determined to fulfill the country's "manifest destiny." Not content with gains resulting from the Mexican War, some wanted to acquire all of Mexico and to annex Cuba, too. And on the commercial front, seeking markets for American goods, diplomats and others moved to "open" various areas to U.S. trade. Around 1853 Argentina agreed to open the River Plate to all flags, and about the same time Perry opened up Japan. But Paraguay demonstrated a reluctance towards meeting foreigners' demands. Paraguayans resented the U.S.S. *Water Witch's* "scientific exploration" of their rivers. They attacked the vessel in the Parana River in 1855, put ten shots in her hull, and killed the man at the wheel. The affair was termed an "outrage" in the American Congress and at country crossroads throughout the nation. To meet the challenge, Commodore Shubrick gathered a force of 15 vessels, 1361 men, 291 Marines, and 76 pieces of ordnance for a demonstration at the junction of the rivers. Here lay

> . . . the warlike *Fulton,*
> The *Water Witch* in her train,
> The *Bainbridge,* too, and *Dolphin,*
> Next comes the *Harriet Lane.*

The cutter carried 82 men, 22 Marines, two 9-inch guns, four 24 and one 12-pound howitzers; she was one of the heaviest-armed vessels of the squadron.

Backed by this threat of force, the American Commissioner at Asuncion, James B. Bowlin, had little difficulty in negotiating a treaty. This agreement provided for "perfect peace and sincere friendship" between

[9] Letter, Captain Faunce to Secretary Howell Cobb, March 24, 1858. In *C. G. Archives.*

the two governments and for the extension of free trading rights to American merchantmen on the rivers of Paraguay.[10]

Commodore Shubrick's report to the Navy Department indicates that the *Harriet Lane* added more than the mere strength of her guns to the success of this expedition. Said he:

> All the vessels grounded more than once and it is proper, and it gives me pleasure to do so, that I should express my sense of appreciation of the skill and zeal with which Captain Faunce has used the very efficient vessel under his command in extricating us from our difficulties. At one time I feared that the services of the *Fulton* would be lost altogether to the expedition and they certainly would have been, for a great length of time if not entirely, but for the assistance afforded by the *Harriet Lane*.[11]

After her arrival back in the United States, early in 1859, the cutter was returned to the Revenue-Marine. The following autumn she patrolled off the Florida coast to prevent violations of the slave trade law, then carried on normal cutter duties out of the Port of New York for about a year.

But normal operations of federal agencies were soon interrupted by the war between the states. Sectionalism shifted its strife from parliamentary fields to bloody battle-fields. And with the swift approach of conflict the *Harriet Lane* again was transferred to duty in the Navy, where she served until captured by Confederates in 1863. Her first orders took her upon another historic mission: to a rendezvous off Charleston with the squadron sent to relieve Fort Sumter. But this attempt came too late. History was in the making, and the expedition arrived to find that war had broken out. Lying off Charleston bar while the bombardment of Sumter was in progress, the *Harriet Lane* hailed the steamer *Nashville*, but the latter refused to show her colors. Captain Faunce then ordered a shot thrown across her bow, and "it had the desired effect." Thus a cutter fired the first shot from any vessel in the long war waged for the preservation of the federal union.[12]

[10] *Compilation of Treaties in Force*, Sen. Doc. 318, 58 Cong. (Washington, 1904), 617-21.

[11] Letter to Navy Department dated January 19, 1859, quoted in *Rec. Movt.*, I, 36.

[12] Army and Navy *Journal*, November 26, 1864. Verified by an eye-witness, Captain (E) J. H. Pulsifer, U.S.C.G. (Ret), in U. S. C. G. Association *Journal*, 1917, Vol. I, No. 1.

CHAPTER VII

The Years Between

SECTIONAL rivalry, nationalism, and a compound of subordinate issues —expressed by no single, simple formula—all boiled together in the cauldron of the great four-year conflict. But amid the confusion and turmoil that followed South Carolina's Ordinance of Secession (December 20, 1860), one single, painful question clearly faced each member of the federal fighting forces—the question of allegiance. The national government moved to assert its authority in the South; the South moved to assert the ultimate authority of states' rights. Each man in federal uniform was forced to decide, and to decide quickly, whether his supreme allegiance lay with a state or with the nation-state.

Typical was the case of Captain James J. Morrison, commanding the cutter *Lewis Cass* at Mobile. This southern skipper had served his country faithfully in both the Seminole and Mexican wars. But like General Lee, who declared himself unable to raise his hand against his native state, his relatives, his children, and his home, and like dozens of others in every service, Captain Morrison determined to cast his lot with the fortunes of the South. He turned over his ship to the authorities of the State of Alabama on January 30, 1861. Third Lieutenant Charles F. Shoemaker, a Commandant of the Revenue-Cutter Service years later, remained steadfast in his loyalty to the national union. With his brother officers and the entire crew of the *Lewis Cass,* Shoemaker made his way through the full length of the hostile South. The party finally managed to reach Northern territory, and Shoemaker reported aboard the *Crawford* in July, 1861, just in time to serve in that vessel as part of Flag Officer S. H. Stringham's naval force in Hampton Roads.

To forestall surrender of the *McClelland* by its southernborn captain, John G. Brushwood, Secretary of the Treasury John A. Dix sent a courier with orders to Brushwood to proceed in the cutter from New Orleans to New York. Brushwood refused, and Dix instantly dispatched to the courier a message whose "determined words reverberated through the North and thrilled all hearts with the hope that the time for delay was past, and that the growing rebellion would be put down with a firm hand."[1] "Tell Lieutenant Caldwell," wired Dix, "to arrest Captain Brushwood, assume command of the cutter, and obey the order [to go to New

[1] W. J. Abbott, *Blue-Jackets of '61* (Dodd, Mead and Company, New York, 1891), 5. For contemporary account, see *Harper's Weekly* for February 16 and March 9, 1861.

York]. If Captain Brushwood, after arrest, undertakes to interfere with the command of the cutter, tell Lieutenant Caldwell to consider him as a mutineer, and treat him accordingly. *If anyone attempts to haul down the American flag, shoot him on the spot.*"

As it turned out, Caldwell was as much a Rebel sympathizer as Captain Brushwood, and the two officers went over to the Confederacy taking the cutter with them. But Dix's heroic sentiment regarding the flag rallied Union morale in a moment of national uncertainty and indecision.

The war, naturally, greatly extended the scope and importance of the Revenue-Marine's operations. Invoking the Act of March 2, 1799, President Lincoln ordered many (but not all) of the cutters to combat duty in cooperation with the Navy. To regulate this association, Congress laid down a precise rule defining relative ranks of naval and cutter officers. The Act of February 4, 1863 (section 4) provided that

> the officers of the Revenue-Cutter Service, when serving in accordance with law as a part of the Navy, shall be entitled to relative rank as follows: Captains, with and next after lieutenants commanding [lieutenant commanders] in the Navy, first lieutenants, with and next after lieutenants in the Navy. . . .

and so on, down the line. (This statute remained the rule for nearly fifty years. It did not, however, raise cutter officers' pay to parity with that of naval officers.)

Cutters assigned to naval forces helped accomplish Union objectives in the war at sea. Basically, these aims were three; namely, economic isolation of the South by seizure of Confederate shipping and ports and by maintenance of an effective blockade of Confederate territory; provision for security of Union shipping; and provision for naval support of Union military ventures.

Cutters assisted with blockade duty along the Atlantic coast, in the Chesapeake, and in the Potomac River. Eight or ten cutters were on duty in the River region and gave especially valuable aid to the Naval Patrol Force operating there. Frequent clashes enlivened patrols along the placid, green-banked stream. Cutters and naval patrol boats made splendid targets for snipers and at night were attractive objects of guerilla raids. These inconveniences, however, were minimized by ceaseless vigilance, and the cutters were able to render "incalculable service" to the Union cause by preventing men, mail, and money from reaching the South.[2]

Other cutters, assigned to normal duties along the coast of federal territory, contributed in their own way to the preservation of the Union.

[2] *Army and Navy Journal,* November 26, 1864.

Assistance to Union vessels in distress now meant direct assistance to the Union war effort, and cruising in protection of shipping now meant cruising against Rebel privateers as well as against natural hazards. Northern trade was vital. In the first year of the war, the North was almost entirely dependent on England for war materials. And, because of conditions in the world market, England was becoming so dependent on America's western wheat that she increased her imports from 17½ millions bushels in 1860 to 62 million in 1862. The United States' ability to supply this demand helped bring in gold to win the war and helped keep England neutral. But Confederate privateers constituted no mere supposititious threat to Union commerce; despite all federal efforts, raiders managed to account for 110,000 tons of Yankee shipping and to scare 750,000 tons (⅓ the fleet engaged in foreign trade) into foreign registry. Under such conditions, every revenue-cutter and every Navy ship that could be spared to cruise along the northern coast increased the safeguard to lanes of necessary trade. Between 1861-65, besides opposing their force to the privateers, cutters assigned to this duty assisted an average of 115 distressed vessels every year.[3]

Further, the work of the cutters in protection of the revenue quickly assumed a new importance. From practically free trade in 1860, the tariff was revised upward by the Morrill (1861) and subsequent (1862, 1864) Acts until, by 1864, the average rate of import duties had advanced 47%. During the war, high tariff was a war measure, a means of financing Union victory. Protection of the revenue, therefore, was a matter of great national concern. To revenue and collateral routine duties, a dozen or more cutters were assigned during the period of the conflict.

When Sumter fell, the Revenue-Marine—like all other services—found itself unprepared for war. The *Harriet Lane* and ten or twelve sailing cutters made up the Treasury's fleet. Before the war was really underway, Confederates seized several cutters at their moorings in southern ports. Almost overnight the Revenue-Marine faced an emergent need for men and ships.

And it needed *steam*-ships, not sailers; even to officials in the national capital—long-time unbelievers—the Civil War demonstrated that the Age of Sail had gone. There was the case of Captain Nones and the revenue-schooner *Forward,* relic of the war with Mexico. In April 1861, Nones was ordered to keep open a course for transports from Perryville to Annapolis in the Chesapeake Bay. He was to "capture or sink any unfriendly craft, after taking out their crews. . . ." But it was evident that the *Forward* was cruising on borrowed time: Nones was ordered to "urge"

[3] On the economic aspects of the war at sea, see esp. G. W. Dalzell, *The Flight from the Flag* (Chapel Hill, 1940); Chapter XXII.

any U.S. *steamer* he met to give his schooner a tow in furtherance of the duty assigned.[4]

No attempt was made to transform the Revenue-Marine into a "little navy"; the vessels acquired by the Treasury were needed first and foremost *for marine safety and law enforcement under war-time pressure.* Naturally, in the early months of the emergency, Navy shipbuilding received priority. The Revenue-Marine fell back upon other methods of acquiring tonnage. Vessels of various types were purchased from private owners, armed, and placed in service. Among these were the *Cuyahoga* and the *Miami,* two seagoing steamers, the former a Mexican War prize and the latter a one-time yacht. A few nondescript units were leased or lent to the Revenue-Marine by private individuals. James Gordon Bennett served as a third lieutenant in command of his own vessel, the *Henrietta,* from June 1861 until he resigned in May 1862.[5]

Most fantastic of all the units acquired from private owners was the *Naugatuck* (sometimes referred to in the records as the *Ironsides* and also as the *E. A. Stevens.*) This vessel was a gift to the government from Mr. E. A. Stevens of Hoboken, a gentleman who had designed her to demonstrate some of the revolutionary theories involved in the construction of his famous "Stevens Battery." The latter was an ironclad which had been a-building for the Navy for twenty years and which, incidentally, was never launched. A contemporary of the *Monitor* and *Merrimac,* the *Naugatuck* was one of the first ironclads ever to go into action. She was semi-submersible; she could take aboard sufficient water ballast in 15 minutes to sink her 2 feet 10½ inches, and she could pump it all overboard again in eight minutes flat. Her twin screws spun her end-for-end in 75 seconds. She was 100 feet long, 20 feet beam, and 7 feet depth of hold. To say the least, she was a rather extraordinary addition to the Revenue-Marine, but she gave a good account of herself in the war and stacked up favorably with many of the other weird naval inventions which the war produced. She remained on active duty until 1890, spending most of her career in Albemarle Sound.

As time went on, the Treasury was able to add to its cutter fleet by a modest building program. Six steamers were built late in 1863: the *Ashuelot, Kankakee, Kewanee, Mahoning, Pawtuxet,* and *Wayanda.* These were single screw, single cylinder, low pressure vessels. They

[4] *Official Records of the Union and Confederate Navies in the War of the Rebellion* (Washington, Govt. Printing Office, 1897), Ser. I, IV, 329.

[5] *Rec. Movt.,* I, 32; II, 470. Bennett succeeded his father as an editor and publisher *(N. Y. Herald, Evening Telegram).* From his Revenue-Marine "service arose his life-long interest in nautical affairs which made the *Herald* long unrivalled in attention to ship, naval, and military news." He fitted out the *Jeannette* Polar Expediton. *Dictionary of American Biography* (Scribners, 1929) II, 199. (This work reports that Bennett was a lieutenant in the Navy.)

averaged about 135 feet in length, 26 feet beam, 350 tons, and cost about $100,000.00 apiece. Each mounted six guns. They had considerable speed, according to Civil War standards, and were useful safeguards against privateers and smugglers. Several of these cutters escorted a "cotton fleet" from Savannah to New York early in 1865 and thus helped reopen the American source of supply for busy Yankee spindles. Capable observers declared the steamers marked a "new era in the history of this branch of our national floating defenses."[6]

The former yacht *Miami* participated in one of the most remarkable episodes of the whole war. In addition to four serviceable brass howitzers, the cutter possessed a well-appointed cabin. In this cabin, cruising down the Potomac on a rainy night in May 1862, sat General Viele of the Union Army, Secretary of War Stanton, Secretary of the Treasury Chase, and Abraham Lincoln. No junket, this was a secret reconnaissance. Its purpose: to discover why the Union Army had bogged down before the city of Norfolk.

Coming up to the Union position the next day, the party helped plan the bombardment of Sewell's Point. This barrage was intended to cover the disembarkation of troops brought from Fortress Monroe. No landing was effected, however, because Yankee Army commanders alleged that the water was shoal for a mile offshore in the vicinity of the projected landing-place. But that night the *Miami* ran close in to the beach, and Lincoln walked on Confederate soil by the light of the moon. Finding the landing not only possible but easy, he and Stanton ordered an attack the next day. When the poorly organized Union attack finally reached Norfolk, the town was found deserted; presumably the party aboard the *Miami* had helped force the vacillating Northern generals into an easy victory.[7]

The *Naugatuck* had a special part in the action against Sewell's Point. The purpose of the cutter's bombardment was not only to silence the Confederate batteries so that Federal troops might land, but also to "draw out the rebel steamer *Merrimac* into a position where she could be attacked simultaneously by the large steamers." These, the Navy's *Susquehanna, San Jacinto, Dacotah, Seminole,* and *Monitor,* completed the attacking squadron under Commodore Lardner. Wrote Lieutenant D. C. Constable, U.S.R.-M., in reporting the affair to Secretary Chase:

> My individual orders from the flag officer were to take a position for the purpose referred to, and engage the battery, and if the *Merrimac* made her appearance to fall back out of the way to induce her to come out into the roads. . . . I selected a position off the battery of the enemy . . . a distance

[6] *Army and Navy Journal,* November 26, 1864.

[7] E. L. Viele, "A Trip with Lincoln, Chase, and Stanton," *Scribner's Monthly,* October 1787 (Vol. XVI), 813-22.

less than that of ¼ of the actual range of our heavy gun [about a mile] from which I threw shell into the enemy's battery with good effect until the *Merrimac* made her appearance . . . when, with the rest of the squadron, led by the flagship we slowly retired towards Hampton Bar.

Everything on board was conducted to my satisfaction. . . .

D. C. Constable, Lieutenant,
Commanding *Naugatuck*.

Although the "Iron Diadem of the South" was not lured into battle, Norfolk fell two days later (May 10, 1862), and on the 11th the *Merrimac* was destroyed by her own people to prevent her capture.[8]

A few days later (May 15), Flag Officer L. M. Goldsborough ordered Commander John Rodgers, U.S.N., to take a squadron composed of the *Naugatuck* and the Navy's *Monitor, Galena, Aroostook,* and *Port Royal* and to "push on up to Richmond, if possible, and shell the place into surrender." This somewhat optimistic venture was undertaken in support of McClellan's Peninsula Campaign. The squadron, led by the *Naugatuck,* ran to a point eight miles below Richmond, where it encountered a double barrier of "spiles, steamboats, and sail vessels" strung out across the river and guarded by rifle pits on the river bank and by a strong battery on Drewry's Bluff. Unable to go up the river, and unsupported by McClellan's troops, the squadron bombarded the battery for four hours and then retired downstream. During the engagement the *Galena* suffered severe casualties. The *Naugatuck's* heaviest gun, a 100-pounder rifled Parrott, burst with the first shot fired, injuring a man and radically reducing the vessel's effectiveness, but "she continued in her position during the entire action, fighting her broadside guns." Wrote Mr. Stevens to Secretary Chase:

On her recent passage up the James River, and in the attack . . . her ability to submerge the whole hull under the water not only prevented her being struck by a single shot, but enabled her to pilot the other vessels of the fleet up the river, as she pumped out her water apartments and in that way got afloat whenever she got aground. The placing of the gun 'en barbette' and the crew below the waterline prevented a large loss of life which otherwise might have followed the bursting of her gun.[9]

Reported Lieutenant Constable:

My officers and crew behaved to my entire satisfaction.[10]

During the war the *Harriet Lane* was doubtless the most famous cutter and Captain Faunce one of the most distinguished officers of the Revenue-Marine. As noted previously, the *Harriet Lane* was inducted

[8] *Off. Rec. Union & Confed. Navies,* Ser. I, VII, *passim.*

[9] J. P. Baxter, *Introduction of the Ironclad Warship* (Harvard University Press, 1933); 217.

[10] *Off. Rec. Union & Confed. Navies,* ser. I, VII; 357.

into the Navy before the fall of Sumter; her speed, light draft, and fighting captain made her a welcome addition to naval forces in many undertakings. She was frequently a member of blockading squadrons; she participated in numerous bombardments; her draft permitted her to work inshore to cover troop-landings with her guns. (She mounted five at this time, an 8-inch and four rifled 32-pounders.) She was often sent on independent missions of considerable importance. For instance, at various times in mid-1861 she escorted thousands of troops in the lower Chesapeake. One interesting little action, typical of the work the *Harriet Lane* was often called upon to do, is described by Captain Faunce himself, in a report to Flag Officer C. J. Pendergrast, U.S.N., Commanding West India Squadron, off Fortress Monroe, Virginia. The date is June 5, 1861:

> Sir: In obedience to orders from General Butler to make a reconnaissance of Pig Point and vicinity, etc., I this morning at 4:50 got underway with my ship from off Newport News and stood towards Craney Island, steaming close in and along the shore. When off Pig Point I observed near the beach a number of men apparently engaged in transporting guns by means of ox teams and wheel carriages, while others were seen near the embrasures of the battery with the secession flag flying over them. At 8:30 a.m. I approached as close to the battery as the flats would allow, a distance of about 1800 yards, and opened fire, which was promptly returned by the rebels, from, I judge, seven guns, four of which were either 42 or 32 pounders and the others appeared to be 24-pounder howitzers. Two of the shot took effect on the vessel, one passing through the plank-sheer forward of the fore rigging on the port side and out through the starboard bulwarks; the other through the fore rigging, grazing the foremast. Several of their heavy shot passed over the vessel and struck some distance beyond. The shell from their howitzers all fell short. Thirty rounds of shot and shell were thrown by us, nearly all of which fell short; some few, however, were observed to strike within the embrasures. [A Confederate gun was struck by one shell and disabled.] The rebels fired about fifty shot and shell. Having accomplished my object of drawing the fire of the enemy, and thereby discovering the strength of their battery, and finding the range of my guns less than theirs, after an engagement of forty-five minutes I drew out of range. From the enclosed report of the surgeon you will perceive that five of our men were wounded. It affords me much pleasure to bear testimony to the gallant conduct of the officers and men under my command. Respectfully submitted,
>
> John Faunce, Captain.[11]

Seamen John Brainard, Peter Woods, Chris Kane, and Charles Johnson sustained splinter wounds, as did Nicholas Payne, captain of the after guard.

Only one serious offensive was undertaken by federal land forces during the early months of the war, and this venture—a frontal attack

[11] *Off. Rec. Union & Confed. Navies,* Ser. I, V, 698.

The United States Revenue-Cutter *Harriet Lane*
(From *Harper's Weekly*, *c.* 1860.)

Harriet Lane Firing First Shot From a Ship in Civil War

(From a mural by Aldis B. Browne, II, in Satterlee Hall, U. S. Coast Guard Academy.)

Lieutenant A. A. Fengar, U.S.R.-M.; Civil War Period

(Official C.G. photo.)

The Yacht *Henrietta*
(From *Harper's Weekly,* August 10, 1861.)

Revenue-Steamer *Hugh McCulloch*
(From a lithograph made during the Civil War by A. Hoen and Company, of Baltimore.)

Departure of the Great Southern Expedition

(The *Harriet Lane* is second from left. From *Harper's Weekly*, September 14, 1861.)

Bombardment of the Forts at Hatteras Inlet

(The *Harriet Lane* is third from left. From a print in the Office of the Superintendent, U. S. Coast Guard Academy.)

The Cutter *Woodbury* (ex-*Mahoning*); Period of the Civil War
(Official C.G. photo.)

Wreck of the S. S. *Bohemian*
(From *Harper's Weekly,* March 12, 1864.)

Model of the Practice Cutter *Dobbin, c.* 1877
(In Chase Hall, U. S. Coast Guard Academy.)

The Practice Cutter *Chase* in '81
(By an unknown artist. From "Tide Rips, '08.")

Lifeboat under Oars
(From a L.-S.S. lantern slide, *c.* 1880.)

Lifeboat under Sail
(From a L.-S.S. lantern slide, *c.* 1880.)

on Richmond—resulted in the Blue army's rout and demoralization at Bull Run (July 1861). The entire North experienced a dangerous psychological slump from which it appeared unable to emerge until a major victory had been won. The capture of Confederate forts at Hatteras Inlet, a few weeks later, restored Union confidence and helped cut off the South from foreign aid.

Flag Officer Stringham's expedition against Hatteras brought units of the Army, Navy, Marine Corps, and Revenue-Marine together in the joint amphibious operation reported below:

The expedition, consisting of the frigates *Minnesota,* Commodore Stringham; *Wabash,* Captain Mercer; the gunboats *Pawnee,* Captain Rowan; *Monticello,* Commander Gillis, and the *Harriet Lane,* Captain Faunce; with the transports *Adelaide* and *George Peabody,* conveying troops [under Major General Butler] to the number of about a thousand, left Fortress Monroe last Monday and reached the rendezvous off Hatteras Inlet on Tuesday morning, the *Minnesota* and *Wabash* coming in in the afternoon, and the *Cumberland* joined the fleet the same day.

Preparations were immediately made to land the troops the following morning, at which time the transports ran near the beach, two miles north of the inlet, and, covered by the *Monticello, Harriet Lane,* and *Pawnee,* about three hundred men were landed through a heavy surf. . . . The gunboats swept the beach and neighboring copse of scrub oaks. All the boats being swamped and bilged in the surf, no more men could be thrown ashore. Meanwhile, the *Minnesota* and *Wabash*—the latter with the *Cumberland* in tow—steamed up to the front of one of the rebel batteries and took position at long range.

At ten o'clock the *Wabash* fired the first gun, the eleven-inch shell striking near the battery. . . . The battery instantly returned the fire [with five long 32's], the shot falling short. The *Minnesota* and *Cumberland* immediately opened fire and rained nine- and eleven-inch shells into and about the battery. . . . The cannonading on our part was incessant, and the air was alive with the hum and explosion of flying shells. But the enemy did not return the fire with any regularity, the battery being too hot for them, from the explosion of shells that dropped in at a rate of about half a dozen a minute.

The enemy ceased firing a little before two, and after a few more shells had been thrown in the Commodore signalized to cease firing.

The troops had meantime advanced to within a short distance of the fort, and before we ceased firing some of our men got in and raised the Stars and Stripes. The place was too hot for the men, but the flag was left waving. Coxswain Benjamin Sweares, of the *Pawnee's* first cutter, stood for some time on the ramparts waving the flag amidst a flight of shells. When the firing ceased the fort was occupied in force, and held afterward.

The *Monticello* had proceeded ahead of the land force to protect them and had reached the Inlet when a large fort to the rear and right of the small battery and mounting ten thirty-twos and four eight-inch guns, which had till then been silent, opened on her with eight guns at short range. . . . The escape of the vessel and crew was miraculous. Until this time we supposed the day was ours, but the unexpected opening of the large battery rather changed the aspect of affairs. Things did not look cheerful at dark. . . .

At early daybreak on Thursday the men went to quarters in the fleet. At a quarter past eight, the vessels having borne down closer than the previous day's position, the action began. The frigates fired nearly half an hour before the battery responded, when it answered briskly. . . .

At twenty-five minutes past ten the *Harriet Lane* opened fire, and soon after the *Cumberland* came in from the offing and joined in the attack. The *Harriet Lane,* with her rifled guns, did good execution, several projectiles from the eight-inch going into the battery and one going directly through the ramparts. The fire was so hot that all of the enemy that could do so got into a bomb-proof in the middle of the battery.

Finally, at five minutes past eleven A.M., an eleven-inch shell having pierced the bomb-proof through a ventilator and exploded inside, near the magazine, the enemy gave up the fight and raised over the ramparts a white flag. . . . We immediately ceased firing. . . .

Articles of capitulation were signed on the flagship by Commodore Stringham and General Butler on the part of the United States, and by Commodore Barron, Colonel Martin, and Major Andrews on the rebel side, and the latters' swords delivered up.[12]

The *Harriet Lane* served under Captain Faunce until the autumn of '61, then under Commander J. M. Wainwright, U.S.N., until 1863, when she was captured at Galveston in a defensive action which cost the gallant Wainwright his life. Captain Faunce commanded several other cutters between 1861-65 and for a while in 1863 served as a member of the Board of Examiners, in New York, occupied with selecting applicants for war-time commissions in the cutter service.

The Lighthouse Establishment as well as the Revenue-Marine played a part in the ultimate victory of the federal forces. During the war 164 lights were destroyed, and nearly all of the lightships south of Chesapeake Bay were captured. Some lightships were sunk to obstruct harbor entrances. The following item from *Harper's Weekly* for December 14, 1861, concerning the lightship at Martin's Industry, South Carolina, shows that the lighthouse men soon learned to go prepared for action:

The lightship . . . will display two bright white lights, which can be seen from a distance of twelve to fifteen miles. Her crew will consist of about twenty persons in addition to the light-keepers. She will be armed with four rifled cannon, and, to prevent the rebels from boarding her, nettings will be placed around her, above the rail.

As the Union pushed southward with its naval operations, the Lighthouse Service assisted by relighting important stations like Martin's Industry and by placing special buoys, lights, and lightships in zones of

[12] *Harper's Weekly,* September 14, 1861.

naval activity, just as the Coast Guard was called upon to do in combat theatres in World War II.

From the people of the United States, the Civil War brought forth an unprecedented demand for news. Technological progress offered improved telegraphs, improved presses, tons of newsprint, and a new journalism to meet the popular demand. As one result of the quickened public consciousness, the Revenue-Marine became better known than ever before. Neither the wartime value of the service's law enforcement and marine safety work nor the cutters' utility as combat units was lost to sight among the larger issues of the day, and the practical benefit of maintaining such a force—adapted to the purpose both of peace and war—received a considerable measure of popular interest and support. One editor, writing in 1864, showed a clear awareness of the service's potentialities and, incidentally, forecast both the motto—*"Semper Paratus"*—and the name destined eventually to mark the corps:

> Keeping always under steam and *ever ready,* in the event of extraordinary need, to render valuable service, the cutters can be made to form a *coast guard* whose value it is impossible at the present time to estimate.[13]

[13] *Army and Navy Journal,* November 26, 1864. (Italics ours.)

CHAPTER VIII

Reconstruction

I

NORTHERN victory was variously interpreted in 1865, but in the long run it meant the victory of American nationalism. The welding of the states into a stable and indestructible federal union was prerequisite to formation of a truly nation-minded people. Gradually, after 1865, consciousness of common nationality came to infuse the vast majority of Americans; in the process, it almost wholly supplanted sectionalism as a major emotional drive. This allegiance to the United States was tinctured by dependence on the national government—a dependence first for aids and favors, later for controls, in the production and distribution of wealth. But whether for aids or for controls, all strata of the population placed increased demands on national agencies after 1865.

It is not odd, therefore, that in post-war years the Revenue-Marine rapidly outgrew many of the early administrative weaknesses to which sectionalism and localism had long condemned it. Indeed, wartime necessity already had tended to centralize and strengthen the service's administration: a sort of general supervision by an Assistant Secretary of the Treasury had been instituted during the war. Centralization was facilitated by the extension of railway mail service and of telegraph lines throughout the country. By 1865, permanent organization of the cutter establishment under centralized control seemed fairly well assured. A short delay arose from official Washington's immediate concern with post-war settlements and with the reconstruction of the South, but the loose system of cutters was on its way toward transformation into a national coast guard.

Before discussing detailed changes wrought in the Revenue-Marine, it is well to note the changes that post-war conditions brought to cutter operations. Mention of the wartime tariff already has been made. Peace brought no policy of reduction in the tax; in fact, such adjustments as were made in it during the remainder of the century were, for the most part, made upward. For better or for worse—depending on one's individual conviction—the country seemed committed to protectionism. But no honest advocate of tariff reduction had any thought of permitting the law to be evaded. With high tariff as a national policy, the demand was for enforcement. However, the higher the tariff, the higher the rewards to smugglers. The situation called for increased vigilance on the cutters' part and for cooperation between the units in adjacent districts. So adequately were these conditions met that eventually the mere presence of a fleet of cutters cruising along the coast constituted an efficient preventive of customs law violation. This deterrent effect was recognized in a statement contained in the Revenue-Marine's *Annual Report* for 1872:

> That . . . withdrawal of the cutters for any considerable period from any portion of the coast would be readily taken advantage of is proved by the extensive operations of organized bands of smugglers discovered last year along the east coast of Florida, between Cape Florida and Saint John's River, a strip of coast unavoidably left for some months unprotected.

Further, a new series of laws began to claim the service's attention. The first enactment curbing immigration was passed by Congress in 1862.[1] This law forbade the importation of coolie labor. Other immigration laws subsequently appeared in the Statutes; from 1862 on, cutters at sea aided in the enforcement of the legislation. Operations involved were, in the main, preventive and were performed collaterally with other preventive and law enforcement activities.

Post-war trends in merchant shipping gradually effected a very material change in the Revenue-Marine's protective work. The wartime decline of the merchant fleet engaged in foreign commerce already has been mentioned. About 40% of the American foreign-commerce fleet had been sunk, burned, or otherwise lost to American registry by the end of the war. The fraction that remained was for the most part old, rotten, or obsolete. Cargoes once carried by American clippers were now freighted in other (mainly British) bottoms. Although American foreign trade was expanding rapidly and although U.S. ships had carried over half a billion dollars' worth of goods in 1860, they transported only $184,000,000 worth in 1864.

Nor were conditions favorable for speedy replacement of American tonnage to recapture the lost advantage. High tariff on iron plates and other shipbuilding materials discouraged American operators (unless subsidized) from purchasing U.S.-built ships to compete with cheaper British-made-and-operated vessels. Foreign-built ships were denied U.S. registry by law; the same prohibition was laid against American ships that had participated in the "flight from the flag" to avoid capture by Confederate cruisers and privateers. And native wooden vessels were out-of-date.

Free capital thus found more inducement ashore than it did afloat in foreign trade. Factories sprang up like mushrooms in the industrial areas, railroads grew into vast imperial networks, and the earth gave up

[1] Act of February 19, 1862 (12 Stat. L., 340, 341).

millions of tons of oil, iron, and coal to be transmuted, at the Midas-touch, into millions of bright new dollars. But men with money found little encouragement to adventure it in so moribund an industry as trans-oceanic shipping. All in all, the glory of the clipper days had vanished. But while American-borne foreign commerce lingered in the doldrums until World War I, the coasting trade, reserved by law to American built-and-operated ships, backed and filled to its old position and then sailed on to greater things.

Conditions were generally favorable to coastwise shipping. Foreign competition was non-existent. Mechanization in industry and agriculture swelled the stream of domestic trade. Growth of textile industries in the North created a home market for the southern staple; tonnage on the Lakes rose with the increasing productivity of soil, mine, and factory; between the Atlantic and Pacific, a trade established back in Gold Rush days by no means was neglected. A chart of merchant marine statistics for the period 1860-1910 shows graphically how American coastal shipping increased, both relatively and absolutely, while American-borne foreign trade declined.

Clearly, increased coastwise shipping meant an increase in the tonnage exposed to dangers of coast-piloting. And these ships in domestic trade—more and more of them, as time went on—were steamers. They were larger and heavier than the coastal schooners of a by-gone day. From the close of the war to the turn of the century, the total *number* of vessels in coastal trade remained about the same, but their total gross *tonnage* nearly doubled. This resulted principally from the widespread acceptance, after 1880, of metal for hulls. Stronger, bigger ships were built. The trend had especial significance to the Revenue-Marine. For instance, while only 20% of the ships involved in marine disasters in 1882 were steamers, the percentage had risen to 25% by 1888.[2] And, obviously, when some heavy iron steamer ran aground not even a Josiah Sturgis could sail up in a revenue-schooner, anchor, pass a line, and haul the ship off by man-power. To be effective in aiding shipping in distress, post-war cutters needed the horse-power of iron and steam.

On the human side, bigger ships could carry more passengers and required larger crews; when trouble came along more lives were jeopardized. Although the number of vessels annually involved in casualties in American waters remained practically constant between 1875 and 1888, the number of persons on board such vessels increased by nearly 40%. Great marine tragedies have always spurred the interest of the American public in the subject of safety at sea. The fact that great disasters did occur led to a humanitarian sentiment among Americans

[2] Statistics on marine disasters cited in this and subsequent paragraphs are taken from sundry *Annual Reports,* U. S. Life-Saving Service.

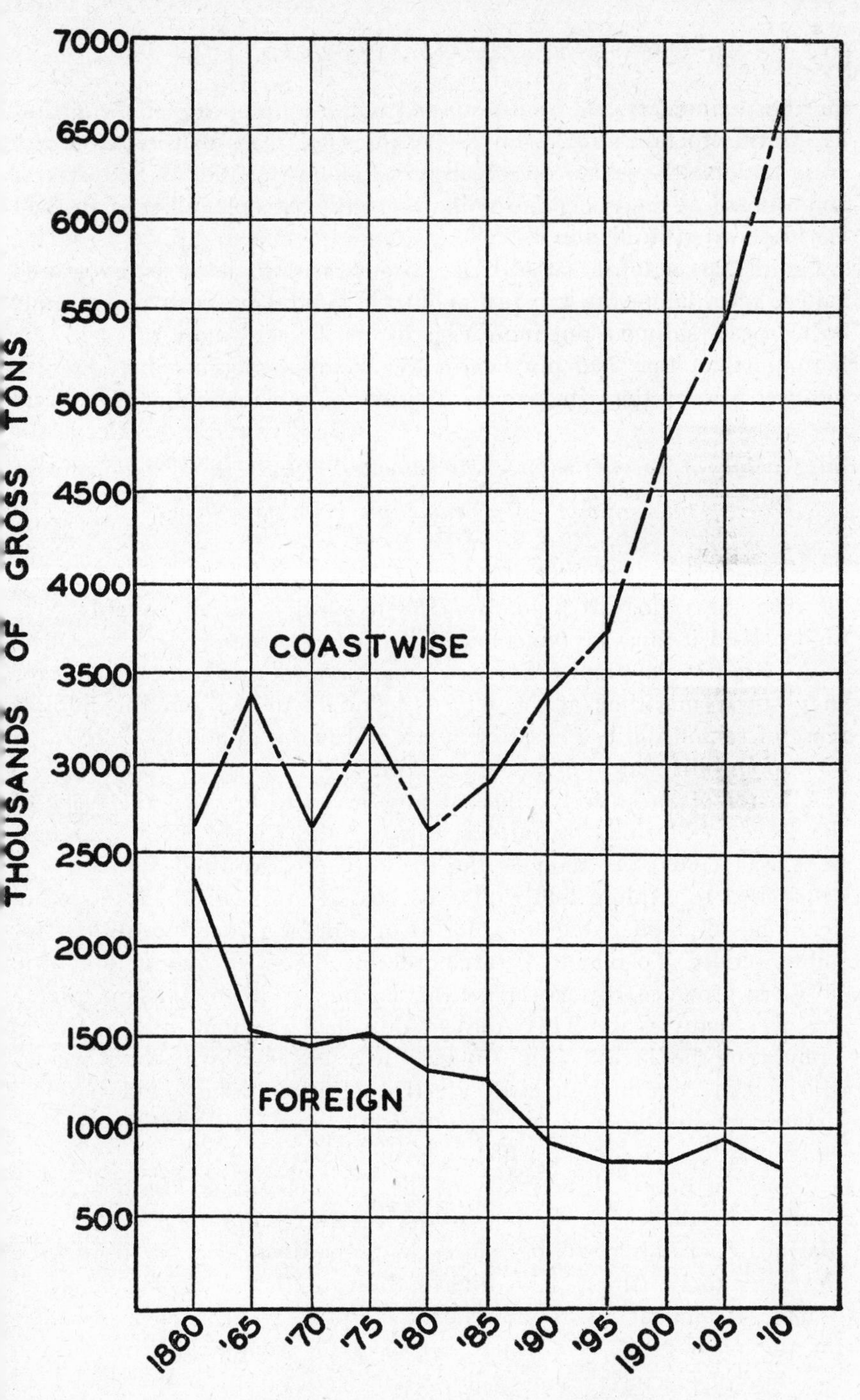

U. S. Foreign and Coastwise Tonnage

(Based on *Merchant Marine Statistics* (U. S. Department of Commerce, Bureau of Navigation; Washington, D.C.; 1931). Tonnage documented for the whale and cod-and-mackerel fisheries is not included in charted figures.)

for the maintenance of well-equipped cutters, life-saving stations, and lighthouses to minimize as far as possible—for ships of their own and every nation—the dangers of ocean travel along U. S. coasts. Self-interest and a practical good neighbor policy merged in this phase of the service's maritime safety function.

Finally, larger ships carried larger cargoes, with higher average insured values, yet a large ship ran just about the same dangers as a small one. So to speak, shippers put more eggs in one basket—more cargo in one bottom—than they had put before. When disaster occurred, the dollar loss was greater than in average disasters of previous years. The ratio

$$\frac{\textit{total value of cargoes aboard documented vessels sustaining casualty}}{\textit{total number of documented vessels involved}}$$

may have only a limited validity, but it serves to indicate this trend. In 1882 the ratio was 5170. By 1888 it stood at 8800—roughly 70% higher. And it must be remembered that every consumer feels the effect both of lost cargoes and of increased marine insurance rates. This factor in post-war maritime affairs served definitely to sharpen the public's sense of responsibility for safety at sea and hence to add to the burden of responsibility laid on the cutter fleet.

A factor of an entirely different sort served to broaden the scope of the Revenue-Marine's operations; this was the United States' purchase of Alaska (1867). As soon as the territory was acquired, cutters were dispatched to explore and police its coastal areas. Probably no other detail has ever offered more colorful or more varied opportunities for public service. To remote waters bordering the great, almost unknown, northern province, cutters carried the flag on a civilizing mission extending over many years. This Alaskan duty had the immediate effect of stimulating the Treasury and Congress to a new interest in the Revenue-Marine; in combination with all the maritime trends and national circumstances outlined above, it climaxed the need for the service's speedy reorganization—a process which was undertaken in 1869.

George S. Boutwell, Secretary of the Treasury under President U. S. Grant, was the prime mover in the reconstruction of the Revenue-Marine. Soon after taking office, he appointed Mr. N. Broughton Devereux to be Chief of an interim Bureau comprising the Revenue-Marine, Steamboat Inspection, Marine Hospital, and Life-Saving Services for the purpose of expediting "measures to promote the interests of each and of placing these four important services on a proper footing."[3]

[3] *Report of the Chief of the Revenue-Marine, Etc., 1869* (Govt. Printing Office, Washington, 1869).

Forthwith, Devereux set up two Commissions to overhaul the Revenue-Marine. Captain John Faunce presided over one, charged with matters concerning personnel. Captain C. T. Patterson, of the Coast Survey, was president of the second, which included Captain Douglass Ottinger, Captain J. H. Merryman, and Charles W. Copeland, of New York. This group was charged with considering and reporting "upon the character of vessels best adapted for the revenue marine service, together with such views and conclusions upon other matters as might appear to them calculated to advance the interests of the service."[4]

These Commissions formulated three basic problems and offered a general solution for each. *Administration,* they reported, should be centralized. Both for efficiency and for economical operations, said the investigators, "the Service should be conducted under stringent regulations, from which the highest authority alone can authorize any departure." *Personnel,* they declared, should be divorced from political influences, and officers should be appointed and promoted on a merit basis. *Floating equipment,* Boutwell was advised, should be designed specifically to meet the peculiar requirements of the Revenue-Marine. Such a policy in earlier days had led to the evolution of splendid sailing cutters. New maritime conditions made sailing cutters obsolete, but few of the remaining war-vintage steam cutters satisfactorily met the service's requirements. The Patterson Commission suggested that replacements be made with smaller, easier-handled vessels carrying smaller crews—vessels built to plans accurately reflecting cutter needs. This policy, followed through ensuing years, produced a new and distinctive type of ship, the power-driven Coast Guard cutter.

To carry out the first of these proposals, Boutwell reestablished a Revenue-Marine Bureau in the Treasury and assigned it the duty of administering both the cutters and life-saving stations. Unlike Secretary Spencer, who had relied upon a cutter captain to head the first Revenue-Marine Bureau, Boutwell appointed a civilian Chief. The choice, however, turned out to be a thoroughly satisfactory one; the post was given to Sumner I. Kimball, a "downeaster," graduate of Bowdoin College, honest civil servant, intelligent and able executive of federal agencies. Having worked up to the position of Chief Clerk of the Treasury Department, Kimball now continued on, to become the real architect of reconstruction for the Revenue-Marine and Life-Saving Service.

Kimball took up his duties on February 1, 1871 and performed them under the Secretary's administrative authority until Congress recognized his office in the Statutes. Under the Act of March 3, 1875 (18 Stat. L., 371, 396), Congress formally established the Revenue-Marine Division,

[4] Reports of Boutwell's Commissions were published as *Senate Ex. Doc. 64 and 93, 41 Cong., 2 Sess.*

and Kimball was confirmed as Chief. (Kimball always referred to his Division as a "bureau.") The Act gave a permanence to the centralized, or "headquarters," plan of organization that Spencer and Fraser had been unable to achieve.

First of all, Kimball set about revising the *Regulations, U.S.R.-M.,* and by August 1, 1871, they were ready for Boutwell's signature. Numerous provisions struck at old evils. Collectors were retained in nominal superintendence over the cutters; for practical purposes, however, they became little more than links between the ships and Washington. Within limits, they were permitted to direct local operations, but use of cutters for purposes other than official was proscribed. Authority over operations, repair, supply, and personnel was centralized in the Department. Control was insured by the rule that Headquarters review all logs and accounts and authorize all funds. As an added safeguard, Kimball introduced the systematic inspection of units. Article 412 announced that a captain would be detailed as inspecting officer for the service, and the same article defined his duties. Among other matters, he was required to investigate whether or not the cutters engaged "actively . . . in cruising, and if the officers have been zealous in the performance of their duties and conducted themselves generally with credit to the Government." As a further measure of economy and good management, it was decreed that no cutter's complement should "under any pretense" exceed the number authorized by the Secretary. Kimball was thus able to reduce the number of enlisted men from 1046 in 1871 to 860 in 1872, a number which he said was found sufficient.

Kimball's *Regulations* carried a long step further the Spencer-Fraser tendency towards giving the service a rational system of discipline. The new *Regulations* insisted that discipline be maintained by legal methods and not by arbitrary or extralegal process, and developed the concept that legal rights, no less than legal duties, define each individual's relation to the service and to the state. On the one hand,

> All . . . persons of the revenue service are required and strictly enjoined to properly observe and obey the orders of their superiors and to use their utmost exertions to carry such orders into effect. . . .

On the other,

> No officer or other person . . . in the revenue service . . . shall oppress, cruelly treat, or maltreat any other person under his command or control. . . . Firm and judicious treatment of officers and men, tempered by kindness, will ordinarily insure discipline and efficiency. . . . The captain only shall order punishment to be inflicted, *which must be in conformity with the law of Congress prescribing the same.*[5]

[5] *Rules and Regulations of the Revenue-Marine Service,* 1871; Articles 78, 81, 230. (Italics ours.)

But although the regulation was sound enough, the fundamental law was not. Because the statutes contained no specific code for revenue-cutter personnel, the service was forced to rely for disciplinary power upon the law governing merchant seamen and upon the custom of the sea. The merchant code was not designed to insure high standards in a military corps, and the custom of the sea, susceptible of wide interpretation by individual officers, scarcely insured the personal rights and dignities of the men. Thus, while Kimball's *Regulations* set a completely reasonable tone for service discipline, they could not remedy the basic defect in the system. And not until many years later (1906) did Congress fill the void by providing specifically a cutter code, with precise definitions of offenses and levels of punishment, needful to a thoroughly rational system of military law.

Even before Kimball promulgated his *Regulations,* Captain Faunce's Personnel Commission had taken drastic measures towards raising professional standards. Faunce's board had been authorized to overhaul the entire list of officers and to weed out undesirables, of whom a number had slipped into the ranks during the service's wartime expansion. Faunce and his fellow inquisitors met for the first time on October 22, 1869 and held sessions at intervals for the next two years. Seven out of 19 captains and 33 out of 103 lieutenants failed to meet the standards set by the Faunce Commission. One second lieutenant, originally appointed in 1864, had no knowledge of charts or instruments; another had a reputation for chronic alcoholism; still another was reported as "not fit for promotion, amounts to nothing."[6] Wrote Kimball, after the board had done its work:

> Those [officers] remaining were given rank and numerical standing [seniority] according to their qualifications. Incompetency was thus eradicated, and the service placed upon a proper basis for the operation of the system of making appointments and promotion upon merit and professional qualifications. Since then all appointments and promotions have been made upon the competitive plan, which, whatever may be thought of the practicability of its application to the civil service . . . has certainly in the Revenue Marine been productive of the best results. It has given the service the best corps of junior officers it ever possessed, and has instituted among them a vigorous competition in the pursuit of professional attainments, productive of diligent application to study and a zealous discharge of duty.[7]

In writing the *Regulations* of 1871, Kimball strove to maintain this high morale. The new rules positively forbade the use of political influence in procuring appointments, promotions, and assignment to

[6] Revenue-Marine Examinations for Promotion of Officers, 1869-71. In *C. G. Archives.*

[7] *Annual Report of the Revenue-Marine* (Washington), 1872.

preferred stations—a policy handed down to the Coast Guard later on. They prohibited the original appointment of officers in any grades other than the lowest (third lieutenant or second assistant engineer). Candidates for commissions were required to possess a stated minimum of practical experience and to pass both a physical and a competitive professional examination. Promotions in all cases were to be based on merit and professional qualifications, without regard to seniority. A tour of duty upon a station was fixed at two years "unless the exigencies of the service should otherwise demand."

Only in a very narrow sense can these reforms be said to have been passed down from above. Kimball was a good organizer, he was something of an efficiency expert for his time, and he had the political support necessary to carry his policies into effect. But officers from Fraser to Faunce and Merryman and many others had recommended such changes for years. To the commissioned corps of the Revenue-Marine, Kimball gracefully acknowledged a patent debt:

> The efforts of the Department to relieve the service of the abuses which oppressed it and to restore it to a healthy condition have generally met with a cordial response from its officers. . . . I have derived the most valuable assistance from the counsel of several of the more experienced . . . and have also, I believe, been cordially seconded in my efforts by every officer now in the service.[8]

The logical next step in the evolution of a modern policy for insuring high professional standards in the commissioned corps was an obvious one, and Kimball took it: he persuaded Congress to inaugurate a system whereby the service might select and train its own officer replacements. It was Kimball's masterwork, the most effective single action ever taken to promote the efficiency of this branch of federal activity. A School of Instruction was established in 1877 under legislation which authorized the appointment and education of cadets and provided for their eventual commissioning.[9] This School was the forerunner of the United States Coast Guard Academy.

Kimball was urged into the cadet training program by three of his closest advisers: Captain G. W. Moore, the Chief Inspector; Captain J. H. Merryman, Superintendent of Construction; and Captain J. A. Henriques. These three must be called the true founders of the Academy; the idea, at any rate, was theirs. In a day when the words "specialist" and "expert" were beginning to take on something of their modern meaning, these captains saw the advantage of training and indoctrinating young men for the especial purpose of performing Revenue-Marine

[8] *Ibid.*

[9] Act of July 31, 1876 (17 Stat. L., 102, 107).

duties. Together they worked out the details of the system, but credit for placing the program in operation must go to Henriques, who was made first Superintendent of the School.

The law specified a two-year period of instruction, and the captains decided that cadets should spend the time aboard a practice sailing cutter. Training in sail, they held, would give cadets a feeling for the sea no other experience could provide. The old *Dobbin* was refitted as a training ship and so served from May 1877 until the late summer of 1878, when she was replaced by the *Chase*. The *Dobbin* was a schooner and bore a close resemblance to the famed *Joe Lane*. The *Chase,* specially designed by Merryman for her particular assignment, was 106 feet long by 26 feet beam; she was a beautiful bark-rigged clipper with a round stern and a graceful clipper bow. New Bedford, Massachusetts, became the practice ship's home port.

With Henriques in the *Dobbin* were First Lieutenant C. L. Hooper, Second Lieutenant D. A. Hall, and Surgeon Irving Rosse. Professor Edwin Emery, of Whitinville, Massachusetts, was engaged to help organize the curriculum and to teach several of the academic subjects. Every subject was oriented towards the needs of a line officer in the Revenue-Marine. Since no engineering cadets were appointed in the first class—or, in fact, for the next twenty years or so, during which period the service continued to obtain its engineering officers direct from civil life—no advanced engineering subjects were prescribed for the original curriculum. Henriques divided the course into a junior and a senior year, with one sea term and two academic terms apiece. For both sea terms he prescribed practical work in Seamanship, Navigation, Signals, and "Exercises Aloft"; some theoretical instruction was included. Among the several academic terms he distributed the following studies:

Algebra
Geometry
Trigonometry
Philosophy (Physics)
Astronomy
History
French
English
Composition

Seamanship (Luce's textbook)
Navigation
Gunnery
Steam Engineering
Law (Kent's *Commentaries*)
Customs Law
Navigation Law
International Law

Kimball's democratic method of appointing officers by competitive examination was extended to cover cadet appointments, and the captains set the examination standard high so as to "secure fairly educated young men" with reasonably bright chances of completing the course. Besides a competitive examination in Arithmetic, Geography, and English, candidates were given marks in General Aptitude. Of the 19 candidates examined by the first entrance board, nine failed the written examination. A tenth failed in General Aptitude because, although "he succeeded in passing to the required standing . . . he made an unfavorable impression on the Board by his general deportment and by his manifest disposition to prevaricate." The nine who "made the grade" received appointments as cadets and went up the *Dobbin's* gangway in May, 1877: the Class of 1879 was entering its "swab year."

These first cadets experienced all the tribulations that are the perquisites of their rank. For the small comfort of later "swabs" (cadet vernacular for "lower classmen"), it may be mentioned that their archetype in misery survived to serve as Commandant. This cadet, Worth G. Ross, of '79, was desperately seasick on his first day at sea, and for the first sea term he managed to lead his class in the accumulation of demerits. But under Henriques and his successors, the School brought something more than tribulation to cadets. By graduation time each year, it had marked its men as members of a distinctive group, selected and trained to become specialists in maritime affairs, indoctrinated with the best traditions of their profession, and keenly appreciative of the social value of their collective work. This thought is best expressed in the Academy's historic "Mission":

> To graduate young men with sound bodies, stout hearts, and alert minds, with a liking for the sea and its lore, and with that high sense of honor, loyalty, and obedience which goes with trained initiative and leadership; well-grounded in seamanship, the sciences, and the amenities; and strong in the resolve to be worthy of the traditions of the commissioned officers in the service of their country and humanity.

II

In carrying into effect the Commission's recommendation concerning floating equipment, Kimball relied for advice chiefly upon Captain Merryman, who had served on the Commission, and upon Consulting Engineer Charles E. Emery, of New York. In five years, from 1871 to 1876, these men contracted for a number of new steamers to replace the more unsuitable or obsolete units of the fleet. Cutters so replaced included eight schooners built in 1866 (the last class of sailing cutters to be used for general service) and about a dozen steamers, including the *Wayanda.* (Four others of the latter class had been sold out in 1867. The *Mahoning,* re-named *Woodbury,* alone of this class enjoyed a long career; she remained in active commission until 1915.) Most of the decommissioned steamers appear to have been jerry-built and either too expensive or too cranky to have warranted retention.

By 1876, the fleet thus consisted of a dozen veterans of the Civil War, no two of which were alike either in size and shape or engine lay-out, and about a dozen new units, built expressly as cutters to specifications checked and approved by Merryman and Emery. The former group included *Woodbury, Seward, Perry, Fessenden, Johnson, McLane, Crawford, Dix, Moccasin, Ewing, Stevens (Naugatuck),* and the *McCulloch;* the latter, *Colfax, Grant, Gallatin, Hamilton, Boutwell, Wolcott, Manhattan* (tug), *Dallas, Rush, Dexter, Corwin.*

Diversity among the older units was largely a matter of chance; for the most part these vessels had simply been picked up by the Revenue-Marine as opportunity came along. They represented no consistent construction policy and no single school of engineering design. But the diversity which showed up in some of the units Kimball added was a planned diversity, indicative of the fact that Kimball and his advisers recognized the service's need for technological re-orientation. From the standpoint of cutter progress, the period of 1871-76 was one of looking around: of judicious experimentation to see which offerings of the new machine era were most suitable for cutter uses.

Experimentation, logically, was directed at fundamentals; refinements could come later. Kimball's officers wanted a small, light-draft, maneuverable, seaworthy cutter, adapted to towing, capable of moderate range and speed under steam, equipped with auxiliary sails for economy, and manageable by a small crew. They had to find the combination of hull and machinery which best met these inter-related demands.

Several possibilities existed. In the war decade, a single-cylinder engine driving sidewheels and served by a boiler at around 45 pounds of pressure had been the dominant marine installation. But the same period had quickened the tempo of American technological progress; for one thing, improvements in materials, lubricants, and machine-shop methods had helped establish the feasibility of screw propulsion. The trend towards general acceptance of propellers had been acknowledged in the *Woodbury* and other *Ashuelot*-class cutters. Concurrently, the compound (multiple cylinder, multiple expansion) engine—developing far higher efficiency than single cylinder types—had begun to prove itself commercially a success. By the time Kimball was ready to launch his new cutter program, then, three general types of steamship offered themselves for his selection. They were: (1) sidewheel, (2) single-cylinder engine, single screw, (3) compound engine, single screw. Which type was best for cutter drive? A direct attempt was made in 1871 to solve the problem on the basis of comparative performance. Three ships, representative of the three types of drive, were built so as to encompass in each as satisfactory a combination of cutter characteristics as possible. One, the *Colfax,* was a sidewheeler. Another, the *Hamilton,* was the first cutter with a compound engine. She had a single screw. The *Grant,* third of the trio, was on the single cylinder, single screw design.

The experiment marked definitely the eclipse of sidewheelers, as far as the service was concerned, but the controversy concerning single *vs.* compound engines ran on for several years. Theoretically the more efficient, the compound was nevertheless relatively new; there were still some "bugs" in its design. However, the *Manhattan, Dallas,* and *Rush* were built with single screws and compound engines. Further, the twin-screw *Boutwell* saw a novel application of the compound principle: her high-pressure cylinder drove one screw and her low-pressure cylinder drove the other. This innovation was a failure and doubtless furnished arguments in favor of the return to single screw, single cylinder machinery which was made a few years later in the *Corwin's* plant. Back and forth swung the controversy, and not until the late 'eighties, in fact, did the compound come fully into its own in the Revenue-Cutter Service. Its final unreserved acceptance was acknowledged in 1894 in a specification for re-engining the *Guthrie:* "The present machinery of the *Guthrie* consists of a single cylinder, inverted, direct-acting, jet condenser engine, built in the year 1882. The engine is . . . of an obsolete pattern."[10]

Prior to the *Corwin,* boilers in general service use had been of the so-called "ordinary flue and return tubular" type. They had been made, during the 'sixties, of charcoal hammered wrought iron plate—with the hope that they would stand a pressure of 45 pounds or so per square inch. Their specifications, in general, had been losely phrased; few meaningful standards were in existence. Only a hydrostatic test, at a little above boiler pressure, had ever been required. For the *Corwin,* however, a Scotch return tubular boiler was built of wrought iron of a *specified* tensile strength (45,000 to 60,000 pounds per square inch) to stand a hydrostatic test of 106 pounds. Boiler pressure increased fairly safely to 50-60 pounds. With this Scotch boiler began the practice of specifying definitely the strength of enginering materials used in cutter installations. The terms became increasingly precise as metals and test methods improved. Higher pressures and higher engineering efficiencies awaited this necessary prelude.

Iron hulls came more and more into favor in the services after 1862, but the Navy built some ships of wood as late as '74, and the Revenue-Marine did not wholly abandon the construction of wooden cruising cutters until considerably later. The *Boutwell* and *Manhattan* had iron hulls, but the *Dallas, Dexter, Rush,* and *Corwin* were built of wood. Not for two decades was iron to be adopted as the standard material for cutters' hulls—and by that time it was time to change to steel.

Some minor notes, of engineering interest, include: the introduction of steam jackets for cylinders, to decrease condensation losses, on the *Corwin;* the first mention of an electric installation for a cutter—a light-

[10] In *C. G. Archives.*

ning conductor tipped with gold and fitted with glass insulators—on the *Wolcott;* the first steam heating plant specified for a new cutter, on the *Manhattan;* the first specification calling for *steel* as the material to be used in the construction of any part of a cutter, for valve stems and crank pins used in the *Boutwell's* engine.

Another interesting "first" was the *Manhattan's* "Cathcart Propeller Attachment." This was an arrangement whereby the propeller was connected to the engine shaft through a universal joint and caused to turn in parallel motion with the rudder. Mechanical difficulties outweighed the expected gain in maneuverability, and no other Cathcart installation was made after the *Manhattan* venture.

No generalization concerning the course of cutter development under Kimball's regime can fail to note the fact that the fundamental problem had been recognized and that practical measures had been taken towards its solution: progress had been made towards creating a specialized cutter type. Reliable steamers had been launched and operated. There was a healthy trend towards the use of more exact specifications, of better materials, of more precise workmanship, and of improved designs. All these were in the direction of producing more efficient, more reliable, and more useful ships. By and large, the re-orientation and advance which had been made in five years represented a very solid engineering achievement.

The effectiveness of Kimball's three-point program for increasing the efficiency of the cutter service was almost immediately apparent. Without doubt, the new policies concerning administration, personnel, and matériél each had a share in the total result, but certainly the existence of a single, powerful, policy-making head was of primary importance. Some one finally was in the driver's seat; this is borne out in the following comparison of statistics for the first year of operation under the Kimball plan with those of the previous eleven years:

	Average, 11 years previous	*Fiscal year 1872*
Vessels assisted in distress	119	219
Vessels seized or reported	114	1,594
Miles sailed	147,599	166,098
Vessels boarded and examined	13,098	24,392

Increased work was accompanied by decreased cost; by rationalizing the organization, Kimball brought expenditures down from an average of around $1,275,000 per year for the seven preceding years to $930,000 for 1872. These generally satisfactory trends continued; Kimball's immediate successor as Chief of the Revenue-Marine, Ezra W. Clark, maintained that all the details of the system had been worked out by 1877, and he commented very favorably upon the success of the entire scheme.

The Life-Saving Establishment underwent a similar overhauling at Kimball's hand. An administrative system of a sort, it will be remembered, had been set up for the stations in 1854. Under this plan, administrative matters concerning stations and lifeboats had passed across the same desk in the Secretary's office that handled the Revenue-Marine; in a sense, therefore, the cutters and stations had formed two branches of the same service even prior to 1871. But in actual fact, the stations had been even more neglected than the cutters, and between 1854 and 1871 the lifesaving system turned out to be no system at all. Writing of the stations, some years later, Kimball said:

> Before 1871 there was probably no other arm of the public service so little held in esteem, as there was none more withered and feeble . . . it was an unconsidered trifle—its central habitat the corner of an office at the seat of government, its coast existence a thin line of weather-broken huts upon the beaches of Long Island and New Jersey—huts scantily furnished with poor equipment and only one of every two provided with men.[11]

It is noteworthy that efforts to build up a life-saving service had died with the outbreak of the war; the equipments and huts Kimball discovered in 1871 were almost entirely the remnants of Captain Ottinger's purchases out of ante-bellum appropriations. During the war, systematic slaughter outweighed systematic life-saving in the public consciousness, and humanitarian interests burned low. With the disappearance of battle-casualty lists from the daily news, however, marine disasters once again found front-page notoriety and aroused public sentiment to the point of action. Congress was called upon to meet the challenge presented by the annual occurrence of a thousand or more disasters in American waters. In 1869, a bill to increase the efficiency of the stations by employing paid surfmen instead of volunteers was voted down, but by 1870 Congress was ready to authorize the "pay of six experienced surfmen to each of the boats at alternate life-saving stations on the New Jersey coast."[12] A half-way measure, the Act proved inadequate. "During the winter of 1870-71 a number of appalling, fatal disasters occurred along the Atlantic coast. These disasters not only revealed the fact that the coast was not properly guarded, but also that the [life-saving] service was inefficient and needed a more complete organization."[13]

To Kimball, who had just become Chief of the Revenue-Marine, the

[11] *Annual Report of the United States Life-Saving Service, 1882* (Washington, 1883); 46-7.

[12] Such service to extend only from December 15 to March 15 each year. Act of July 15, 1870 (16 Stat. L., 291, 292).

[13] J. W. Dalton, *The Life-Savers of Cape Cod* (The Barta Press, Boston, 1902); 28.

situation was a stimulant to action. He soon discovered the existence of the stations and, through Captain Faunce (whom he sent to inspect them), he received detailed data on their sad condition. Administration, personnel and matériel, all showed the effects of neglect and lack of suitable directives. Kimball, "convinced that the [Life-Saving Establishment] . . . was capable under proper development of effecting great good," immediately set about the work of rehabilitation. An Act which authorized the Secretary to "employ crews of experienced surfmen at such stations and for such periods as he may deem necessary" was steered through Congress.[14] Another Act allotted $200,000 for the supply and repair of equipment. Kimball assigned Revenue-Marine officers to supervise the reorganization in the field; they inspected the stations, repaired the existing plant, bought new equipment, drilled the crews, instituted beach patrols and lookouts, introduced a system of signaling to ships offshore, and helped draw up regulations for the whole establishment. Captain Merryman and Captain John McGowan were made superintendents of construction for stations. Congress authorized stations for Rhode Island in 1871 and rapidly extended the system to other portions of the coast; within ten years, 189 stations were in operation—139 on the Atlantic, 37 on the Lakes, 7 on the Pacific, 5 on the Gulf, and one at the Falls of the Ohio. For administrative purposes, these stations were grouped in districts (of which there were 12 by 1882), under district superintendents. The latter were generally appointed from among the keepers in the districts concerned. Control was centralized in Washington and insured by district inspectors, Revenue-Marine officers detailed to train the crews and check up on operations in their areas. Captain Merryman acted as Chief Inspector of the entire system.

Of all the foregoing reforms, none had more lasting effect than the laws authorizing payment for the full-time services of professional crews. Volunteer surfmen, men willing to risk their lives with little thought of personal gain, were appealing and romantic figures—but they were not always on the job. Until professional crews were installed at stations reliable service could not be guaranteed, training was haphazard, and standards in all but courage remained low. Employment of paid men led rapidly to the development of *esprit de corps* and of a proficiency with life-saving equipment unsurpassed anywhere in the world.

Employment of full-time surfmen had another effect, one seldom any longer called to mind: it ended in the United States the ancient and barbaric profession of ship-plundering. Wreckers could no longer show false lights along the shore and draw ships into disaster—not with beach patrols keeping constant watch. The awful boast of a Barnegat pirate of the 1870's:

[14] Act of April 20, 1871 (17 Stat. L., 5, 12).

> No man or woman was ever robbed on this beach till they was dead. Of course, I don't mean their trunks and sech, but not the body. The Long Islanders cut off the fingers of living people for rings, but the Barnegat men never touch the body til it's dead, no sir![15]

echoes weirdly from the past; credit for carrying law to lonely beaches must go to the professional station crews.

Although Kimball kept the life-saving branch within the Revenue-Marine for awhile and filled its higher administrative positions with Revenue-Marine officers, it must not be supposed that these cutter men stole the show. They worked behind the scenes. The life-savers from their own ranks produced hundreds to play the really dramatic parts—men who gave their strength, sometimes their lives, that others might go on living. Kimball called them "hardy, able-bodied surfmen . . . native fishermen and beachmen . . . familiar with the habits of the surf." They knew how the surf looked from seaward. They could pull their weight in a boat. They were quiet, unassuming men. Some were middle-aged, be-whiskered, family men. Men whose uniforms never seemed to fit. Unromantic. But the show, played out most often against a back-drop of black seas in fury running, was altogether theirs.

The record of the re-invigorated service had a certain magic quality. Within the scope of station operations during the first year of Kimball's administration, not a single life was lost by shipwreck. In the later 'seventies, casualties to American ships in all parts of the world brought death to one out of every 48 persons on board. But from 1871 to 1882, death came to only one out of every 306 persons wrecked on coasts patrolled by U.S. Life-Savers. In the same period, the station crews saved $18,000,000 worth of property and rescued over 14,000 lives. Three thousand more, "brought to the stations drenched, frozen, starving, or nearly spent from the torture of the breakers," were sheltered and given aid. And the total cost of the whole life-saving program was no more than half a million annually. Here was a record that gave every citizen ample cause for pride. No wonder the stations' prestige grew; as Kimball said, it was based on success that had succeeded.

Kimball bossed both the cutters and the stations from 1871 to '78. In the latter year, Congress erected the Life-Saving Service into a separate bureau of the Treasury.[16] Kimball accepted the position of General Superintendent of the new agency, and the post of Chief of the Revenue-Marine went to another civilian, the above-mentioned E. W. Clark. But the two services were never completely divorced from each other; in fact, for a number of years there were more Revenue-Marine officers performing staff duties for the Life-Saving Service than there were in comparable

[15] Reported by Rebecca Harding Davis in *Lippincott's*, Vol. XVIII, 305 (1876).
[16] Act of June 18, 1878 (20 Stat. L., 163).

positions in the Revenue-Marine. The Act of 1878 authorized Kimball to set up a separate administrative and clerical force in Washington and reaffirmed the existing system of district superintendents for local administration, but, at Kimball's instigation, it retained cutter officers on the staff for construction and inspection duty. The Life-Saving Service remained so organized until 1915, when it re-joined the cutter branch in the U. S. Coast Guard.

Besides outlining the organization and reaffirming the duties of the Life-Saving Service, the organic Act of 1878 struck a note or two of innovation. Section 9, arming the service with the means for self-criticism, directed the General Superintendent to cause an investigation to be made of each maritime disaster attended by loss of life and occurring within the scope of the stations' operations. Other passages required the General Superintendent to collect and compile statistics of marine disasters, to acquaint himself with life-saving methods in use in foreign countries, and to insure the proper investigation of all plans and devices for the improvement of life-saving apparatus. The last-mentioned led to the appointment of a "Board on Life-Saving Appliances" (so-called after 1882), which met about once a year and performed the very valuable work of testing and reporting upon the large number of inventions submitted to it. Many of these have been impractical, a few have been ludicrous, but some have been the means of advancing ship and shore lifesaving equipment to a relatively high state of effectiveness. Improved surfboats, line-throwing guns, pyrotechnics, and breeches buoys, all were segregated from hundreds of less practical appliances and brought into active service via the Board.

The Revenue-Marine lost its most capable civilian Chief when it lost Kimball. Mr. Clark was aided by another civilian, Assistant Chief C. S. Trevitt; these two men with a dozen clerks constituted Headquarters in 1878. But whereas Kimball had placed great dependence on the advice of senior officers, Clark did not seem to have the same understanding of the functions of a military staff. He retained C. E. Emery as Consulting Engineer in New York, but no commissioned officer appears to have been either formally or informally on the Headquarters staff. This was especially unfortunate from the point of view of cutter development, as will be noted in a later chapter; however, the tradition of a central Headquarters did persist to serve as a keystone later on.

After the Kimball regime, civilian bureaucrats did nothing to improve the service further, but the officers, freed from their worst troubles by Kimball, retained their high morale, and the cutters continued to turn in records of valuable accomplishment. Service progress was resumed, however, after the appointment of a military Commandant in 1889.

Plainly, the Reconstruction Period had produced great changes in the

Revenue-Marine's organization, personnel, and ships, changes aimed at improved performance of the cutters' manifold duties. The latter were expanding gradually to meet changing maritime conditions, and the service itself was being transformed into a close-knit, centralized, self-conscious force. In carrying out the varied functions assigned them by the Congress and the President, cutters made news which the press willingly retailed to the public. The concept of a *national arm for maritime law enforcement and marine safety* colored every service report, news item, and magazine article, especially those dealing with operations in Alaska, and favorably influenced the emergence of a rational attitude towards the service's place in the governmental structure. The next chapter tells a little about the cutters' pursuit of national interests along this new frontier.

CHAPTER IX

Policing a New Frontier

I

RUSSIAN America meant little to the people of the United States before the Civil War or in the period immediately following. Closer home there were abundant subjects for consideration: carpet-bagging, deflation, homesteading, factory-building, stock-watering, Jim Fisk, and the price of wheat, were just a few. To most citizens of the U.S., Alaska was as far away as Aldebaran—and quite as unrelated to contemporary concerns. Certainly no imperialistic clamors urged acquisition of the territory. Alaska was a geographical expression covering 590,000 square miles of well-nigh unknown land. Of the gold, copper, tin, oil, coal, lead, tungsten, sulphur, gas, and platinum the land contained, the world as yet was unaware.

But Russia had supported the Union cause, and the Russian minister, offering the whole tract to the United States for $7,200,000 in 1867, found in Secretary of State William H. Seward a customer more than willing to be sold. The bargain was struck, and the Senate ratified a treaty of purchase on April 9, 1867. However, the requisite Appropriation Act experienced a rougher passage. Notwithstanding the fact that the purchase could be interpreted as repayment for Russia's previous support and, at the same time, that it would rid the continent of a potential threat to the Monroe Doctrine, the appropriation called forth a wave of ridicule in Congress. Some persons scoffed at "Seward's Ice-Box"; others balked at buying "a pig in a poke." For awhile it looked as though the entire business might bog down. According to Fernando Wood, chairman of the Committee of Ways and Means of the 44th Congress:

> When the proposition to purchase the Alaska Territory from Russia was before Congress, the opposition to it was very much based on alleged barrenness and worthlessness of the territory to be acquired. It was supposed that though there might be many political reasons for this addition to the American Pacific possessions, there was not commercial or revenue advantage.[1]

Opposition of this sort was unreasoning and blind. Alaska's maritime resources, certainly, were not unsuspected in all quarters. It was well-known, for instance, that in '65 the ubiquitous Rebel cruiser *Shenandoah*

[1] *Report,* dated June 3, 1876. Copy in *C. G. Archives.*

had caught a considerable number of Yankee whalers and traders in the Bering Sea—and Yankee sailormen seldom swarmed in wholly unprofitable parts. The Russians themselves had exploited the territory's fur trade for years. Salmon were known to abound. In the face of such facts, opposition to the purchase stood firm. It weakened only when the Russian minister, according to reliable reports, scattered part of the purchase money in Washington to sweeten up the deal.[2] Suffice to say, the appropriation finally was made (July 14, 1868) and the purchase carried out.

Seward's judgment soon proved sound. Politically, the purchase "locked America's back-door," to use the current phrase, and as a financial venture the territory paid for itself many times over before the century wore to a close. As early as 1877, a single Alaskan product was pouring into the federal Treasury a 4½ per cent per annum return on the cost price of the entire territory. This commodity was the fur-seal, special ward of the cutter service.

Extension of U.S. sovereignty over Alaska, a sparsely-settled region ten times the area of the British Isles, posed unique problems. As late as the 'eighties, barely a thousand whites and possibly 30 or 40 thousand natives and mixed breeds lived in the entire area. Most of the white settlers congregated in southeastern Alaska, although a few transients and traders ventured farther north. Whatever of stable commerce the land possessed lay almost entirely in the southeast around Sitka. Here, too, the need for protection against Indians was greatest; "from Chilkat to Tongas are the fierce people," said one old Sitka resident. For ten years after the purchase, the federal government was represented in the new lands by a few troops in scattered garrisons, by a collector of customs at Sitka, and by cutters cruising along the full sweep of the coasts. Commenting on this period, William Gouverneur Morris, Treasury investigator and a very careful observer, wrote:

> The revenue cutters . . . have been the safeguard and life of the Territory.[3]

The first cutter to visit Alaska after the purchase was the *Lincoln*. (One cutter had visited Russian America as early as 1865. In that year Captain C. M. Scammon took the *Shubrick* north to act as flagship for the six vessels that composed Western Union's expedition. The telegraph company's project of stringing a line overland to Bering Strait and thence across the Strait and overland to St. Petersburg (Leningrad) was abandoned, however, when the Atlantic cable finally was laid, and the

[2] Memorandum of a conversation between Andrew Johnson and W. H. Seward, Johnson Papers, Library of Congress, Washington, D.C.

[3] W. G. Morris, *Report on Alaska*, 1879 (published as *45 Cong. 3 sess., Senate ex. doc. 59)*; 12.

Cutter *Lincoln* Anchored at Victoria, B.C., after First Alaskan Cruise
(Official C.G. photo.)

U.S.R.-C. *Oliver Wolcott, Jr., c.* 1875
(From a painting by Joseph Lee. Official C.G. photo.)

Captain Charles M. Scammon, U.S.R.-M
(Official C.G. photo.)

Corwin, 1876-1900
(Courtesy of the artist, Mr. C. J. A. Wilson, and "Tide Rips.")

The Cutter *Dallas, c.* 1875
(Official C.G. photo.)

The Cutter *Forward, c.* 1885
(Official C.G. photo.)

Offshore Light
(Official C.G. photo.)

Launching the Surfboat, *c.* 1885
(Official C.G. photo.)

Shubrick returned to the United States.) Immediately following ratification of the treaty in 1867, the *Lincoln* was dispatched north to carry the flag. She transported to Sitka the government's special representative, Lieutenant George W. Moore, U.S.R.-M., the first U.S. agent to establish headquarters in the provincial capital, and then proceeded upon a long reconnaissance of the coast. In 1867-8-9, Captain J. W. White in the *Wayanda* scouted the coast from the southeastern islands to the Aleutians, the Pribilofs, and north to Bering Strait. In 1868, the revenue-schooner *Reliance* was stationed at Sitka, which was her home port until 1875; her cruising ground extended to the Bering Sea. The *Lincoln* made additional cruises of reconnaissance in 1869 and '70. Other cutters from West Coast ports came to be well-known to Alaskan natives, traders, and immigrants during the early period; among these were the *Wolcott, Rush,* and famous *Corwin.*

Army occupation was discontinued in 1877. No one appears to have been particularly sorry to see the troops move out. Protection of settlers through the southeastern islands necessarily had to be provided by sea. But without transports or gunboats the soldiers were practically marooned in their garrisons and were unable to undertake swift expeditions of the sort necessary to check Indian unrest. And the soldiers themselves added fuel to the unrest which lay always glowing: it is said that "from the first sergeant down to the drummer-boy" they moonshined on their own account and "taught the secret to the natives." Thus the Act of July 27, 1868, barring liquor traffic with the Indians, was effectively circumvented. Taking its name from Kootznahoo, a place near the Sitka garrison where it was manufactured in quantities, the native liquor "kootzenoo," or "hoochenoo" (whence "hootch"), contributed in great measure to social disorders among the tribes. Hoochenoo hot from the still was in great demand at "potlatches." The native still, composed of a tin tea-pot attached to a coil of seaweed, was a vivid caricature of the impact of civilization on a primitive culture. And although some white men and squaws were content enough to hibernate together through the winter months, both Indians and whites became aggressively race-conscious when full of hootch. Far-sighted men demanded teachers and missionaries to give the Indians better lessons than those learned from an idle soldiery, and they asked that swift and mobile justice be provided to keep all men within the law. Wrote I. C. Dennis, plain-spoken man-on-the-spot, Deputy Collector of Customs at Wrangel, in 1877:

> A revenue cutter has a pacifying effect upon both whites and Indians—more effect toward suppressing the liquor traffic and preserving order and quiet than forty regiments of troops without means of transportation.[4]

[4] W. G. Morris, *op. cit.,* 25.

When the troops moved out, according to Commodore Byron L. Reed, U.S.C.G. (Ret.), "correspondence between the Secretaries of War and Treasury shows that the exercise of authority for the preservation of law and order would devolve upon collectors of customs and the commanding officers of Coast Guard [Revenue-Marine] vessels." Thereafter, cutters made frequent cruises from West Coast ports to the southeastern islands; for instance, the *Corwin,* Captain J. W. White, spent considerable time in those waters in the late summer of 1877. Although the Indians made no sign of violence, Morris was convinced that the *Corwin's* visit "had a very healthy effect and quieting influence upon the natives and prevented any outbreak." The *Wolcott's* visit the following spring added to the general sense of security and, according to Morris, led the Alaska Gold and Silver Mining Company to undertake "the pioneer mining venture of any magnitude in the Territory," on Baranoff Island. As a matter of fact, says Commodore Reed, the cutters found little evidence of impending Indian war, although they did uncover numerous individual cases of crime. Only once was it necessary to take action against an entire tribe. The Commodore tells the story thus:

> The outstanding instance of disorder occurred several years later, in October, 1882. It appears that a native Indian chief, or shaman, a medicine man, was killed by the accidental discharge of a bomb on a whaling boat in the vicinity of Killisnoo, on inland waters eastward of Sitka, and that the Indians retaliated by seizing the boat and two white men on board, threatening to kill them and burn the buildings of the whaling company unless a ransom of 200 blankets should be paid. An appeal was made to the naval commander at Sitka, who proceeded to the scene on the *Corwin* with a small detachment. As the Indians were defiant and apparently warlike, forty canoes of their leaders were destroyed and their summer village destroyed by the guns of the cutter. It does not appear that lives were lost. Peace followed. . . . The lesson was salutary.[5]

But in Sitka, apprehension of a general Indian uprising reappeared whenever the cutters cruised to other points, and in 1879 a naval officer with a small detachment of Marines (mentioned in the foregoing account) was sent to reestablish the Sitka garrison and ease the minds of Sitka residents. When Congress in 1884 created the nucleus of a civil government for Alaska and extended the laws of Oregon to the territory, the naval garrison was retained for the administration's local reinforcement. A territorial civil government was established in 1912.

From 1867 on, cutters supported the authorities and governors seated in the southeastern section. In the more remote, thinly-settled coastal regions, these ships generally were the only representatives of lawful

[5] B. L. Reed, "The Contribution of the Coast Guard to the Development of Alaska," in *U. S. Naval Institute Proceedings,* May, 1929.

government. Some of them were assigned permanent stations in eastern Alaskan ports; others cruised from West Coast ports on special northern cruises. The Bering Sea Patrol Force, composed of four or five cutters under a force commander, was inaugurated in the middle 'nineties and thereafter patrolled the Bering Sea and the Aleutian chain from April to November every year. Commencing in the 'eighties, one cutter made an annual summer cruise in the Arctic north to Point Barrow. For a few weeks in summer, easterly winds force the Arctic sea-ice off the American shore and open a narrow passage for ships between the ice and shore; this lane leads to Barrow, northernmost settlement under the flag. And for fifty years the *Bear* carried the flag to Barrow. All in all, a great many famous cutters have patrolled their thousands of foggy Alaskan miles.

Thus from '67 towards the century's close, cutters in Alaska traced a pattern of work which in broad outline was to continue for many a day. Any attempt to log their cruises in a single chapter would most surely fail; a simple list of cutter actions in the north would fill a book. But their chores may be grouped under four familiar headings, namely: investigation, law enforcement, protection, and prevention. In this chapter a few specific cases of each general class of operation will be recorded. Since all classes of operations were generally carried out collaterally, no special attempt will be made to keep them separate in the telling.

Back in 1867, the U.S. needed information about its new domain. What was the country really like? Who were its people? Was it barren as bone or was it a natural treasure chest? Just what had Americans gained by extending their frontier towards the Pole? To answer such questions the *Lincoln* made her first Alaskan cruise, and many of the miles logged by later cutters have been devoted to scientific investigation of far northern areas. As a contribution to the development both of Alaska and of science, this work has been of inestimable value.

The *Lincoln* sailed from San Francisco in July 1867. She was only 165 feet in length; her double oscillating engine required a great expenditure of lubricating oil, and her undersized boiler required a great expenditure of fuel—faults typical of cutters in that period. On the long northern voyage she found it necessary to sail whenever the wind was favorable and to carry extra fuel in sacks on deck. Her skipper was Captain W. A. Howard, with thirty-seven years in cutters to his credit. In addition to her regular crew and to Lieutenant George W. Moore, the *Lincoln* was provided with a surgeon and carried a party of Coast Survey men headed by Mr. George Davidson.

Thus loaded and manned, the *Lincoln* bore away through the fog, rounded Flattery, skirted British Columbia, and entered Alaskan waters.

Her orders were comprehensive beyond word. After touching at Sitka to land Lieutenant Moore she was to proceed on a general reconnaissance of the coast, north and west to the Aleutians. Captain Howard was directed to make local surveys, investigate locations for lighthouses and coaling stations, determine suitable points for customhouses, search out probable haunts of smugglers, locate fishing banks, inquire into the physical characteristics and resources of the coastal areas, and collect specimens for the Smithsonian Institution. The *Lincoln* cruised from July to November and returned with a wealth of information. Innumerable soundings had been recorded. Fishing banks extending 700 miles across the North Pacific had been located. At Unalaska, one haul of the *Lincoln's* seine had brought up 2,500 salmon and herring. Captain Howard had found Unalaska ideal for a coaling station. Indications of coal deposits had been discovered elsewhere in the Territory. The Coast Survey group had secured data for charts. And the surgeon had collected many botanical specimens for the Smithsonian staff.

In the same year, the *Wayanda,* Captain White, commenced her long-drawn voyage of survey and discovery. The *Wayanda* entered Cook's Inlet and found that "it extends to nearly 61° north and broadens into a sea in some parts." "But," said Captain White, "geographers plot it as an unimportant arm of the sea! They are wrong. It is a large body of water. Its shores, though in part mountainous, [rim] several valleys and plains and forests with large and various resources."[6]

To investigate these resources, Captain White sent expeditions ashore at various points and dispatched an exploring party by boat up the Kukuy River. They found much to interest them. Commodore Reed recalls, for instance, that "the commanding officer reported the east shore of the inlet was a fine agricultural country, capable of supporting a dense population." Three-quarters of a century later, this area was to become famous as the locale of the New Deal's Matanuska Valley experiment. Captain White found good coal at Kenai and charted the harbor. Said he: "I have seen coal-veins over an area 40 by 50 miles, so thick that it seems one vast bed. It comes out in cube blocks, bright and clean. It does not coke. It has an excellent steam quality and leaves a clear white ash."

The *Wayanda's* report on the codfish bank jibed with the account given by the *Lincoln*. Among Captain White's reminiscences of Alaska was this beautiful fish story:

> I sounded the shores 700 miles by log northwest of Sitka, and found the entire length a codfish bank (with plenty of halibut also). The smaller codfish are in the shallower waters near the shore, of 20 or 30 fathoms; but the best fisheries are farther out, in 70 or 80 fathoms. For example, one day,

[6] White's remarks are quoted from Morris, *op. cit.*, 150.

when sounding south of Kodiak, wishing to lay in a store of codfish, I ordered the sails set back and the lines prepared. What bait? I had a barrel of Puget Sound clams salted for me with this purpose. I took my lead-line as large as my thumb, attached five hooks above the lead, with a clam on each, and fastened it to the davit. Soon the bites, one, two, three, often five were felt. I threw the line over the pulley and put four men to pull, and up would come two, three, and sometimes five cod, weighing 30 to 40 pounds apiece. We had out about 20 lines and caught 250 fish in two hours.

Authoritative reports given out by the *Lincoln* and *Wayanda* undoubtedly spurred the development of Alaska's fishing industry. Within 75 years or so, the northwestern fisheries were supplying some 400 million pounds of food annually to the American larder. Congress at an early date began to enact legislation to conserve this vast national resource. The first Act was for the protection of the salmon fisheries. It was passed in 1889, and the work of enforcement was delegated to the Revenue-Marine.[7] Subsequent legislation extended protection to other fisheries. In supporting these statutes, cutters worked in close cooperation with the Bureau of Fisheries and performed the general cruising necessary to the enforcement of fish conservation laws as a collateral to their many other patrol duties. Thus the federal government was spared the expense of setting up within the Bureau of Fisheries an extensive off-shore patrol service, or "fish guard."

No assurance from cutters was necessary, however, to induce private enterprisers to venture into the sealing trade. The Pribilof Islands, in the Bering Sea, were known to be the rookeries of the world's largest herd of fur seals. Evacuation of these islands by Russian authorities signalled a free-for-all scramble by fur traders to get all the skins they could while the getting was good. When Captain White arrived at the islands on his cruise in the *Wayanda,* he found "four or five companies killing seals as fast as they could hire Aleuts" to do the work. The companies, Captain White soon discovered, were not only annihilating the seal herd but also were luring the Aleut people towards death and destruction. The Aleuts' normal summer work was to catch and cure fish to provide their winter food supply. Traders (including "one eastern firm too religious to work on the Sabbath," according to Captain White), induced the Indians to go sealing instead of fishing; further, instead of paying off in food, this company and others paid in liquor. Said White:

I knew that when the ships were gone the Aleuts would be left without food, and that the great slaughter of the seals would soon destroy all. Following my general instructions to care for our country's interests, I put a stop to the slaughter and I broke every whiskey-barrel and poured the contents on the ground. The Aleuts thought I did wrong. They were so eager

[7] Act of March 2, 1889 (25 Stat. L., 1009).

to get it that some of them laid down and sucked the ground and the puddles and got drunk. But I saved them. I would not allow the traders to kill any seals except a limited number of the two-year old males, and I required them to pay the Aleuts in provisions, clothing, and other needful articles. I reported my action to Secretary Boutwell, and my course was approved.

Captain White recommended that the islands be made a reservation of the federal government, in order to insure protection both of islanders and seals. In 1870 this suggestion was carried into effect. The sealing companies' cutthroat competition (which, said the Captain, would in the end "have destroyed the business and the Aleuts too") was smashed. The government leased the sealing privilege to a single concern (the Alaska Commercial Company), established suitable regulations for the killing of seals on the islands, made provision for the Aleuts' welfare, and assigned an agent to hold the company to the contract. And to cutters fell the job of protecting the herd from poachers.

The lot of the island Aleut, in matters of education, health, and material well-being underwent a marked improvement, and by 1876 the A-C Company had paid into the federal Treasury $1,722,813.67 in rent and taxes. But as far as the seals were concerned, the new dispensation proved inadequate. The cutters easily cleared poachers from the three-mile zone (territorial waters) around the islands, but waters outside this zone were technically "high seas," where federal regulations had no force on foreign ships. The seals, moreover, knew no international law. They cruised, willy-nilly, beyond their protected area, in search of the herring and the cod, and they became easy prey to pelagic sealers sailing under every flag. Soon more seals were being shot at sea than were being taken legally ashore. The pelagic catch in 1890, the year the North American Company succeeded the A-C as legal sealers in the islands, was estimated at 40,000 skins and represented an immediate loss in federal revenue of about $100,000. The United States tried, unsuccessfully, to secure recognition of the Bering as a "closed sea," subject to the laws of the U.S. In 1891 a *modus vivendi* was established with England; under this, the Royal Navy undertook to help protect the seals from British poachers. In 1894 and again in 1897, Congress extended the zone within which American ships were forbidden to catch seals.[8] The Revenue-Marine sent additional cutters north in '95 to form the Bering Sea Patrol Force, first commanded by Captain C. L. Hooper, U.S.R.-M. In three years, this fleet cruised a quarter of a million miles, and its officers examined nearly a hundred thousand skins for the brands indicative of legal catch. Said Professor David Starr Jordan, a member of the Seal Commission:

[8] Act of April 6, 1894 (28 Stat. L., 52, 55); Act of December 29, 1897 (30 Stat. L., 226).

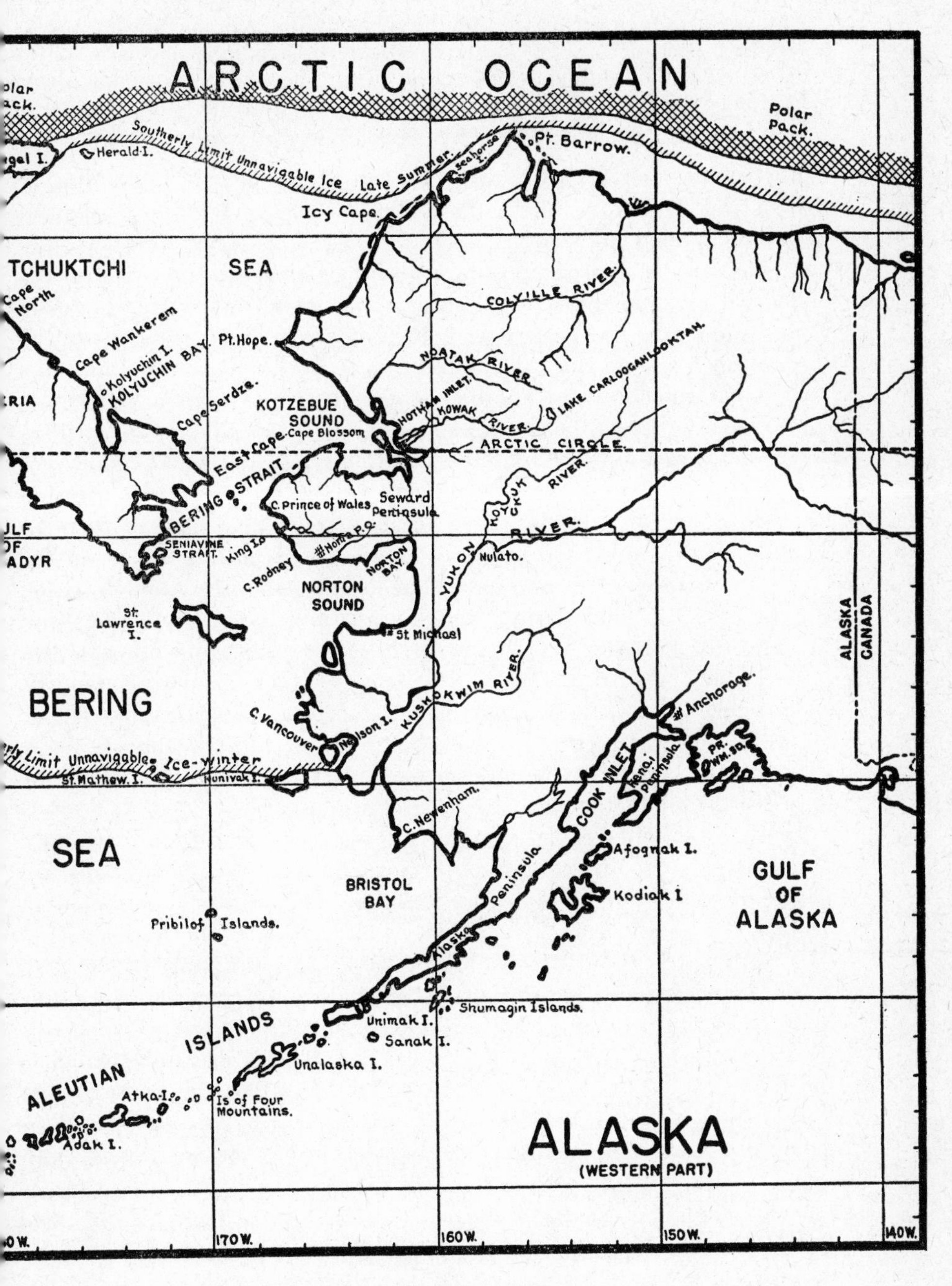

Alaska (Western Part)

> This work has been performed with the greatest faithfulness by the admirably organized fleet of United States revenue cutters. How unpleasant and even dangerous is the continuous cruising in this rough and foggy sea those who have not visited this region can hardly appreciate, while the work of examination and seizure is a task extremely unpleasant.[9]

But while such activities served to diminish pelagic operations of British and American sealers, they failed to protect the seal herd from slaughter by men under other flags. As the century drew to a close, the herd was rapidly approaching the vanishing point—and so was a source of federal revenue which in those days was quite impressive. The Seal Commission and the cutters were fortunate to conserve a remnant of this national resource for the 20th century to work with and restore.

Information concerning another resource native to Alaskan waters was contributed by Captain C. M. Scammon. In 1874 this officer published his *Marine Mammals of the North Western Coast,* in which he brought scientific treatment to the subject of whales. Scammon was born in 1825 in Pittson, Maine. In 1850 he sailed for California and engaged there in whaling. He discovered the haunts of the grey whale in a bay on the California coast called Scammon Lagoon. During the Civil War he entered the Revenue-Marine, and, as mentioned previously, he took the *Shubrick* north in 1865. Cruising in the *Shubrick* and other cutters in Pacific and Alaskan waters, he continued to observe marine *mammalia* and to amass knowledge of their habits. Not the least valuable parts of his work were the accurate sketches he drew for illustrations. His book served as the standard reference on its subject for decades, and brought him distinction in the ranks of natural scientists.

Emphasis should be placed upon the work of the cutters in making soundings, charts, hydrographic observations, and, in general preparing sailing directions for Alaskan waters. Before the territory could be safely opened, someone had to chart the way. Existing charts and hydrographic data were based on old Russian surveys and on running surveys made by a few American and British naval officers; details were scant and often faulty. The charts in common use, said Captain White, were more guesses than surveys. The vast extent of the waters and coastlines to be mapped, the frequency of fog over the area, and the fact that the Coast Survey was already loaded down with work, were factors which promised to delay any American attempt at a comprehensive Alaskan survey. The

[9] *Report of the Chief of the Division of Revenue Cutter Service* (Washington, Govt. Printing Office, 1897); 22-3. On seals and sealing, see also A. C. Laut, *The Fur Trade of America* (Macmillan, New York, 1921); and *U. S. Fish and Wildlife Pamphlet No. 131735 (I-77),* February, 1941. Pelagic sealing, or the killing of seals at sea, is destructive both of males and females and is an economic waste. Many seals so killed cannot be retrieved. Also, when a nursing female is destroyed, her pup dies of starvation, as the other seals refuse to adopt the orphan. Only young males can be slaughtered without endangering the survival of the herd.

work of the cutters in transporting and assisting Coast Survey parties and the long-continuing work of cutter personnel in making innumerable special surveys on their own, therefore, were of special value in opening Alaskan harbors and seaways to safe navigation.

II

Another phase of Alaskan duty began in 1880, when the *Corwin,* under Captain C. L. Hooper, inaugurated the service's systematic cruising in the Arctic Ocean. Other cutters had worked north of 66°30′ North upon occasion, but with the *Corwin's* voyage adventuring in high latitudes became for the Revenue-Cutter Service a regular routine. From the first, cutter operations in the Arctic included such varied activities as exploration, law enforcement, protection of shipping, and care of natives and settlers along the Arctic American shore. On these lines, innumerable specific missions in support of human safety and well-being have been carried out.

Hooper's prime objective in 1880-81 was to find the famous exploring steamer *Jeannette* and two whalers, *Mount Wollaston* and *Vigilant.* These ships had been unreported for many months. The rumor regarding them most widely accepted along the Pacific Coast and in the American press declared that they had been locked or crushed in the polar ice-pack. The *Jeannette,* commanded by Lieutenant Commander G. W. De Long, U.S.N., had been outfitted and sent north by James Gordon Bennett, of the New York *Herald.* Her voyage received considerable publicity, and the mystery of her disappearance focussed national attention on the waters north of Bering Strait and on the *Corwin's* cruise.

Several features of the cutter's operations in '81 hold especial interest. The 145-foot steamer arrived at Unalaska from San Francisco that year in May. Hooper was forced to remain a week in the Aleutian harbor, while his resourceful crew—far from drydocks and shipyards—careened their wooden ship upon the beach and repaired the oak ice-sheathing on her bow. By June, the cutter was at sea again, cruising at the southern limit of ice on the Siberian side, near Cape Serdze.

There was a chance that if any of the missing ships had been caught fast or broken up their crews might have escaped to the icebound Asian shore. If this had in fact occurred, a single day saved in getting help to the men might have meant the difference between life and death; Hooper realized that he could not afford to wait for the ice to break so that he could scout the shore in the *Corwin* at his leisure. He therefore dispatched a sledge party over the frozen ocean and northwest along the coast to carry aid to the men without delay.

First Lieutenant W. J. Herring, Third Lieutenant W. E. Reynolds (a later Commandant), Coxswain Gessler, and two natives made up the rescue party. These men loaded a quantity of relief supplies aboard four dog sleds and on June 2 struck out from the vicinity of Kolyuchin Island towards Cape Wankerem. They were to be gone a month. Their trail probably seemed longer than it was, for they were inexperienced at northern travel and the necessity for speed made the going all the harder. Most of the time their landmarks were obscured by mists and snow, and the searchers were forced to grope their way along the rugged shore. Their sleds broke down. Their dogs' rations gave out, and the dogs, vicious with hunger, proved difficult to handle. Herring and his companions were alternately "assailed with blinding snow and drenched with chilling rain." Still they mushed steadily on, over the rough terrain, putting a few more miles daily between their camps. Along the way they watched for signs of the explorers and whalers, and they stopped in every deerman's hut to ask for news of wrecks and castaways. But neither news nor signs rewarded them.

At last, wearied by fruitless effort, the party came to Wankerem, and found that native Tchuktchis at the Cape had a grisly tale to tell. Their hunters, said the Tchuktchis, had sighted a derelict drifting in the pack at the time of newly-forming ice the previous autumn. They found the helpless ship dismasted, broken, quiet, as though spent in some titantic Arctic battle. Their every instinct warned that hidden dreads and evil spirits might lurk on board, but experience taught that loot might be there, too. Not without foreboding, therefore, the bravest men began to search the ship. Tchuktchi morale faded when four frozen, blackened corpses were discovered in the cabin, but the hunters kept their courage long enough to snatch a little booty before they dashed ashore.

Lieutenant Herring listened to this Tchuktchi saga and examined the articles taken from the ship. This evidence identified the wreck as the *Vigilant.* It also sealed the *Mount Wollaston's* fate and left little hope for the safety of any member of the crews. But of DeLong's *Jeannette,* the men of Wankerem had no tidings good or bad. Having completed his mission, Herring and his party rejoined the cutter at a rendezvous near Cape Serdze.

Throughout the season of open navigation, the *Corwin* searched the Arctic shores and islands and the edges of the ice-cap. Once, struggling with the ice up there in a wilderness of white, she lost her rudder. ("The situation was anything but pleasant," reported Hooper, "caught without a rudder in the end of a rapidly closing lead, 120 miles from open water, in a howling gale and driving snowstorm.") From the momentary danger of being crushed and from the dreary hazard of being imprisoned in the pack and doomed to endless polar drift, the cutter was rescued by the seamanship and teamwork of her crew. Bosun Hallahan's gang rigged a jury rudder so that the captain could work the little vessel clear—in the very nick of time. The seamen then proceeded to carpenter together a regular rudder out of odds and ends and managed to get it shipped at sea; the *Corwin* once more was ready to steer handily through the fogs and floes.

Back and forth she shuttled, following leads in the ice between America and Asia. Up the Alaskan shore to Icy Cape. Aross to Cape North, as the ice receded a little, and south to Wankerem. Thence to Herald Island and Wrangel Land and on to Barrow. Watching for signs and signals, interviewing natives, hailing whalers, keeping out an eye for wreckage: so the cutter searched. But these efforts brought to light no trace of De Long's men, and the *Jeannette's* ill fate remained a mystery till autumn. Then a remnant of her crew, led by the Navy's great Melville, won through to the Lena Delta and gave the world the story of her drift in the solid pack, past and far beyond Wrangel Island, to the fatal spot where she went down.

In connection with the *Corwin's* search, however, one more episode must be reported: the landing on Wrangel Island. Because "De Long had directed any vessel that might be sent to look for traces of him" to search the eastern end of that bleak country, Hooper was determined to comply. Four times in 1880 he bore down upon the "blue hills of Wrangel," but each attempt was thwarted by heavy ice floes which extended far offshore. Attempts early in the season of 1881 met similar conditions and were abandoned, but on August 12 the cutter forced her way close enough to the beach for Captain Hooper and a small party to go ashore.

Hooper was confident his landing was the first ever made on Wrangel Island by the representatives of a recognized government. In his report he was able to offer considerable historical evidence to support the claim. He therefore directed Lieutenant Reynolds to plant the flag, and in the name of the United States he claimed possession of the country, which he called "New Columbia." Reynolds built a cairn upon the Island in 71°04′ North, 177°40′ West, and left there a copy of the New York *Herald* and a record of the visit, but little else was ever done to establish U.S. sovereignty. Sixty years later, the Chairman of the Senate Military Affairs Committee could write of Wrangel Island: "As aviation progresses into easy Arctic flying it may become a base of immense importance."[10] But in 1881 such a pronouncement would have been utterly

[10] Senator Robert R. Reynolds in *The American Magazine,* Vol. CXXXII, No. 3, September, 1941. On the Wrangel incident, see also C. L. Hooper, *Report of the Cruise of the U. S. Revenue Steamer* Thomas Corwin *in the Arctic Ocean* (Govt. Printing Office, Washington), for 1880 and 1881; also, *Bulletin of American Geographical Society,* No. 3, 1883; also, Harper's *New Monthly Magazine,* Vol. LXIII, No. 438, November, 1886; 909.

fantastic, and the ceremony of planting the flag seemed little more than a patriotic gesture. An eyewitness declared:

> Possession was formally taken of the ice-clad territory amid enthusiastic cheers and a salute from the guns of the cutter. . . . The acquisition of this remote island, though of no political or commercial value, will serve the higher and nobler purpose of a perpetual reminder of American enterprise, courage, and maritime skill.

Thus on August 12, 1881 the flag flew on Wrangel, and Captain Hooper, back aboard the cutter, ordered all hands aft to splice the main brace in celebration. Then he set a course for Barrow to check up on the safety of the whaling fleet.

Before returning to San Francisco, the *Corwin* spent another month or two patrolling between the latitudes of Point Barrow and the Pribilofs. She enforced the laws, aided whalers, sheltered destitute castaways, assisted an Army Signal Corps expedition, gave medical attention to seamen and natives whom she found in need, and, in general, extended the protecting arm of the United States to all men along the maritime frontier.

Perhaps of equal value, in the long view, were the scientific achievements of the *Corwin's* cruise. Several naturalists made the voyage aboard the crowded little ship, to collect and systematize knowledge of the regions visited. Aiding the work of accredited scientists in this way, whenever possible, is a traditional cutter practice; in a later day, for instance, many Coast Guard men gave their affectionate cooperation to the great Aleš Hrdlička as he journeyed and dug in the north country, piecing together the remarkable story of the earliest Americans. To the scientists who accompanied the *Corwin,* Hooper showed every consideration and to their projects offered every aid he could.

Most famous naturalist with Hooper in '81 was Professor John Muir. Muir's chief contribution was an article, *On the Glaciation of the Arctic and Sub-Arctic Regions.* Therein he first demolished a belief then held by many men: that each of the Aleutian Islands was the result of a distinct volcanic upheaval. He then proceeded carefully to marshal the evidence of his own observations and from it to induce a new and sweeping theory: that, prior to the last Glacial Period (geologically, not long ago), the continents of Asia and America had been connected by a land bridge extending from the Arctic to the Aleutian ridge, and that the Bering Strait, Bering Sea, and the passes through the Aleutian chain had been formed by *glacial erosion.* Here was a concept startling in its simplicity and in its implications, a starting-point for the work of many later scientists, a part of the foundation of modern theories of the world.

Less famous but no less competent than Muir was E. W. Nelson, another voyager in the *Corwin.* Nelson's report on *Natural History Collec-*

tions Made in Alaska served as a fitting companion-work to Professor Muir's *Botanical Notes.* Nelson drew on his cruise in the *Corwin* for some of the data which went into his later works on anthropology.

Captain Hooper and the ship's surgeon, Dr. I. C. Rosse, were additional members of the *Corwin's* erudite fraternity. These men had sailed together before, in the schoolships *Dobbin* and *Chase,* and they had many mutual interests, including scientific ones. Since both were filled with "enthusiasm for humanity," as Rosse put it, they naturally directed their investigations principally along humanistic lines.

Rosse was a genial medico and a top-notch shipmate for an Arctic cruise. As ship's doctor, he preserved both the health and good humor of the whole ship's company, and he examined and treated suffering Innuits (Eskimos) by hundreds. He easily won the natives' confidence and was thus enabled to turn loose his inquiring intellect upon their physical character and culture. His *Medical and Anthropological Notes* on the Innuits was an authoritative and valuable report.

Captain Hooper, as might be supposed, was first of all a geographer and hydrographer. At the time of his first passage north the region above the Bering Strait was almost mythical; his explorations and careful calculations cleared up many uncertainties as to the country's physical characteristics. In addition, Hooper's sympathies and scientific interests reached into the past, present, and future of the northern people. Many of the anthropological notes which he crammed into his cruise report were the results of his own keen observations.

Captain Hooper regarded the semi-civilized Alaskan natives as special objects of federal interest and protection. This may account, in part, for the care with which he carried on his researches and for the life which Innuit anthropology took on at his touch. He continually directed his work to the practical end of helping the federal government meet fundamental native problems. In summary, he wrote:

> To the three thousand Innuits who inhabit the Arctic coast of Alaska, and who are entitled to the protection of the American flag, the origin and past history of the Innuit race are not of such vital importance as the present and future. Although for more than twelve years these people have been the wards of the American Government (made so through the voluntary act of the Government itself, and as such, by all the laws of humanity, entitled to a chance to develop into civilized beings, if they will), not one step has been taken looking towards the improvement of their condition. On the contrary, they are sinking each year lower and lower . . . at the mercy of the whisky-seller. This is a great wrong, and unless remedied will prove a lasting disgrace to our country.
>
> I believe the Innuits could readily be civilized if any opportunity were given them. They are great imitators; they must be taught by example. They have little confidence in mere verbal statements, especially in matters which they do not comprehend. A missionary going among them to preach the

doctrines of some particular sect and to levy assessments would fail, but one who would teach them by example to build better houses for themselves, to be more cleanly in their habits, to treat their women with more consideration, to be industrious and provident, truthful, and honest, point out to them the evils of intemperance, and teach them the rudiments of self-government, is the kind of missionary they require. Create in them a desire for knowledge by showing them its benefits, and it will be gladly received.

Here was a straight-forward piece of social thinking, surprisingly advanced in its general tone. Reports of this sort, which came out of the Arctic from the hands of Hooper and a few other men of good will, laid a new grip on "The White Man's Burden" and achieved the cumulative effect of bringing Congress within a few years to make positive provision for the welfare of Alaska's aboriginal population. This humanitarian work was undertaken in 1884 under the federal Bureau of Education, a civilizing agency that provided the "kind of missionary" Captain Hooper had in mind. Thenafter, cutters assisted the Bureau (later, the Office of Indian Affairs) by transporting agents, wards, equipment, and supplies throughout the length and breadth of the northern littoral.

Like all cutter captains, Hooper seemed to feel that the best safeguards for inter-racial comity in the North were fair dealing, swift justice, and strict enforcement of liquor laws. He found the Innuit, for all the latter's barbarity, "cheerful and exceedingly good-natured . . . inclined to laugh at what he does not understand . . . disinclined to quarrel." He found also that "in the few instances where trouble has occurred between Innuits and white men, it appears to have been the fault of the latter." And the fault generally was mixed with whisky. All observers insisted that the natives could not be civilized unless this one ingredient of civilization could be withheld. Here was something Hooper himself had power to do. He took a personal satisfaction in curtailing the flood of liquor which threatened to engulf the simple Arctic people and sweep them into crime and conflict with the whites. One vessel he seized for violating the liquor regulations was the American schooner *Leo;* she had on board 50 gallons of alcohol, slightly colored, labelled "Bay Rum," "Florida Water," "Pain Killer," and the like. This cargo, dumped into yearning Innuit bellies, would have precipitated enough concentrated hell to detonate a thousand murders.

But Captain Hooper had little sympathy for the President's regulations prohibiting the sale of modern rifles to the natives. The regulations, issued under authority of the same Act which prohibited the sale of liquor, were supposed to protect the whites against the tribes. Hooper believed that sober natives could be trusted with firearms. In his reports he ably presented the case for the hunting tribesmen.[11]

[11] The scientific notes and papers cited in the foregoing paragraphs were published

While Hooper was thus engaged aboard the *Corwin* in the Arctic, First Lieutenant Michael A. Healy, in the *Rush*, patrolled Alaska's Pacific coast. Healy's experience in the territory dated back to 1868, when, as a young officer, he had made his first trip north. By '81, "Cap'n Mike" was known from Attu to the Farallones as a brilliant seaman. By 1895, when his Pacific cruise was done, he had become one of the Northwest's truly legendary figures. Newssheets across the country headlined his passage from the scene. In a feature article, the New York *Sun* interpreted the colorful old Captain's reputation:

> Capt. Mike Healy is a good deal more distinguished person in the waters of the far Northwest than any president of the United States or any potentate of Europe has yet become. He stands for law and order in many thousand square miles of land and water, and if you should ask in the Arctic Sea, "Who is the greatest man in America?" the instant answer would be, "Why, Mike Healy." When an innocent citizen of the Atlantic coast once asked on the Pacific who Mike Healy was, the answer came, "Why, he's the United States. He holds in these parts a power of attorney for the whole country."
>
> For twenty years or more Capt. Healy has been the sole representative of legal authority in much of the territory north of Port Townsend. To the Indians of that region he stands for the United States government. To the whalers of the Arctic he is by turns a beneficent providence and an avenging Nemesis. Everybody in San Francisco knows him. He has time and again suppressed disorder and prevented crime in regions a thousand miles from any legally constituted authority. He is the ideal commander of the old school, bluff, prompt, fearless, just. He knows Bering Sea, the Straits, and even the Arctic as no other man knows them.[12]

This was the officer who succeeded Hooper in command of the *Corwin*. Healy and the *Corwin* were well-matched. Even as seen through the Captain's matter-of-fact reports, the cutter's Arctic cruises in '84, and '85 glistened with salty romance. Healy wrote of such things as rescuing a ship from a closing ice-lead as though the feat were merely boat drill, and he spoke of Arctic exploration as casually as one might mention marlinspikes. This is the traditional literary style of sailors, especially in reporting their own achievements. But anyone who has smelled sea-water can sense through Healy's official log-entries the full flavor of the experiences they so blandly describe. Several follow.[13]

---

as Treasury documents by special Congressional resolutions, as were Hooper's cruise reports. Nelson was an employee of the Signal Service, and his report was published as No. 3 of the *Arctic Series of Publications of the Signal Office, U. S. Army*. Muir's work was released through various scientific channels and also in Muir, *The Cruise of the Corwin*. (Houghton Mifflin Company, Boston and New York, 1917).

[12] N. Y. *Sun*, January 28, 1894.

[13] Healy's reports were published as Treasury documents by special Congressional resolutions. Quotations are from Healy, *Report of the Cruise of the Revenue-Marine Steamer Corwin in the Arctic Ocean in the Year 1884* (Govt. Printing Office, Washington, 1889), and *Report, etc., in the Year 1885* (G.P.O., 1887).

The first concerns one of the *Corwin's* operations on a day that Healy called "the most eventful" of the 1885 season. The cutter and about thirty vessels of the whaling fleet lay anchored a little north of Icy Cape. They were close inshore, to clear the ice, which was moving swiftly northward. Squalls whipped up around noon, and in an hour or two a violent sou'-sou'west gale was fuming into the anchorage. Work for the *Corwin* blew out of every gust. Ships' boats capsized; crews floundered about in the water until hauled in by the cutter's surfboat or cast up, dead or half-dead, on the shore. Yawing wildly, ships dragged their anchors and came crashing into each other, causing considerable damage. Most of the whalers, with superb seamanship, eventually managed to get sail on and work clear, but the bark *George and Susan* snapped her cable and struck hard on the beach. The *Corwin* then undertook a most hazardous operation. Healy described it thus:

> . . . we steamed down toward the *George and Susan* to see if we could render any assistance. . . . Observing that the bark *Mabel* [which had been fouled and damaged by the *George and Susan*] was in an extremely dangerous position, we entered the breakers and anchored near her in four and a quarter fathoms of water with ninety fathoms of chain. While in the breakers the *Corwin* shipped a very heavy sea over her starboard quarter which swept clear forward to the forecastle. Our surfboat was made ready with a picked crew, and then, steaming ahead to windward of the *Mabel* to a full scope of chain, the boat was lowered, with Mr. Douglas in charge, to run a small line to the *Mabel*. Notwithstanding the heavy sea and the strong wind and tide, he succeeded in running the line in a most admirable and seamanlike manner. A large hawser was bent to the running line, but before it could be hauled on board the *Mabel* she parted her cable and drifted towards the shore. Her head sails were hoisted and every endeavor used to work her into deep water. Before she could be got about she struck very hard on the bar and then went ashore broadside on. The sea broke over her from stem to stern, and in less than thirty minutes her masts were gone, she bilged and filled with water, and became a total wreck.

The crews of the *Mabel* and *George and Susan* were picked up by the cutter and transported to safety.

Healy's matter-of-factness held out when he reported the *Corwin's* own troubles. One such report is tragic evidence of the beating small cutters sometimes take:

> About 2 a.m., Francis McCauley, the seaman on lookout, was suddenly thrown overboard by the motion of the vessel, which was rolling deep in the trough of the sea. The engine was immediately stopped and reversed, a life-buoy was thrown overboard, and two boats promptly lowered to rescue him, but all without avail. Our boats pulled to and fro for four and one half hours, and then we steamed ahead for Ounalaska. The deceased bore a most excellent reputation, and his sad death cast a gloom over the ship for many days.

The *Bear* in the Ice
(From a painting by an unknown artist. Official C.G. photo.)

The *Bear,* Close-hauled
(Official C.G. photo.)

The Men Who Sailed the *Bear* in '95
(Official C.G. photo.)

In Distress
(From a L.-S.S. lantern slide, *c.* 1880.)

Rescue by Breeches-Buoy
(Official C.G. photo.)

Cutters at Anchor, Sitka Harbor, 1895. *Left to right: Wolcott, Rush, Grant, Corwin*
(Official C.G. photo.)

Officers Buying Deer from Tchuktchis, Baronkoff Bay, Siberia, 1895
Center group: 2nd Lieutenant Harry G. Hamlet *(left),* and Dr. Alamson Weeks, of the *Bear;* a representative of the Russian Government *(right).*
(Courtesy of Vice Admiral H. G. Hamlet, U.S.C.G. (Ret.).)

Here he describes another near thing for the *Corwin* in the treacherous northward-flowing ice:

> [Near King's Island] At 8 a.m. the ice by an erratic movement swung around to the southward of the vessel, completely inclosing us in the pack. . . . Finding our position growing more serious, as the vessel was drifting to the northward in the pack at the rate of one and one half knots, I made a determined effort to work out under a full head of steam, but after three hours of hard work I was obliged to desist, as the vessel could not be moved in any direction. At midnight another attempt was made under steam and sail, and, although the gain to the southward was hardly perceptible, we gradually entered weaker and more open ice, and at 8 a.m. of the 13th, to the satisfaction of all and to my intense relief, clear water was reached. The thumping of the vessel against the heavy ice as she was being forced through it was terrific. At times it seemed hardly possible that she could hold together under the pressure . . . [in] her perilous situation.

But even Mike Healy could get steamed up over a high-tail race with the Arctic ice:

> During the afternoon of the 24th the wind had been freshening up from the westward with snow squalls and overcast, threatening weather, and by the time I had reached latitude 71°17′ north (ten miles distant from Point Barrow) I found further progress impossible. The pack was now moving inshore, and the leads began to close so rapidly that I found it necessary to order increased speed and to carry all sail to escape from the imminent danger that threatened us [of being crushed between the solid ice-pack and the shore]. Just before we turned, the steam-whalers that had ventured to the northward with us became alarmed and an exciting race of twenty miles between ice and steam commenced.
>
> The leads most clear of ice were sought with as much care as the necessity for haste would permit, but large cakes of ice frequently almost blocked up the way. Down through the narrow passages, with rapidly turning screws, long streams of black smoke stretching out over the quarters, and all fore-and-aft sail bellying to a stiff southwest breeze, the steamers were pushed for a position of safety. Now one would go full speed into some large piece, and when the vessel was almost brought to a standstill, the cake would split and the two parts shoot from each other. Again, some vessel would come to a standstill in an unruly piece, and a following vessel would shift her course and strike the binding ice with such judgment and skill as to loosen the former and yet not stop her own progress. Now one vessel would slide broadside up on a huge piece and roll covering-boards under, while another would force her bows high up out of the water until the ice broke and the pieces were forced up from under her bottom. On board these ships little noise was heard except the orders of the officers. When conversation was carried on it was in an undertone, the excitement being so intense. Each sailor saw and appreciated the danger, and with one accord drew a long breath of relief when a place of apparent safety had been reached.

Captain Healy, like Hooper before him, offered the *Corwin's* protection as readily to Eskimos as to whalemen and traders. He felt that the same flag covered all. In characteristically blunt words he continued to plead the case Hooper had made for the natives, and he took a professional pride in pointing out signs of the *Corwin's* civilizing influence among them. By '84-'85, these signs were especially hopeful. Shamanism (cult of Innuit medicine men) had declined, wrote Healy, as the faith of the natives in the cutter's doctor had increased. As a result of determined efforts by the *Corwin,* the whisky traffic in northern Alaska had almost entirely ceased, and the cutter herself had earned the name *"Oomiak-puck-pechuck-tonika"* ("no-whisky ship"). Captain Mike was "happy to state that . . . a changed condition of the Eskimos" closely followed curtailment of the liquor trade. "Sickness has decreased," he went on, "and the people are better clothed. More attention is paid to their boats. Food is plentiful; furs, bone, and ivory for trade are abundant. And the large number of healthy young children in every village dissipates former fears that the race might become extinct."

Under Healy's command, the *Corwin's* principal work of scientific importance lay in the exploration of the Kowak (Kobuk) and Noatak Rivers, from their mouths, on Hotham Inlet, to their headwaters, several hundred miles up in the Alaskan hinterland.

A glance at the map will show that Hotham Inlet reaches east of Kotzebue Sound. Before the *Corwin's* explorations, few white men had ever ventured across Hotham Inlet's shallow bar, and none had ascended the tributaries more than a dozen miles or so. In fact, the whole vast tract north of the Arctic Circle and between 135° and 165° West longitude, lay practically unexplored.

Captain Healy's interest in tracing the winding Kowak to its source was attracted in 1883, when Lieutenant George M. Stoney, U.S.N., then a passenger in the *Corwin,* reached a point 50 miles up the river in a boat manned from the cutter's crew. Stoney's report flashed an idea to the captain. Healy knew that the Colville River flowed north and emptied into the Arctic Ocean at a point east of Barrow. He knew also that the Koyukuk River, in roughly the same longitude as the Colville, flowed south and emptied into the Yukon near the village of Nulato. Now, Stoney had steered east up the Kowak, and the Kowak was about midway in latitude between the mouths of the Colville and the Koyukuk. Healy jumped to the hypothesis that the headwaters of the three rivers lay in proximity to each other.

One way to check this hypothesis was to send an expedition up the Kowak. If it were found that the rivers did in fact rise in the same locality, Healy hoped to determine the feasibility of a route from the mouth of the Colville upstream to the river's source, thence by short portage to the Koyukuk, and downstream to Nulato. Such a route might offer escape to whalemen caught in the ice or cast away on the barren coast east of Barrow, where they sometimes ventured in the short summer season. Nor was Healy blind to the scientific and commercial interest that would be attracted by even a superficial survey of people and resources in the unknown hinterland. Such conceptions became definite objectives for the Captain and induced him to send an expedition to the Kowak in 1884.

The explorers were led by Third Lieutenant John C. Cantwell.[14] The party included Second Assistant Engineer S. B. McLenegan, Quartermaster Horace Wilbur, Fireman Frank Lewis, Mr. James Miller (an experienced miner), and Fernda and Natorak, interpreter-guides. Cantwell planned to go up the river in the *Corwin's* steam-launch as far as possible, then by canoe to ascend to the river's source.

Cantwell and his second in command, McLenegan, made an odd team. The leader was young and buoyant. For him, the ascent of the Kowak became a trip into never-never land, a search for a legendary Jade Mountain veiled by the tabus of forgotten men. The shamans told him that spirits guarded the mountain, and the mountain guarded the river route. The shamans' stories, the wild beauty of the country, the perilous rapids, the exhilaration of filling in blank spaces on the map: these things had a glamour which Cantwell, with true explorer's instinct, appreciated to the full. McLenegan, on the other hand, was somewhat dour and inclined to take a work-a-day attitude towards the whole project. Neither man had had much formal training in geology or anthropology, valuable as those sciences might have been to them, but each had a scientific turn of mind, a sailor's eye, and an unquenchable desire to see around the next bend in the river. Healy was fortunate in having such officers to entrust with the expedition.

Cantwell wrote his log in considerable detail; it is much too long to include in this book. A few extracts, however, will serve as fair samples:

> July 13, 1884. . . . All day long the river grew narrower and the current more rapid. The bends were more abrupt and around the longest sides of the bends the water swirled into eddies too strong for the launch to overcome. Foot by foot the little craft crawled up in the backwater, and we took advantage of every projecting point to get ahead. We experienced much trouble in keeping steam. During the afternoon we ran into a reach of the river extending NE for about six miles; the vista was one of surpassing loveliness. Both banks were low and green in the sunshine, while beyond and partly hidden by a light mist a range of rugged mountains could be

[14] Exploration of the Kowak was only one of Cantwell's many Alaskan exploits. Best-known was his work in command of the *Nunivak,* policing the Yukon River during the Klondike gold rush. See Cantwell, *Report of the Operations of the U. S. Revenue Steamer* Nunivak *on the Yukon River Station, Alaska, 1899-1901* (Govt. Printing Office, Washington, 1902).

seen, lying cool and tranquil in the distance. At the end of the reach we came upon a succession of high bluffs formed by the foot-hills of the mountains running in on the river. Their sides were clothed with the sweet-smelling pine and juniper, and a narrow, rocky beach lay at their bases. Here we pitched camp. The sides of the hills were dotted with many species of wild flowers, and under the pines the moss-covered ground was like velvet to the touch. We would have called the place Utopia, had not the mosquitoes nearly driven us wild. As it was, we named the halt Highland Encampment. Today we added 24.9 miles to the distance already made.

July 18. . . . Shortly after leaving the [Innuit] village we came to a part of the river where . . . the shoals extend in all directions. The velocity of the current was about seven knots, and it was only by bottling up our steam and getting out warps ahead that we managed to get through. We struggled on, sometimes finding the current almost too strong for us to stem. Wood along the banks became scarce. At seven o'clock a high serrated mountain was discovered ahead, and Natorak told us it was the Ashiganok, the greenstone mountain.

July 19. . . . Our expedition wound its slow way along the banks of the river, sometimes getting ashore in shoal water and then miraculously escaping being dashed onto the rocks, which were only to be discovered by a peculiar ripple on the water; many jutting rocks lie just beneath the surface. All day we have been steaming towards the mountain of the mysterious green stone; sometimes standing up plain to our sight and sometimes obscured by heavy masses of clouds, its presence was ever felt, and it seemed to me to hold within its shadows some charm, some fascinating secret which must be wrested from its grasp. As the day closed and the soft light of night came on, we pitched our tent on the side of a woody hill. Today we made 16.3 miles. Average temperature, 95°.

July 22. . . . Towards noon the Indians held a consultation. Andre informed me they would not go with me as the summer was too far gone and they must fish. I knew this was a trivial excuse, as the women do all the fishing. . . . They then demanded half their pay in advance, which was granted, but this did not satisfy them, for they now came back and said I must make deer very plentiful and close to their homes this winter. This remarkable request was occasioned by the fact that they thought I was a shaman, from seeing me work with the sextant and artificial horizon. . . .

August 2. [About 300 miles from the expedition's goal.] . . . So far as the launch was concerned, I found she was scarcely in condition to go *down* stream, and it would be useless to attempt to make her stem the current. I saw with alarm the rapidly falling river, and I considered it best to make our way back to the mouth of the river while we yet had time. . . .

August 4. . . . We now settled ourselves steadily to the oars, knowing that the 225 miles of river before us must be traversed in this way. . . .

In 1885, at the head of a second Kowak River Expedition, Cantwell had better luck. His steam-launch (which had been overhauled and remodeled in the meantime) on its second attempt managed to stem the current far upstream, until shoals barred its further passage. From this point Cantwell proceeded by canoe and then on foot to Lake Carloogahlooktah, the river's principal source. He describes his discovery of the lake:

> . . . we struck out across the tundra and in a short time climbed up the sides of the hill and looked away to the north. Four or five miles away, and almost completely surrounded by mountains, the blue sparkling waters of the long-sought lake burst upon my view. The sensations of pleasure and triumph which took possession of me as I gazed upon the waters, now for the first time seen by a white man, amply repaid me for the long tedious journey. As the last rays of the setting sun gilded the rugged peaks and the shadows of approaching night crept silently upward, the Indians set up a wild chanting of joy.

The same year, McLenegan and one companion, Seaman Nelson, paddled a three-hatch bidarka (native skin-boat) up the Noatak, winding endlessly through mountains and Arctic moors to its source amid small lakes and snowbanks. In contrast to the beauty of the Kowak region, McLenegan found the Noatak country drear and barren, a treeless and a cheerless land, in summer swamped with rain and in winter lost in snow. July brought insufferable heat to the wooded sections of the Kowak, but along the Noatak bitter gales continued lashing down as though heedless of the season.

The river itself seemed to possess a studied treachery. It often rose or fell six, seven, even eight feet in a day, depending on the duration of the daily deluge, and its current whipped over shoals and down deep gorges at a reckless rate. To McLenegan and Nelson, the river gradually assumed a distinct and definitely unpleasant personality; it became a thing which must be fought and cussed into submission. Extracts from several days' entries in the log of the bidarka follow:

> . . . the current seemed to increase in strength every mile of our journey, and before we had proceeded very far above the camp we were obliged to abandon the paddles and place ourselves in the tracking harness. The river banks at this point were such that tracking was next to impossible; the dense growth of bushes along the shores made our footing very precarious. Shortly after starting we reached a very dangerous rapid, and I directed Nelson to adjust the tracking harness preparatory to passing around it. When all was in readiness I took the steering paddle and sheered the bidarka into the midst of the flood. The strength of the current, however, was greater than I anticipated, and catching the canoe under the bow, in an instant whirled it into the torrent. While vainly endeavoring to check its mad career, Nelson was dragged into the river and narrowly escaped drowning. . . .
>
> . . . The heavy protracted rains of the past few days had now caused very high water, and we found that the current had nearly doubled in strength. . . . It was impossible to stem the river with our paddles, and even in places where the tracking line could be used it required our utmost exertions to drag the bidarka through the water. . . . The constant succession of rapids rendered our work exceedingly hard, but the amphibious qualities of our

nature made it a matter of little importance whether we were in or out of the water. . . . At times it required the united exertions of Nelson and myself, up to our waists in water, to control the unruly canoe, and then we were by no means always successful. . . . In addition, the drenching rains [and] cold winds continued. . . . Notwithstanding, we made fairly good headway, although both were thoroughly fatigued at night. . . . After going into camp for the night, our chilled blood, again put in circulation, produced a most peculiar burning sensation, which caused no little pain and utterly precluded the idea of sleep.

. . . The mountains now seemed to approach the river again, and the lofty summits towered hundreds of feet above it. The stream again pursued a very tortuous course, winding in and among the mountains, through deep canons and gorges, . . . The fresh breeze of morning had increased to a gale which fairly whistled through the chasms, and, hoisting our sail, we were driven rapidly forward, notwithstanding the current of the river. The work now became exciting in the extreme. To Nelson I intrusted the steering paddle, while I held the sheet and employed every faculty in avoiding the submerged rocks, which seemed to threaten us with destruction. In the afternoon the bed of the river began a most remarkable ascent, resembling in appearance a heavily-graded railway through a mountain district. With the assistance of the favoring gale and our united exertion with the paddles we succeeded in stemming the flood and finally gained the smoother water above.

. . . Behind us the dark wall of mountains through which we had just passed towered upward until their summits were lost in the clouds; they seemed like an impassable barrier, shutting us off from the outside world. . . . The almost entire absence of life is one of the characteristic features of this region. The sense of loneliness which frequently took possession of the mind was, indeed, difficult to throw off, and its influence was depressing in the extreme. . . . Before us lay the level plains of the interior, stretching away in the distance, unrelieved by a single object upon which the eye could rest with any feeling of pleasure. . . .

. . . the bidarka fouled with a sunken rock . . . whirled broadside to the current and capsized, by which everything was more or less damaged. We righted the craft . . . and our next impulse was to indulge in a hearty laugh, although there was nothing ludicrous in the situation. The only serious loss was that of our footgear . . . I directed Nelson to cut some of the spare seal-skin . . . to be made into a rude moccasin which might at least serve as a protection against the sharp rocks, and before nightfall we were shod and ready to advance. . . . With a determination not to be baffled, we prepared ourselves to meet anything short of utter annihilation.

. . . The utmost economy of provisions was now absolutely necessary, and the limited allowance per day was beginning to make inroads upon our strength. I succeeded in shooting a few curlew, which Nelson incorporated into a kind of soup, almost as thin as the celebrated "Shadow" brand. . . .

. . . The Noatak was now a mere chain of rapids following in quick succession, and each seeming to surpass its predecessor in dangers. . . .

. . . Nelson was now suffering from a high fever. . . . Towards evening he improved somewhat and declared himself able to move on. I did not consider it prudent to allow him to track, so put myself in the harness and we started forward. . . .

. . . We had now gained a point about five hundred miles from the coast, having accomplished the distance in 27 days' time. . . . We had passed the head of boat navigation . . . I determined to leave the canoe and proceed on foot as far as circumstances might permit. . . . Early the following morning we resumed our journey, taking with us a small quantity of provisions, together with the instruments. Driven by the fierce blast, the rain now turned to sleet. . . . Late in the day we gained an eminence on the right bank. I clambered up the steep sides, taking with me only the compass. I stood on the height, pelted by the storm. . . .The scene which met my gaze was one of utter desolation. Not a vestige of life was to be seen; even the hardy waterfowl seemed to have forsaken the region. In every direction, as far as the eye could reach, the dreary expanse of tundra, covered with small lakes and half-frozen marshes, stretched away in the distance. The Noatak, no longer the stately river which flowed into the sea, had degenerated into a mere rambling creek. . . .

Besides having opened up and mapped a large tract of territory previously unknown to white men, Cantwell and McLenegan returned from their expeditions with extensive anthropological notes on the inland tribes, with natural history collections for the Smithsonian, and with valuable information on the resources of the region.

A winter sledge route south from the Colville to the Kowak, Koyukuk, and Yukon was found feasible, but in McLenegan's opinion travel in summer over the boggy tundra lands between the river valleys was the next thing to impossible. Since the whalemen could get into the dangerous reach east of Barrow only in the summertime, they particularly needed a summer route to safety in case of disaster to their ships. Such a route, unfortunately, did not lie along the rivers and inland trails.

Along the wild Noatak, McLenegan discovered few resources of commercial interest, but the Kowak proved to be by no means barren. In both rivers salmon were found in abundance, and the surrounding country was filled with silver fox, marten, land otter, and other fur-bearing animals. But chief interest centered on the Kowak's minerals. Halfway up this river Cantwell found fairly large deposits of coal and fire-clay. Here and there he discovered traces of silver. And in almost every stream in the Kowak basin the explorers washed out the color of gold. McLenegan feared that mining could not be carried out with profit in so remote and generally cold a region, but within a few years hundreds of prospectors were following their luck over the route blazed by the Revenue-Marine.

III

The *Corwin* returned to California late in 1885 and cruised along the coast during the winter season. On February 21, 1886, while at anchor off Santa Barbara, Captain Healy called away his gig and pulled over to welcome another vessel to the Pacific station. This was the cutter *Bear*, soon to be the best-known ship in the service and eventually to hold the same relation to the Coast Guard that "Old Ironsides" bears the Navy. The *Bear* is more than just a famous ship; she is a symbol for all the service represents—for steadfastness, for courage, and for constant readiness to help men and vessels in distress.

The *Bear's* reputation as a cutter was won in Arctic waters, where in '86 under Captain Healy she took over the *Corwin's* many police duties. The *Bear* was especially well-fitted for a northern career. She had been built as a whaler (in Greenock, Scotland, in 1874), with massive beams, heavy oak frames, reinforced bow, and Australian iron-bark sheathing to enable her to work in safety in the ice. She was considerably larger than the *Corwin* and consequently was much better able to take down from Alaska the motley and numerous gang of castaways, federal agents, destitutes, missionaries, lunatics, scientists, and prisoners that each year on the homeward voyage to San Francisco had taxed the *Corwin's* limited facilities. The new cutter's dimensions were: length, 200 feet; breadth, 32 feet; depth, 18 feet 2 inches; 703 tons net. She was a barkentine with auxiliary steam power; she could sail at eight knots and steam at nine.

This ship had received her first test in the Far North under the U.S. flag as a member of the Navy's Greely Relief Expedition in 1884. Commanded by Lieutenant W. H. Emory, U.S.N., she had proved her ice-worthiness and her suitability for Arctic cruising by beating all other relief vessels to Greely's aid. Upon her return from this expedition she had transferred to the Revenue-Marine and, cruising annually to the Arctic, served as a cutter until 1927, when she was relieved by the diesel-electric *Northland* and laid up under the guardianship of her old boatswain, Thurber, a man who had attended her for many boisterous and windswept years. Later the distinguished relic served quietly as a museum-ship for the City of Oakland, California, where she received a pledge of perpetual care.

But these tender rewards at the end of a long career came too soon for the ancient wanderer, and at the first opportunity she parted her mooring-lines and sailed away, the *Bear of Oakland,* towards the South Pole with Richard Byrd. Later, when the country sent out its call for volunteers to help fight World War II, the *Bear,* nearing seventy years of age, came back home to join up for active duty in support of U.S. forces in Greenland, along a new and fateful maritime frontier.

If this rapid sketch takes the Coast Guard's story far ahead of itself, it is only because the *Bear* is, in truth, one of the Coast Guard's bonds with a storied past. Back in the 1880's, the cutter had a long future ahead, and she lost no time in filling her log with work-reports of the sort that eventually defined her proud tradition. She stayed in the North long enough to witness many changes. The whaling fleet sailed out of the Arctic fogs into the mists of memory. Miners flocked to Kotzebue and Nome, and traders followed with supplies. As the country opened up, various federal agencies established themselves ashore to help provide governmental controls and law and education and other civilizing influences. Before the *Bear* went south from her final Barrow cruise, radio and airplane had begun the annihilation of distance between all terrestrial boundaries. Life at the frontier was rapidly becoming much like life elsewhere.

All this the *Bear* witnessed, and in quite a bit of it she had a part. Her job, like the *Corwin's,* was to protect life and property and to extend American ways to the nation's Arctic province. The protection she offered and the other services she performed were themselves aspects of American civilization. At every stage of culture, men seek *security* as a fundamental goal, and security the *Bear* helped to provide. Other federal agencies in Alaska were working with the same end in view; the *Corwin* in her time had helped a few of these, and the *Bear* was able to extend the *Corwin's* work by assisting many more.

For example, in 1891, she made a special voyage of 5,000 miles for the Department of Justice to secure witnesses in the Hemingway murder case. Captain Healy declared that "everything desired by the judicial authorities was carried out to their satisfaction, and at the same time such revenue duty as came our way was not neglected." On the same cruise, the cutter transported the Governor of Alaska on an inspection of the westward islands otherwise inaccessible to him. As soon as these jobs had been completed, the *Bear* sailed north again. En route, she transported the U.S. Geological Survey's Mount St. Elias Expedition, under Professor I. C. Russell, to its advanced bases. (In landing a boatload of the Expedition's supplies through the dangerous surf at Icy Bay, Third Lieutenant L. L. Robinson disobeyed his orders—to lie off and carefully observe the surf before attempting to land. His boat filled in the breakers, and he and five of the boat's crew were drowned.) The cutter then continued north and aided many other agencies during the remainder of the season. She carried supplies and lumber for government and mission schools in the Bering Sea and Arctic regions. She transported the teachers, protected them from local dangers, and helped them get established in the rough new land. She carried the mails for the Post-Office Department, cooperated with Treasury agents stationed on the Pribilofs, and gave assistance to members of the Coast and Geodetic Survey. All these incidental activities she accomplished in addition to her normal Arctic cruising.

In cooperation with Dr. Sheldon Jackson, of the federal Bureau of Education, the *Bear* undertook one of her most far-reaching enterprises: the introduction of domesticated reindeer into northwestern Alaska.

Although there were wild reindeer in the territory, none of these had ever been corralled. Tchuktchi deermen across in Siberia kept great herds, but in Alaska the natives' livelihood always had depended on the hunt. As firearms came into wide use in Alaska, however, the tribes found that the game they had hunted for centuries (principally seals, walruses, and wild deer) became increasingly shy and scarce. Some long-range measures had to be taken to insure the Eskimos against eventual starvation.

Captain Healy believed that "the introduction of deer seems to be the solution of three vital questions of existence in the country—food, clothing, and transportation." In this he was doubtless influenced by Captain Hooper, who in one of his early cruise reports had included a great deal of information regarding the feasibility of such a project, and by Charles H. Townsend (an employee of the U.S. Fish Commission and one of Cantwell's companions on the second Kowak River Expedition), who suggested that the introduction of reindeer would contribute more towards the Innuits' welfare than anything else the government could do. And everyone who had travelled overland in the north country could see one advantage of deer transport over dog-sled—the deer lived on tundra moss and were self-sustaining on a trek, while dogs had to be provided for and their rations took up valuable cargo-space on every dog-sled.

In agreement with Healy point by point, Dr. Jackson took up the project as a definite cause. Four obstacles were involved: (1) the reindeer had to be procured from Tchuktchis, who had a superstitious aversion to selling live deer; (2) once procured, the animals had to be transported across the Bering Sea and landed in Alaska; (3) the Alaskan Innuits had to be re-oriented from a hunting to a pastoral mode of life; and (4) the Washington government had to be persuaded to bless the whole proceeding. Healy was ready to negotiate with the Tchuktchis and to transport the deer, Jackson was eager to teach the natives how to be successful herdsmen, and Jackson's influence in Washington won governmental approval of the scheme. In 1891, Captain Healy took the educator on a short cruise in the *Bear* to Seniavine Strait, Siberia, and there the two men bought 12 reindeer from Quoharie, a Tchuktchi deerman. They landed these at Unalaska.

During the next ten or eleven years, cutters procured and carried to Alaska some 1,100 animals. Jackson's Bureau of Education took charge of the deer on landing and distributed them among government and mission schools which trained the Innuits in reindeer-culture and then gave a nuclear herd to each "graduate" deerman. Although few people seem to have realized it at the time, this rather unexciting piece of business was one of the most remarkable social experiments the world had ever seen, for by it, deliberately planned, a whole people was shifted from one stage of civilization to another. Paleolithic man had required several hundred thousand years to ascend from the huntsman's to the herdsman's level; Healy and Jackson hoped that with Uncle Sam's benevolent guidance the Innuits could clamber up the grade within a generation. By 1930, domesticated deer herds in Alaska had multiplied to 600,000 (estimated) head, and 13,000 natives drew on them for their simple life's essentials.[15]

Aid to federal agencies, missions, ships, and whole tribes of Eskimos was aid on a fairly sweeping scale, but this was not the only sort of help the *Bear* offered. The individual could always call upon the cutter and be assured of a friendly hand in time of trouble. In assisting private persons, neither class, race, nor creed made any difference to the *Bear;* degree of stress was the sole controlling factor. The cutter's skipper judged each case upon its merits and gave such relief, within reason, as the *Bear* was able to provide.

For instance: the case of William Brown, sometime whaleman—a typical case recorded in the *Bear's* log in '91. Partly frozen, half-starved, and wandering near the Noatak in mid-winter, Brown was found by another whaleman. He was helped by his rescuer to a shanty near Point Hope, where he clung miraculously to life. On the *Bear's* next cruise, Captain Healy heard of the man and sent Surgeon S. J. Call to investigate his plight. Call submitted the following report:

> In accordance with your instructions I accompanied the whalers to their station, distant about ten miles, where I found the patient in a most pitiable condition. He was lying on a rickety bunk in a small, dirty room. His clothing consisted of a deerskin covering for the extremities and a shirt for the body. The shirt had been worn continuously for almost four months. His finger nails were from a quarter inch to a half inch in length. Vermin covered his body. The man's left foot, almost to the heel, was a mass of distorted, foul-smelling, gangrenous tissue. Three fingers of the left hand were mere stubs. . . . I find it necessary to amputate his left leg and three fingers of his left hand. These operations will seriously endanger his life, considering that through neglect, no medical treatment, little food, and bad quarters, his vitality is much reduced and his pulse and temperature are below the normal. The patient has been informed of his condition and has consented to the operation, knowing that he may not survive it, and that it is his only chance for life.[16]

[15] On the introduction of reindeer and their effect on the life of Alaskans, see: Hooper, *Report of the Cruise of the Corwin,* etc., for 1881, *passim;* Healy, *same,* for 1885, *passim; Annual Report of the Revenue-Marine Service,* 1891 (Govt. Printing Office, Washington, 1891), *passim;* Sheldon Jackson, *Annual Report(s) on Introduction of Domestic Reindeer into Alaska* (for various years, commencing 1891) (Published as Senate documents by Govt. Printing Office, Washington); Dr. Sheldon Jackson, "The Arctic Cruise of the Revenue Cutter *Bear,*" in *The National Geographic,* January, 1896; and Anderson and Eels, *Alaska Natives* (Stanford University Press, 1935).

[16] *Annual Report of the Revenue-Marine Service, 1891* (Govt. Printing Office, Washington, 1891).

The patient did survive, and the *Bear* took him down from Alaska in the autumn. His case bore out the service's traditions, in which there lives a deep conviction of the innate worth of individual men and in which the words "the general welfare" have always been interpreted to mean the welfare of each and every lawful person touched by the shadow of the flag.

A spectacular mass-rescue, performed in 1897-98, brought international fame to the already nationally-famous *Bear*. Late in the autumn of 1897, reliable reports reaching the outside world confirmed fears that the whaling fleet, composed of 8 or 10 ships and nearly 300 men, had become caught in the ice near Barrow. No hope of escape could be entertained for the vessels until the following August—ten months off—the time for the annual break-up of ice along the coast. It was known that the ships had insufficient food to keep their crews alive for such a lengthy period, and it was feared that if meagre stores belonging to traders and natives at Barrow were commandeered the result would simply be that everyone eventually would starve together. Under the circumstances, violence, disease, and bitter misery could be expected to precede starvation's end.

Over the wires to the presses and thence to the people of America went news of the whalers' sorry situation. The popular reaction was a demand for practical measures, and President McKinley determined to send relief. He handed the problem to his Secretary of the Treasury, Lyman Gage, who selected Captain Francis Tuttle (the *Bear's* new captain) to carry relief to Barrow without delay.

Captain Tuttle manned the cutter with a crew of service volunteers. Knowing that the *Bear* would be prevented by ice from approaching the whaling fleet closer than a thousand miles or so, Tuttle planned to push north as far as possible and then dispatch an expedition overland. Along its way, the land party would draw on government reindeer stations and private owners for domesticated deer to drive as food-on-the-hoof to Barrow. First Lieutenant D. H. Jarvis, Second Lieutenant E. P. Bertholf, and Surgeon S. J. Call volunteered to take the trail. Tuttle's plan called for the *Bear* to winter in Unalaska after landing the expedition, then to proceed to Jarvis' support when August opened Arctic navigation.

The *Bear* took her departure from Port Townsend, Washington, about the first of December, 1897. Two weeks later, when only 85 miles from Cape Nome, she was forced to turn back on account of ice. On December 16, still running the risk of being caught, she ploughed through drift-ice and landed Jarvis and his party on Nelson Island, near Cape Vancouver. The *Bear* then headed back towards Unalaska.

For the three officers who composed the Overland Expedition, a great adventure had begun. Their projected mid-winter's journey from below the timber-line to well above the Circle was a well-nigh unheard of thing. Fifteen hundred miles of snow and ice and wintry peril stretched between them and their goal. Whether or not deer owners could be persuaded to part with Arctic wealth so recently bestowed by Washington was a question which left Jarvis little peace of mind, for failure to collect the deer would mean the expedition's fruitless end. And even if the party managed to drive the herd to Barrow, only Heaven knew what conditions waited to be confronted there.

Jarvis' log is contained in the *Report of the Cruise of the U.S. Revenue-Cutter Bear and the Overland Expedition for the Relief of the Whalers in the Arctic Ocean.*[17] This tells in detail how the little party pushed its way, sometimes with deer-sleds, sometimes with dogs, "through what at times seemed impassable obstacles, across frozen seas, and over snow-clad mountains, with tireless energy until Point Barrow was reached and the object of the expedition successfully accomplished" (Tuttle).

On a not unusual day:

> The blizzard was still on when we started this morning and grew worse as we went along. As though to make amends for his performance of yesterday, my deer kept up alongside Mikkel's [a herder's] sled, and we two soon were far ahead of the others, and were greatly relieved when we picked up the village of Opiktillik—at least, the deer led us there, for it was beyond us to find the way in the blinding snow. It was now blowing so hard that we could scarcely stand. In an hour the others came along. They had been compelled to pick their way on foot, one of the natives going ahead on his hands and knees. It was hard to think of losing the day, for we had made only about 5 miles, but there was no help for it. It was impossible to go on in that wind, so we crowded into an already overfilled native hut and tried to wait patiently for the storm to let up . . . the natives and whites all agreed that it was dangerous to venture out, and I reluctantly fell into line, though I resolved that no amount of wind would keep us there another day.

Sometimes no one in the party was sure of what lay ahead:

> Our mountain climbing for the day was not over, for there was still another portion of the range to be crossed, which was even higher and steeper than the one we had just come over. Refreshed by our rest and lunch, we started for the second ascent in good spirits. In course of time, after much tugging and pushing of sleds and urging of dogs, we reached the summit, where we found ourselves in the midst of a furious storm of wind and snow so thick that it was some time before Alexis (the guide) and the natives could decide upon the proper direction. There was some danger of our taking the wrong course and going over a precipice into the sea. They finally came

[17] Dated "From November 27, 1897 to September 13, 1898." *Treasury Department Document No. 2101, Division of Revenue-Cutter Service* (Govt. Printing Office, Washington, 1899).

> to a decision and preparations were made for the descent, which Alexis told us was so steep that the dogs could not run fast enough to keep ahead of the sleds. The dogs were turned loose, small chains (brought along for the purpose) were wound around the runners to impede the rapid descent, and we proceeded to coast down the side of this mountain, which, as near as I could judge, was some 2,000 feet high. The additional weight of two people seated on each sled gave us a momentum that nothing short of a solid obstacle could stop, and we flew along at such a rate that in about ten minutes we reached the gentle slope at the base. Here we waited for the dogs, for the little fellows had come down on foot and were far behind.

Many days, like the following, called for almost superhuman effort and endurance:

> . . . a rough road . . . here were all the crushings of the straits shoved up against the mountains that ran down abruptly into the sea, and over this kind of ice we had to make our way. Darkness set in long before we had come to the worst of it, and a faint moon gave too little light for such a road. It was a continuous jumble of dogs, sleds, men, and ice—particularly ice—and it would be hard to tell which suffered most, men or dogs. Once, in helping the sled over a particularly bad place, I was thrown 8 or 9 feet down a slide, landing on the back of my head with the sled on top of me. Though the mercury was $-30°$, I was wet through with perspiration from the violence of the work. Our sleds were racked and broken, our dogs played out, and we ourselves scarcely able to move, when we finally reached the cape. . . . I have not dwelt upon the personal part of the travel with any intention to magnify the dangers or trials, but simply to show some of the difficulties . . . which all people travelling in that country have to contend against.

In another place, Jarvis gave his philosophy of Arctic travel:

> If you are subjected to miserable discomforts, or even if you suffer, it must be regarded as all right and simply a part of the life; like sailors, you must never dwell too much on the dangers or sufferings, lest others question your courage.

In this spirit, the expedition slogged northward. It pulled into St. Michael trading station by the thirtieth of December. There it refitted, and Bertholf separated from the main party to go by short-cut across the Seward Peninsula with flour and dry provisions obtained from St. Michael traders. Jarvis and Call crossed the ice-clogged Norton Bay and skirted the Peninsula. At Cape Rodney, on Jarvis' pledge of eventual restitution, Eskimo Charlie Antisarlook agreed to drive all his deer (133 head) to the white men at Point Barrow. At Cape Prince of Wales, Mr. W. T. Lopp, an American missionary, gave up all his mission's deer (292 head) to the same humanitarian purpose, under a similar agreement. Lopp's wife courageously urged him to help herd the animals to Barrow (which he did, to Jarvis' great satisfaction), although such action meant that Mrs. Lopp and her children would be left unprotected, the sole whites in a village of 500 barbarians. A few deer were obtained from other sources, and the massed herds, 448 beasts in all, crossed the frozen waters of Kotzebue Sound about the middle of February.

Bertholf rejoined the caravan near Cape Blossom and continued with it to Point Hope, where he cached his provisions and took station to await such whalemen as Jarvis might decide to send south by land.

Jarvis and Call raced on ahead by dog team towards Barrow while the herders made their slow way up the Arctic coast. From here on, the temperature was generally around $-20°$ but sometimes it plunged to sixty below zero. Gale after gale streamed off the polar ice-cap to harass this portion of the journey. The officers drove on. On February 26, Jarvis sighted the first of the imprisoned ships, the *Belvedere,* jammed in the ice near the Sea Horse Islands. Three days later, he and Dr. Call drew up at the settlement at Barrow. "All the population came out to see us and wonder what strange outfit it was," wrote Jarvis, "and when we greeted some of the officers of the wrecked vessels, whom we knew, they were stunned; it was some time before they could realize that we were flesh and blood. Some looked off to the south to see if there was not a ship in sight, and others wanted to know if we had come up in a balloon. Had we not been so well known, I think they would have doubted that we really did come in from the outside world. All was excitement and relief in camp." And the next day, Lopp and Antisarlook brought the deer herd to the end of its long trail.

But the expedition's work was by no means finished. Jarvis' orders required him to "take charge in the name of the Government and organize the country for mutual support and good order . . . to deal firmly and judiciously with every situation . . . bearing in mind that he represents the Government on the spot." No federal statute but simply the law of stern necessity could be invoked to support so all-inclusive a commission; it is fortunate Jarvis was able to bolster such authority with the power of his own personality. None of his decisions was ever questioned. Probably the leadership he took to Barrow was equally as important as the food.

Preliminary survey disclosed that about 100 refugees from wrecked whaling ships were crowded together in the settlement. Eighty of them lived in an old hut, 22 feet wide by 55 feet long, lighted by a single window and unventilated except through the door and cracks. So much floor space was taken by the berths and stove that there was scarcely room for the men all to stand up. Jarvis found that:

> [the steam generated in cooking the scanty meals] gathered in frost overhead and on the sides of the hut, and the drippings from this kept the floors and

walls continuously wet and filthy. Lower down on the walls ice had formed 3 or 4 inches thick, and the drippings and meltings ran down over this into the berths, and even what little bedclothes the men had were never dry. In the endeavor to keep warm some of the men had boxed in their berths, and in these boxes kept improvised seal-oil lamps burning. The soot and smoke from these lamps covered everything, their clothes and bodies, with a black, greasy coating, so they were scarcely recognizable as white men. Some hardly left their berths at all, and all were in such a low, demoralized condition that only the cold weather prevented a serious outbreak of sickness. Filth and vermin were everywhere, and those men inclined to keep clean and live decently could not accomplish it in such a place and under such conditions. The masters of the two crews had done nothing for them in any way, either in seeing they were provided with food and quarters or in exercising necessary control . . . so far there had been no deaths, but Surgeon Call reported four cases of scurvy and all hands more or less affected. They were much debilitated and run down, and if something was not done quickly the weaker ones would soon die from general debility and serious sickness attack all. We had no antiscorbutics but the fresh meat we brought with us, but I determined that changes must be made at once: the men were moved from their present quarters, their clothes and bodies cleaned, and proper rules of discipline, health, and exercise enforced.

In meeting these conditions, Jarvis worked a minor miracle. Within a few days the Barrow situation was under his complete control, and he and Surgeon Call were free to visit the outlying ships. These were strung out between the Sea Horse Islands and a position some hundred miles east of Barrow. Their crews, like the men at the settlement, required food, a steady hand, and medical attention. On all the whaleships, Jarvis' stabilizing influence was felt. He decided questions between the officers and crews, acted as food and housing authority, supervised relations between the whalemen and the natives, and acted as a sort of extra-legal judge in disputes of every kind. In this regard, he wrote: "After I once assumed the authority, the men would be amenable to no one but me, and while I was away [on circuit of the ships] reserved all their disputes for my return." The result of the lieutenant's many-sided activities in the fleet and at Barrow was a speedy return of the whalemen to health, orderliness, and a measure of contentment. These conditions the *Bear* found prevailing when she arrived at the Point in August 1898. The cutter helped the whaling ships out of the ice, took the Overland Expedition and the stranded whalers on board, and headed home to receive the world's "well done." Wrote President McKinley:

I commend this heroic deed to the grateful consideration of Congress and the American people. The year just closed [1898] has been fruitful of noble achievements in the field of war, and while I have commended to your consideration the names of heroes who have shed lustre upon the American

> name in valorous contests and battles by land and sea, it is no less my pleasure to invite your attention to a victory of peace.

In response, Congress awarded special gold medals to Jarvis, Bertholf, and Call for "heroic service rendered."[18]

[18] Act of June 28, 1902.

CHAPTER X

The Home Fleet

WHILE they brought romance and renown to the Revenue-Marine, the captains and crews of Alaskan cutters by no means carried the entire burden of service operations; their activities, in fact, represented only a fraction of the organization's total effort. Most of the fleet remained on home stations, where demands for maritime police work of every sort mounted in phase with the continuous upswing taken after 1880 by coastwise tonnage figures. Upon these cutters fell most of the increased load; their faithful attempt to meet the situation is borne out by the service's total cruising record, which shows a 50% increase between the decades of the 'seventies and 'eighties to an annual average of over 300,000 miles.

But even by straining men and ships to the utmost, the Revenue-Marine was unable to keep up with the maritime requirements placed upon it. Almost unchanged in personnel and equipment since Kimball's time, the service was forced to struggle along for ten years or more, doing the best it could with what it had. The mass of useful work accomplished by the little cutters was out of all proportion to their actual strength.

The best source from which to dig the record is Headquarters' old log-book file. Not only do these dusty manuscripts give the day-by-day account of the hard-pressed outfit's operations, but also they reveal the secret of the cutter men's ability to carry on. As one fans the dimming pages, it becomes quite clear that the personal satisfaction of doing hard jobs well was the force that motivated every rank and rate.

This traditional service attitude sustained cutter personnel in the late 19th century as in other stressful times before and since. Aboard every ship out on patrol—comes snow or blow—the lookout aloft kept watch for vessels in distress. His cry of "Sail ho!" would send his cutter away on an intercepting course to determine whether or not the sighted ship was safe and sound. There was always a chance—too good a chance—that distress signals would be flying. One researcher, digging into the record of the *Gallatin,* found that this cutter's log,

> especially throughout the winter months, constituted a continuous roll-call of rescue operations . . . along the rugged coastline of Massachusetts.[1]

[1] Arthur Tourtellot, "C. J. Soong and the U. S. Coast Guard," in *U. S. Naval Institute Proceedings,* February, 1949. In this sidelight on service history, Tourtellot recalls that Captain Gabrielson, struck by the loyalty and intelligence of his cabin-boy, Chai-

To the *Gallatin's* crew, from the commanding officer, Captain Eric Gabrielson, to the young Chinese cabin-boy, one Chai-jui Soong, there can be little doubt that life-and-death battles with disaster at sea were only normal anticipations, occasionally borne out in multiple measure; for instance:

> On the day of the famous March gale in 1879 . . . when every ship along the New England coast was battered . . . by winds and high seas, the *Gallatin* alone went to the rescue of no less than five widely scattered vessels. Not waiting for distress signals, she went out in search of the vessels, which Captain Gabrielson knew would inevitably meet with troubles. In quick succession, the *Gallatin* steamed to the aid of the *Emma L. Gregory,* the *S. J. Lindsey, Neptune's Bride,* and the *Aliston.* Due to her ubiquitous efficiency, not a soul was lost. Then the *Ligure,* a huge schooner heavily loaded with lumber, en route from Calais to Bridgeport, ran into trouble between some shoals. All day she had beaten her way through the storm, out-fighting as fierce a wind and heavy a sea as ever tested New England shipping. Then as the night approached the strain of the fight began to tell on her. All day the sea had made a clean sweep over her. And although her pumps had been working steadily throughout the day, she began to fill with water. Finally, she rolled over on her beam ends.
>
> In the darkness of the night and as the gale continued, the *Gallatin,* four rescues behind her, was still seeking out vessels in distress. But somehow she missed the *Ligure.* With the crew all but exhausted, she continued her search, and every man of the crew was on the alert. It was sometime after daylight when the *Ligure* was sighted.
>
> In the heavy seas and after great difficulty, a boat from the *Gallatin* was sent alongside the stricken ship, which had righted itself. The *Gallatin's* men learned that the *Ligure's* masts had been cut away and that her people had spent the night in open boats under the lee of the schooner as she lay on her beam ends. The mate had died of exposure during the night.
>
> The *Ligure's* crew had boarded her again when she righted herself in the morning, but the wreck was slowly sinking and the *Gallatin's* men took them and the mate's body off in the *Gallatin's* boat. In the heavy sea the boat was stove in before it could be taken upon the *Gallatin's* davits, and all hands had to be hauled aboard the cutter.[2]

But the *Gallatin's* score was not especially unique: in a single week in winter, 1881, the *Grant* logged the following incidents:

> February 2.—Towed the American brig *Atlas* to New York, a distance of 90 miles, her crew being in a frost-bitten and exhausted condition.
> February 3.—Quelled mutiny on the American ship *Criterion.*

---

jui Soong, encouraged and counselled the youngster to acquire an education. After leaving the service, according to Tourtellot, Chai-jui attended Trinity College, in North Carolina, and then graduated from Vanderbilt University; later, in China, he founded a great fortune and a famous family: his daughter Ching-ling became the wife of Sun Yat-sen, founder of the Chinese Republic; Mei-ling became Madame Chiang Kai-shek, wife of the Generalissimo; Ai-ling married Dr. H. H. Kung, who, with Chai-jui's three sons, T. V., T. L., and T. A. Soong, became outstanding in Chinese and world finance.

[2] *Ibid.*

February 8.—Extricated three American schooners from dangerous positions in ice near Delaware Breakwater.
February 9.—Supplied the American schooner *Louise P. Meloy,* near Delaware Breakwater, with provisions and medical assistance. She was unable to communicate with the shore on account of ice.
February 9.—American schooners *Frank Norton* and *Andrew Nebbinger,* being pressed with heavy ice and in collision near Delaware Breakwater, were extricated and assisted to get underway.

Every cutter took its part in reducing the toll levied on ships and seamen by Davy Jones' old partners, Fire, Collision, Grounding, Ice, Famine, Mutiny, Plague, Gales, and Sudden Death. On a three weeks' cruise out of Newport, the *Dexter* easily matched the *Grant's* record by logging the following cases:

December 30, 1880.—Found sloop *Peerless* in distress near Warwick Neck Lighthouse; in dangerous position, leaking, crew frost-bitten, sails split, center-board and pumps frozen. Towed her within a few miles of Providence, R.I.
December 31.—Assisted steamer *Wyoming* off Beaver Tail.
December 31.—Found schooner ashore in Coasters' Harbor. Hauled her off and towed her into Newport.
January 6, 1881.—In company with the revenue-steamer *Gallatin,* rendered assistance to 32 vessels beset in the ice in Hyannis Harbor.
January 11.—Found American schooner *F. L. Richardson* seven miles SSW from Montauk Point; leaking badly and in danger of sinking. Towed her into New London.
January 16.—Found schooner one-half mile SW of Halfway Rock; ashore on a rock. Hauled her off and towed her to Bristol Ferry.
January 18.—Rendered necessary assistance to Italian bark *Machiavelli,* four miles NWxN from Montauk Point; 131 days from Alexandria, Egypt; out of provisions.

The entire fleet of 25 cruising cutters was able to assist more than 300 vessels in 1886—an average of almost one per day. And in any normal year during the period, the service's one thousand officers and men could expect to aid about four and a half million dollars' worth of ships and cargoes; aboard these hapless hulks there would be more than 2300 human lives.

Distress work along the shore frequently brought cutters and life-saving stations into close cooperation. Revenue-Marine officers continued to be assigned to the Life-Saving Service as inspectors and instructors, and the liaison thus established no doubt facilitated joint operations of the sort typified by the *Ada Barker* case. This American schooner's sails were blown away in a gale on January 11, 1891, and she struck a reef beyond Green Island, Maine, that same evening. Completely gutted by the impact, she heeled over and laid her foremast against an off-shore rock, to which her crew of six barely managed to escape. Half-frozen, spray-soaked, and hungry, they clung there for forty hours, until rescued in the skillful action described below by Captain Fengar:

U. S. Revenue-Steamer *Woodbury*.
Rockland, Maine. January 14, 1891.

The Secretary of the Treasury,
Washington, D.C.

Sir:

I have the honor to report that I left Portland, Maine, in the *Woodbury* on the 12th instant, as soon as the prevailing gale abated and the dense fog lifted enough to see our way out, in search of vessels in distress.

Shortly after noon a signal was discovered from a small outlying rock near Green Island. In approaching nearer, the remains of a wrecked vessel were discovered in the breakers, and perched on the rock above the reach of the waves were six shipwrecked men. A heavy southeast sea was running, and the rock being surrounded by jagged boulders and spurs, caused a tremendous breaker, running at least thirty feet high. The force of such a sea was so great that no boat in existence could have lived for a moment in its clutches. We encouraged the imperiled crew as best we could by steaming about in the vicinity all day, vainly hoping that the sea would abate sufficiently at least to enable us to drift a line to the rock and pull one or more of the unfortunates through the breakers.

Darkness coming on, we were obliged, reluctantly, to abandon any attempt at rescue until morning. I steamed to Portland, procured two dories from a fishing vessel, conveyed the tidings of the wreck to the Cape Elizabeth Life-Saving Station, and proceeded again to the scene at an early hour on the morning of the 13th. Fortunately, during the night a fresh gale from the west had sprung up, reducing the sea considerably. We laid by until daylight, and then determined to make a strenuous attempt to save the men. I sent in the first cutter [one of the ship's boats] in charge of Second Lieutenant W. S. Howland, also the two dories manned by four of our crew expert in the handling of these boats.

The Life-Saving boat also arrived at this time, and followed our boats in through the breakers. Their boat became unmanageable, but with the aid of our cutter's crew, who had landed, was extricated from her perilous position. Five of the wrecked sailors were bundled into her. Meanwhile, the dories had rescued the sixth man, and all succeeded in dashing out through the seething waters safely, reaching the *Woodbury* without accident and greatly to our relief. The half-famished men were properly cared for, fed and clothed, and conveyed to Portland.

Without detracting from the excellent conduct of every officer and man attached to this ship, I desire particularly to commend the heroism of Cadets Scott and Van Cott, who begged to be allowed to take the post of danger in place of two of the crew at the after oars in the first cutter, in going to the rescue through the breakers in an open, unprotected boat, and acquitting themselves in a splendid manner. Such mettle cannot fail to produce the right kind of officers.

Very respectfully,
A. A. Fengar,
Captain
United States Revenue-Marine.[3]

[3] In *C. G. Archives.*

Each case of assistance successfully rendered added a line to the Revenue-Marine's enviable tradition and boosted the service in the public's estimation. Courage and skill colored the whole story and helped make it an ample cause for patriotic pride. Historically, national agencies devoted to the humanitarian principle of *Safety at Sea* were rare. Probably it was only natural that such an agency should achieve highest development among a people to whom the welfare of individual men was a matter of deep concern.

Marine disasters could be so horrible that exceptionally meritorious assistance jobs sometimes called forth waves of national satisfaction and acclaim. Such was the case of the *City of Columbus,* reported voluminously throughout the contemporary press. A magazine version follows:

> Not less hardly than the rough-and-ready surfmen who patrol our coast day and night are the officers and crews of the cruising cutters, who look so fine in sunny ports. It is the purpose of this article to recall a few of their adventures and heroic deeds.
>
> [These officers] have a strong love for the life they have chosen, and a characteristic coolness in time of danger. Such an officer was Second Lieutenant John U. Rhodes, of the cutter *Dexter*. His matchless courage in the disaster to the *City of Columbus,* off Gay Head (the westernmost cape of Martha's Vineyard), won him the plaudits of a continent and promotion in his profession. No brighter instance of the valor and seamanship of the Revenue-Marine officers may be found than that exhibited by the men of the *Dexter* at this memorable wreck.
>
> The *City of Columbus* left Boston for Savannah on January 17, 1884, with 82 passengers and a crew of 45 persons; she was a staunch iron vessel of nearly 2000 tons and was commanded by Captain S. E. Wright, who had made innumerable passages through the treacherous waters of Vineyard Sound and was familiar with their every reef and shoal. Many of the steamship's passengers were invalids, going south to escape the rigours of a northern winter and win back lost health. The night was quiet, and here and there in the quiet sky stars were visible. A gale was whistling out of the west, lashing up a high head sea. When the vessel was within half an hour's sail of the promontory of Gay Head, and less than an hour from the open ocean, Captain Wright went below, leaving the quartermaster and Second Mate Edward Harding in charge of the pilothouse. The course of the steamship was SWxS.
>
> Less than a minute before she struck, the man on lookout forward rushed into the pilot-house and exclaimed tremulously that the Devil's Bridge buoy was close on the port bow. Devil's Bridge is a double ledge of submerged rocks abreast of Gay Head light. The outer ledge is an eighth of a mile from the mainland, and on either side is very deep water. It has been the scene of many wrecks, the most recent of which was that of the United States war-vessel *Galena*.
>
> When the two men in the pilot-house of the *City of Columbus* realized the proximity of the terrible reef, they were for a moment nearly unnerved. The lookout had barely told the danger before the keel of the steamship grated on the ledge. The second mate ordered the quartermaster to put the wheel to port. The order came too late. Again the vessel's keel thumped on

the reef. The force of the impact was so slight at first that only a few of the passengers were awakened. Captain Wright felt the gentle jar, and supposing he had run down some small sailing craft, he sprang from his bed and ran to the pilot-house, repeating the order of the second mate, "Hard aport!" the moment he saw what had happened.

It was about three o'clock in the morning. The Captain saw the Gay Head light on the port bow through the land haze. He believed at first that he was not so fast on the reef that he could not work off. He signalled the engineer to back at full speed and threw the wheel over to starboard. The effort was unavailing. Then he ordered the men forward to hoist the jib, hoping to cant the vessel's head to starboard into deeper water. She swung off a few points and then swerved back again.

While these attempts were being made to release her from the deadly grip of the reef, not a dozen of the passengers knew what had happened, and few of the crew realized their danger. As a last resort, Captain Wright determined to try to pass over the obstruction, and he gave the engineer the signal to go ahead. The steamship only pounded more on the reef. By this time, all the passengers had been awakened. The purser and his assistant had gone around knocking on their stateroom doors, ordering them to get up, saying that the vessel was ashore.

Supplementing the verbal warnings, the passengers heard the roar of the wild sea on the reef. Throwing around them whatever outer garments were nearest, they hurried into the saloon. Many were congregated there with grave faces, mutely looking questions that they feared to ask, when the captain, who had abandoned the pilot-house, came down among them and told them what all captains of sinking ships tell their passengers . . .

The captain calmed the fears of many, but he was hardly through talking when a cataract of freezing water poured down the companionway among them and created a panic. They crowded up the stairs and rushed out on the deck. At this instant a towering sea roared athwart the ship, and every woman and child and half the men aboard were swept away.

Before the giant wave struck her, about 40 men had climbed into the rigging. Living on deck was impossible afterward. There was a great gash in the ship's port side, and sea after sea broke across her. Two boats were launched and dashed to pieces against her iron sides. Now and then a body floated out of the cabin and was borne away on the foamy waves. The benumbed men in the rigging watched the Gay Head light, gleaming like an evil eye, until it was lost in the whiteness of the coming day. Their hearts beat high with hope for a little time just after daylight, when they saw a steamer three miles away, bound to the westward. She was the *Glaucus*. Her captain did not notice that there were men in the rigging of the wreck, and he kept on his course. Hope in the hearts of some of the men vanished with the *Glaucus,* and they let go of their hold on the ratlines and dropped into the sea.

Those who remained in the rigging saw a boat coming out from Gay Head Point at half-past ten o'clock. It was manned by the Indian life-savers. They dared not approach near, as their boat would have been smashed by floating wreckage or against the ship itself. They shouted to the men in the rigging to jump. Six of them accepted the invitation and were picked up by the Indians. The boat returned to the wreck and saved others in the same way.

While the brave Indians were working at the wreck, the *Dexter* was laboring to the eastward through the heavy seas. She came within sight of the high land of Gay Head soon after dawn. It was Lieutenant Rhodes' watch. He saw through his glass the dim outlines of a vessel's masts, slanting, as if she were ashore. He reported his discovery to Captain Gabrielson, and the *Dexter* was headed in the direction of Gay Head under all steam.

As she drew nearer to the wreck, a score of men were discerned clinging to the rigging above water. All hands were called, and preparations were made for lowering the boats. The *Dexter* steamed to windward of the wreck, and the cutter [one of the *Dexter's* boats] was swung out on the davits and lowered into the turbulent water, with Lieutenant Rhodes in command. It flew to leeward on a tall wave, towards the wreck. The boat's crew pulled carefully, and when just under the lee of the rigging to which some of the survivors were clinging, the lieutenant ordered them to jump, assuring them that they would be saved.

Thirteen men trusted their lives to him. Every one was picked up. Two men, apparently unconscious, remained dangling in the rigging. The plucky lieutenant determined to save them, if they had enough vitality left to stand transference to the cutter. It would have been courting death to have gone near enough in the boat to take off the exhausted men in the rigging. There was only one other way to help them. Lieutenant Rhodes adopted that. He fastened a line around his waist and boldly plunged into the riot of frigid waters. A piece of wreckage struck him, and the men in the boat, fearful for his life, dragged him back on board. He was undismayed by the accident, and went overboard again. This time he reached the wreck, got the men from the rigging, and brought them with him to the cutter, but they died after being put aboard the *Dexter*.

After launching her boat, the *Dexter* steamed to leeward of the wreck and anchored, in order to pick the cutter up. Her anchor chain was tough and her holding ground good, or she would have been unequal to the task of facing the heavy seas, into which she dipped her prow at frequent intervals.

Lieutenant Kennedy had gone out in the *Dexter's* gig with a volunteer crew to assist his daring brother-officer. He could not get near the wreck because of the lightness of his boat, but he saved men who had drifted to leeward of Rhodes' boat and picked up several bodies.

The gallantry of the *Dexter's* officers and crew received ample recognition. The Legislature of Connecticut, Lieutenant Rhodes' native state, thanked him; the Humane Society of Massachusetts gave him its gold medal; the President of the United States ordered him to be advanced 21 numbers in his grade. Captain Gabrielson also received a medal from the Humane Society, and certificates were awarded to the other officers. Each of the crew received a money reward. Congress recognized the rescue in joint resolutions, and the Secretary of the Treasury made it the theme of a congratulatory circular, which was read at muster on every vessel in the service.[4]

The *City of Columbus* and many another similar incident kept public interest focussed on federal measures for accident prevention. These gradually became more and more effective as engineering and public administration became more advanced. The Lighthouse Service—a purely

[4] ——, *Some Typical Rescues by the Revenue-Cutters,* in an old volume of magazine and news clippings in *C. G. Archives.*

preventive agency—in the years from 1870 to 1890, increased its major lights from 528 to 1,243 and installed 1,745 minor lighthouse stations. In the same period, the number of buoys (about 2,500 in 1870) was nearly doubled. Lighthouse equipment kept fairly well abreast of technological progress: the first lighted buoy went into service in 1881, and an incandescent electric lamp was installed in Sandy Hook (New Jersey) Beacon in '89.

The Life-Saving Service also had one distinctly preventive function: its *Regulations* required beach patrols to keep a watch for vessels standing into danger and to warn them clear by appropriate signals from the shore. This form of aid to navigation, together with the rest of the life-saving work, was considerably extended between 1882 and 1900 by the establishment of new stations; the total in operation increased from 189 to 269.

Although cutters had cooperated with the foregoing agencies for many years, this phase of Revenue-Marine work expanded and acquired more significance as coastwise navigation grew. Contemporary cutter log-books make reference with increasing frequency to such odd jobs as transporting inspectors, personnel, and stores to out-of-the-way lights and lifeboat stations; reporting buoys which had parted their moorings and drifted out of position; and giving notice of rocks, shoals, and shifts in channels discovered by cutters on patrol. While no great consequence should be attached to isolated cases of this sort, the totality of the work (performed collaterally with the cutters' major functions and therefore entailing no great additional expense) considerably facilitated the operations of the agencies concerned.

To these numerous preventive duties must be added at least one more, derelict destruction, which during the 'eighties and 'nineties became recognized as an important phase of the cutters' maritime safety function. Disasters caused by derelicts frequently crashed the headlines and dramatized the menace of these floating deathtraps. Steamships ripped open by fog-lurking hulks represented losses which many men considered not entirely unavoidable. Cutters customarily swept their cruising grounds for such hazards—a simple, commonsense measure of prevention. As the derelict problem became more widely recognized, mainly through the medium of the press, the cutters' direct approach found widespread approval. Their work of "removing dangerous obstructions to navigations along their cruising grounds" received special mention in the *Annual Report* for 1891.

Derelict destruction was by far the most thrilling preventive job on the cutters' list. Some floating dangers could be towed to port and salvaged, others could be towed to shore and beached, but, depending on the circumstances, many had to be demolished where they lay. This could be accomplished only by mining the obstructions and blowing them apart. Aboard the cutters it was considered no more than ordinary routine for a boat's crew to pull through rough seas with a heavy load of explosives for the gunner to lash, as best he could, to some dismasted and water-logged old wreck wallowing and heaving in the swell—but nevertheless it was a ticklish business. The matter of attaching the mines often called for ingenuity and vast amounts of seamanly skill, especially if the hulk were riding bottom up—a very normal situation. And the maneuver of pulling away from the mined wreck while paying out electric firing cable until a more or less safe firing point had been reached was one which, in a heavy sea, held hazards all its own. A slip of the hand or a joggled firing mechanism could be fatal. Premature explosion, flying wreckage—a dozen dangers—eliminated every vestige of montony from this type of preventive operation.

The enforcement of all categories of maritime law remained throughout the period a primary concern of cutters. Cruising and boarding were the tactics commonly employed in the enforcement of the navigation laws. Statutes in this category had become so complex by 1884 that an Act of Congress in that year established a Bureau of Navigation in the Treasury Department to have general supervision of the administrative details they involved.

This Bureau's function in many respects was closely allied with that of the Steamboat-Inspection Service and was aimed at promoting both the country's seaborne commerce and the safety of navigation. In general, the Bureau was entrusted with many details of an administrative and statistical nature, such as the documentation of vessels, the preparation of annual tonnage reports and lists of merchant vessels, the supervision of the shipping and discharge of seamen, and the collection of tonnage dues. The Steamboat-Inspection Service, on the other hand, concerned itself chiefly with that portion of the navigation laws relating to the inspection and certification of vessels and their equipment and the examination and licensing of merchant officers. (The two Bureaus merged in 1932 to form the Bureau of Navigation and Steamboat Inspection, re-named "Bureau of Marine Inspection and Navigation" in 1936. The latter was abolished during World War II, when most of its duties and personnel were transferred to the Coast Guard.)

It will be recalled that the cutter establishment's lack of a shore organization in 1838 had been at least partly responsible for the development of the Steamboat-Inspection Service as a separate agency; the same lack in 1884 doubtless discouraged any serious thought of consolidating the administrative work of the new Bureau in the hands of the Revenue-Marine, although a close relation between the administrative and enforcement phases of maritime statutes might have made such a move seem quite logical. Nevertheless, except for inport boarding and dock-side enforcement, carried out by Customs men, Steamboat Inspectors, and Bureau of Navigation personnel, the Revenue-Marine remained the chief agency for the enforcement of all navigation laws.

These statutes increasingly after 1885 emphasized *safety at sea.* An International Marine Conference, held at Washington in 1889, proposed many notable safety measures and succeeded in standardizing the "Rules of the Road" (seagoing traffic regulations) used throughout the world. Sumner I. Kimball helped represent the United States at this important affair. Other suggestions and movements for improving conditions at sea preceded and followed the Conference, as the American Congress turned more and more of its attention towards maritime affairs, especially the *prevention* of maritime disasters.

Among specific enactments around this period were the first federal anchorage laws; they opened a new phase of activity for the Revenue-Marine. Anchorage regulations for crowded New York Harbor were established under the Act of May 16, 1888, and the harbor cutter *Manhattan* was detailed to enforce them. A similar act, in '96, directed the Secretary of the Treasury to prescribe rules for the movement and anchorage of ships in the St. Mary's River, Michigan, a busy thoroughfare, and further directed him to assign such cutters as might be necessary to enforce the traffic rules so made.[5] Anchorage work was dull enough, from the cutter men's point of view, but it required considerable local activity and it kept the harbor channels safe. In New York Harbor alone, the *Manhattan* in one year cleared 1,375 ships from anchorage within prohibited areas; she assisted 809 of these offenders by towing them to proper grounds.

Another safety measure adopted in 1896 extended the cutters' traffic-control operations still further by authorizing the Secretary of the Treasury to assign cutters to enforce rules for insuring the safety of life and property at regattas and marine parades and to render aid in case of accidents at such affairs.[6] Statistical estimates of the value of such work through the years are impossible to make, but the willing cooperation and sincere friendship that cutters traditionally have drawn from the yachting fraternity as a result of the operation of the Act of '96 are testimony of a sort that statistics scarcely could improve.

The customs laws, too, continued to call for enforcement by the cutter fleet. Sporadic attempts to divest the tariff of its strong protective bias in the post-Civil War era failed dismally. Republicans, carrying

[5] Act of March 6, 1896 (29 Stat. L., 54).
[6] Act of May 19, 1896 (29 Stat. L., 122).

the banner of economic liberalism in one hand and the umbrella of protectionism in the other, viewed with loathing and alarm each low-tariff movement, and against spokesmen for reduction (who contended that American industry had outgrown its ante-bellum infancy) they levelled their heaviest political artillery and all their forensic skill. Led by Cleveland in '92, Democrats fought the presidential campaign mainly on the tariff issue. Their party platform denounced "the Republican protection as a fraud, a robbery of the great majority of the American people for the benefit of the few . . . the culminating atrocity of class legislation." But when the roar of battle quieted down, Cleveland's sweeping victory was able to induce no more than half-hearted and totally ineffective Congressional action towards reduction of the import duties. Even so slight a breach of the Republican battlement was quickly closed by GOPoliticians. The tariff remained high, and revenue evasion continued to be a problem for the Revenue-Marine to solve with the old, familiar tactics of cruising off the coasts and boarding all suspicious vessels found.

One phase of these operations, at least, received considerable popular support. A section of the press was just beginning a crusade against the evils of narcotics, and the public conscience was beginning slowly to awaken to the need for suitable restrictions on the trade. Because there was a tax on drugs, drug-running constituted a violation of the customs laws, and thus, although fully adequate narcotic controls were lacking, the cutters were able to stand with the Customs Bureau between the country and a flood of relatively inexpensive, smuggled drugs. West Coast ports were centers of operations for the dope rings, and cutters in Pacific waters were a first line of defense against the ugly business. The *Wolcott*, stationed in the Straits of Juan de Fuca, in a boarding operation carried out on August 31, 1890, found on the American steamer *George E. Starr* a quantity of undeclared opium, which she seized (together with the vessel) in one of the first recorded battles of the campaign.

The country's increasing maritime needs thus fostered an expansion of the cutters' *protective, preventive,* and *law enforcement* duties both in scope and number, and the service's position as the federal government's principal agency for maritime law enforcement and marine safety attained wide recognition and support. Meanwhile, however, no comparable expansion of the service itself was effected, and although every cutter evidently was driven hard there was always more work than the organization possibly could accomplish with the means at its disposal. In fact, as time wore on, the Revenue-Marine's ability to maintain its past level of operations definitely declined. By 1890 or so, cutters were assisting only 75% as many distressed vessels as in 1880, and during the same interval the number of vessels boarded declined from 33,000 to 27,000 per year. These figures were not parallelled by proportional decreases in the incidence of distress or in the total number of documented U.S. vessels.

Such straws in the wind of diminishing returns apparently failed to urge the civilian Chief of the Revenue-Marine Division to effective action, yet they gave fair warning of the simple fact that the Revenue-Marine was wearing out, both in man-power and in matériel. Lack of an energetic administrator who could and would present its needs to the Secretary and the Congress in a businesslike, well-reasoned way had brought the Revenue-Marine to the verge of pauperism. Its ships, whose average age increased from 9 years in 1878 to 15 in 1887, were largely junk and frequently required extended in-port periods for repairs. Underpowered and slow when they ran at all, they were ridiculously inadequate to their work. A prime example was the *Forward,* a 155-footer powered by one single cylinder. After a year's lay-up for alterations and repairs, she could wheeze back to her station at a maximum speed of only about six knots.

Like the cutters, the commissioned corps was aging, too. Civilian Chiefs of the Division apparently failed to interest Congress in retirement legislation which would have enabled them to maintain a fairly constant age level for each officer grade. Without such legislation, age levels moved sharply upward—five full years, for the second lieutenant group, between '78 and '87. Under such circumstances, aged and aging skippers held up the promotion of younger men. So few vacancies for third lieutenants occurred in '89 that in 1890 the School of Instruction was forced to close; it was argued that if the Revenue-Marine needed only one or two third lieutenants every year or so it could draw them from the Naval Academy's overflow. In brief: the course of cutter progress had been allowed to peter out, and the source of the service's vitality—its pool of young, enthusiastic officers—had been permitted to dry up. The price of administrative incompetence had been very high.

With the system thus running in reverse at a time when the country needed it to go ahead faster than ever, something obviously had to be done. The *Army and Navy Journal* sponsored one concrete suggestion, whereby the Revenue-Marine was to be given a Commandant of its own and made a separate corps, with a status similar to the Marine Corps, in the Navy. Many officers favored the idea as a way of escape from the maladministration then prevalent in the Treasury. The pros and cons were argued in Washington for several years, and an enabling bill was introduced in Congress. Although the bill failed to become law, the controversy brought out one point on which agreement was quite general. As one *Army and Navy Journal* correspondent expressed it:

> An experienced, nautical, military head, with fixed prerogatives, seems the only relief for the Revenue-Marine, one of the most useful services under the government but one whose life blood has been tapped by the greed of the selfish.[7]

Such agitation had the effect of bringing Secretary of the Treasury William Windom finally to the same decision Secretary Spencer had arrived at fifty years before: the logical person to lead the cutter branch and direct its operations—regardless of the executive department to which it might be attached—was a cutter captain, a man trained and experienced in maritime law, expert in the field of safety at sea, and imbued with the high standards of the commissioned corps. Accordingly, he ordered Captain Leonard G. Shepard to Washington and installed him as Chief of the Division on December 14, 1889.

[7] *Army and Navy Journal,* vol. for 1889. See also *The National Democrat* (Washington, D.C.), vol. for 1889, and *The Marine Journal,* December, 1889.

CHAPTER XI

New Departure

HISTORICALLY, reasonable changes in governmental agencies and functions seldom have been made on time; the policy of appointing cutter captains to the Revenue-Marine's top command was approximately ninety-nine years overdue. But in 1889, public disgust with the Spoils System and clamor for the replacement of political spoilsmen in public office by qualified technical experts reached so high a pitch as to induce considerable cleaning of the federal house. Windom had been forced to reinstitute the long-neglected Spencer-Fraser plan calling for a military Commandant, and this time Congress gave the stamp of its approval by a statute passed in 1894, requiring that "a captain of the Revenue-Cutter Service . . . shall be Chief of the Division."[1]

Shepard and his successors were career men. They were trained leaders, holding their posts by merit and ability alone. Bound not by partisan politics but by their corps' traditionally high sense of duty to the nation and to all humanity, they were free to pilot their agency along ever-broadening channels of public usefulness.

Captain Shepard, the crucial figure, initiated many modernizing trends. Like every succeeding Commandant, he was meticulous in advising the executive and legislative branches continuously and completely as to the potentialities of the service for meeting current national needs. Shepard knew all too well that the current need for maritime law enforcement and safety operations far out-stripped his neglected little organization's facilities and strength, and in his plain-spoken *Annual Report of the U.S. Revenue-Marine Service for 1891* he gave the Secretary and the Congress an unvarnished picture of what was wrong.

On the subject of floating equipment, he said:

> The policy pursued for many years past, of making extensive repairs to the old vessels, is a mistaken one. Had the same amount of money, with a little more added, been judiciously expended in the building of new vessels of a modern type, the Service would now have a much more efficient force. . . .
>
> . . . New vessels are urgently needed. . . . The rapidly increasing commerce on the Great Lakes, the Pacific Coast, and Puget Sound, . . . the enormous quantities of opium believed to be smuggled into the United States from contiguous foreign territory, and the additional service required of revenue cutters in protecting Government interests in Alaska, all demand

[1] Act of July 31, 1894 (28 Stat. L., 162, 171).

new and more efficient steamers. The present vessels . . . are entirely too small to meet the enlarged duties of the Service.

On another vital matter he continued as follows:

The improvement of the condition of the personnel has of late become a matter of grave necessity. Its importance is as great as that of improvement in the materiel and demands early and liberal legislation on the part of Congress.

This relief is indispensable to the best interests of the Service. . . . Legislation has been denied or neglected from year to year until the present condition of the Revenue-Marine is little short of actual stagnation and promotion is practically at a standstill. Both officers and men are deprived of the benefits that would result from the enactment of such laws and regulations regarding retirements, longevity pay, and pensions as are in force not only in the strictly military services but to a certain extent in some of the civil branches as well. . . .

There are at present on the active list some [captains] who are over eighty years of age, who have served faithfully and with credit in every naval war since that of 1812, who have been and are refused the well-merited recognition of their services such as was long ago accorded their brother officers-in-arms serving under other departments of the Government. . . . These old and faithful servants are deserving of the care of the Government, and the absence of a suitable provision in law for their honorable retirement seems a manifest injustice to them, is a source of great embarrassment to the Department, and works detriment to the efficiency of the Service. . . . The higher grades contain so many of these officers that promotion is well-nigh blocked and generally an officer is well past his prime before he can attain the rank that would entitle him to command. This manifestly detracts from the energy and efficiency of the corps. . . .

While awaiting Congressional action on his main proposals, the Commandant went ahead with other projects, one of which called for speedy resumption of the cadet training system. A one-time captain of the practice cutter *Chase,* Shepard could not agree that the pinch-penny policy of procuring officers from the Naval Academy's overflow served either the best interests of the cutter branch or any true economy. For one thing, there was naturally a better chance that the Navy would tap its overflow from the bottom of graduating classes than from the top, and thus the cutters could rely only upon luck to send them better than mediocre men. Further, Shepard was convinced of the necessity of providing cutter officers with a distinctive indoctrination as well as an up-to-date professional training. Therefore, when rapid expansion of the Navy finally closed off the Naval Academy's overflow in 1894, he welcomed the opportunity of recommissioning the cadet training ship. No new Act of Congress was required for this action, since the original authority granted by the Act of 1876 had never been withdrawn.

The next year Congress brought relief to the commissioned corps by retiring certain officers (specifically named in the Act) who by age or infirmity were incapacitated for further duty.[2] (Subsequent Acts granted authority for retiring aged or incapacitated personnel generally.) Resultant promotions left vacant the entire grade of third lieutenant. With junior officers at a premium, the *Chase* was lengthened 40 feet to accommodate a total of 25 cadets, and a new impetus was given to the training program. Captain Oscar C. Hamlet was assigned in command of the cutter, and Lieutenant E. P. Bertholf was detailed as executive officer. With the Department's approval, these men raised cadet entrance requirements so as to admit only candidates who had completed their general scholastic work. Under this plan, the two-year line cadet course could be concentrated almost entirely on technical and professional subjects. For a time, the *Chase* moored in various southern ports through the winter months, which the cadets devoted to classroom work; in 1900, regular winter quarters for the School were established at Arundel Cove, Maryland. Summers were always spent by cadets in cruising in the *Chase* to foreign ports. By reopening the School of Instruction, Shepard insured to the service a steady supply of specially trained and selected, enthusiastic line officers. No change was made at this time, however, in the method of procuring junior engineers; the latter continued, for several years, to be drawn direct from civil life. Eligible candidates with "at least six months of practical experience with marine engineering in seagoing vessels" were selected for commissions by competitive examinations.[3]

During Shepard's administration, the strength of the cutter branch stood at 144 line and 78 engineering officers, 1000 enlisted men.

Captain Shepard was as solicitous of enlisted men as of commissioned personnel, and he was ever conscious of the relationship which exists between the welfare and the efficiency of a crew. Remembering that the enlisted men's daily ration allowance had remained unchanged since the Civil War—notwithstanding a general upward trend in American living standards—he soon sought and obtained authority to increase the allowance and bring it into line with current living costs.

Shepard's next step was so obviously necessary that it needs no explanation here: he provided the service with the nucleus for a technical staff to advise and assist the Commandant in several specialties. Besides hiring two naval constructors, Mr. James Lee and Mr. John Q. Walton, he detailed Captain Russell Glover to be superintendent of construction and repair and Chief Engineer John W. Collins to act as consulting engineer. Eventually commissioned, Walton became the service's first chief constructor. Collins had served as an engineer in the Navy from

[2] Act of March 2, 1895 (28 Stat. L., 920).

[3] *Annual Report, U. S. Revenue-Cutter Service,* 1897 (Govt. Printing Office, Wash.), 9-10.

1864 to '65 and had entered the Revenue-Marine as a second assistant engineer in 1866. He was promoted to chief engineer December 31, 1891 and assigned as consultant. The same Act (1894) which provided for a military Commandant provided also for an Engineer-in-Chief, and, upon passage of the Act, Collins was so appointed with the rank of "captain of engineers."

Under these men and their successors, Kimball's old policy of developing the cutter as a distinctive type of ship designed to meet the service's special needs was reinstituted and carried steadily forward. The first vessels launched under the auspices of the new staff were the cutter *Windom* and the harbor cutter *Hudson*. Both were built of steel and powered with triple expansion engines driving single screws. Designed especially for patrolling, the 171-foot *Windom* could make 15 knots; she was one of the fastest ships afloat. The 96-foot *Hudson,* somewhat slower, transformed most of her 160 pounds of boiler pressure into power. The technical staff's influence was manifested in the precise, scientific language of the two vessels' specifications, which left very little to chance or to the contractors' judgment. Modern design in cutters, as in every field of engineering, followed the application of exact and tested knowledge to engineering problems. The *Hudson* thus could carry high boiler pressure in safety because her specifications laid down precise metallurgical standards for her boiler plates. Shepard's successor called these ships "the first and only effort at modern cutter construction up to 1895."[4]

Reorganization of the field administration appears to have been one of Shepard's most difficult tasks. It will be recalled that collapse of the Spencer-Fraser system had given collectors of customs an opportunity to reestablish themselves in considerable authority over cutter operations; even Kimball had been unable to break their hold completely—a most unfortunate circumstance. Collector control, often inefficient and sometimes abusive, became more and more incongruous as time brought the cutters more and more duties totally unrelated to the work of enforcing the customs laws. While in 1790 protection of the revenue had absorbed almost 100% of the cutters' efforts, by 1890 it represented only a relatively small fraction of the total job. With this apparently in mind, one of Shepard's assistants searched for a general term descriptive of the service at that date and hit upon *"the maritime constabulary of the nation."*[5] But although the Act of 1894 had recognized the necessity of placing an expert at the head of this force, the full effect of the

[4] *U.S.R.C.S. Annual Report,* 1897; 12, 15.

[5] *History of United States Revenue Cutter Service,* a typewritten brochure, unsigned, 42 pp., dated April 1, 1890; file No. 554. In Commandant's Office Library, C. G. Headquarters.

Act had been discounted by retention of politicians in the secondary posts. Not only were many collectors inexpert in general maritime affairs, but also—and equally important, from the Revenue-Marine point of view—they were civilians exercising a degree of military command. The situation was illogical, to say the least: interposed between the Commandant and the cutter captains were civilian agents who, while not legally responsible to the former, exercised at least a nominal control over the latter. The chain of command was badly fouled.

The best Shepard could do towards clearing this politically dangerous tangle was to demonstrate a saner administrative plan. The opportunity came within his reach with the current necessity of cracking down on seal-poaching in Alaska. It was obvious that unity of command over the group of cutters then about to sail for the Bering Sea would be an operational asset, and it was well-known that in the Bering Sea area there would be no collector of customs near enough to exercise control. Shepard thus was free to appoint a cutter captain to the military post of Commander, Bering Sea Fleet, and thus to establish a true military chain of command between Headquarters and units in the field. Between all elements in this chain there existed precise duties and responsibilities, both up and down the line, as defined by law and fundamental military doctrine. The success of the Fleet as an operational unit facilitated the ousting of civilians from intermediate control posts and the rebuilding of the service as a thoroughly military organization within the next few years.

Captain Shepard persevered in his reforms until 1895, when death brought to a close his notable career. Before he died he might well have looked with satisfaction upon his handiwork, for he had turned the service definitely into the current of a new, fast-moving age.

His successor, Captain Charles F. Shoemaker, made no deviation from the course. The new Commandant obtained from Congress all the personnel legislation Shepard had requested and then proceeded to carry out the balance of Shepard's plans. It was Shoemaker who placed into effect the reorganized system of cadet training, previously referred to, and who in 1900 gave the School of Instruction its first quarters ashore by assigning the *Chase* a permanent base, at Arundel Cove, Maryland. Here Shoemaker, with a $30,000 appropriation from Congress for a starter, was beginning to build up a cutter depot and boatyard, and here the School remained until 1910.

Like Shepard, Shoemaker saw clearly the scope of the over-all job confronting the "coast-guard navy," as he once called the cutter branch, and he realized that antiquated methods and tools could not meet the demands of the nation's maritime interests in the 20th century. In renewed calls upon Congress for up-to-date ships—specialized cutter types—he based his argument on the changes being wrought by technology at sea:

> The multifarious duties placed upon the Revenue Cutter Service . . . and the rapidly growing scope of its operations imperatively demand that an efficient class of vessels be provided in which to do the work. The cruisers should be able seagoing vessels, swift runners, of modern type as to construction, equipment, [and] motive power . . . and of such weatherly qualities as to fit them to keep the sea upon occasions which are constantly arising. These demands have been emphasized in recent years by the steady advance made in the size, draft, and superior speed of vessels employed in the Merchant Marine. The ocean-carrying trade is now done chiefly in large steamships, including the huge ocean liners as well as the "ocean tramp"—about all steam now, where nearly all were sail a generation ago.
>
> This is equally true of our coastwise commerce. The sail vessels now employed are huge in comparison with what the same trade knew twenty years ago, and it is by no means rare in this day to meet vessels, both steam and sail, in the coastwise trade, of more than 3000 tons burden. . . .
>
> It follows that in case of disaster to such vessels, requiring steam assistance, the cutter on the station should be of size and motive power to render it effectively.[6]

Influenced by the common sense of this view and by a new stirring of the public's awareness to America's maritime heritage, Congress authorized Shoemaker to embark on a cutter-building venture that soon gave the Revenue-Cutter Service half a dozen new and able vessels, including some of the most famous cutters ever launched. Before 1900, the *Manning, Gresham, McCulloch, Algonquin,* and the *Onondaga* had been completed. These ships, all slightly more than 200 feet in length, had modern hulls, Scotch boilers (160 pounds steam pressure), triple expansion engines, single screws capable of driving the ships at nearly 18 knots, and generators (the first ever installed in cutters) to supply current for lights and call bells. Said Shoemaker, with no little pride.

> The construction of these cruisers marks a new and radical departure from the methods which have always prevailed in the Revenue Cutter Service. The entire work—the preparation of the plans and specifications, and the construction—has been executed under the immediate control and supervision of officers of the Service, resulting not only in a considerable saving to the government but in securing a type of swift and, in all particulars, modern vessel.[7]

These splendid vessels were reliable, seaworthy, and fast; their architects had achieved a fairly satisfactory synthesis of the ship-characteristics required in cutters of the day. *McCulloch* (219 feet overall, 1440 tons) was the largest cutter built up to that time. *The Manning,* more typical

[6] *U.S.R.-C.S. Annual Report,* 1897; 10.
[7] *Ibid.,* 13.

of the group, was 205′ 6″ overall, 32′ 10″ beam, 12′ 3″ draft (trial). She cost $175,000. Her lines were the fine lines of ancestral clipper-cutters, but, in the fashion of the period, she had a plumb bow instead of the more graceful clipper stem. They were the last cutters ever rigged for sail. As a class, they were suitable for scouting, for rendering assistance, and for cruising at moderately long range. They so successfully measured up to their designers' expectations, in fact, that they furnished the general pattern for cutter construction for the ensuing twenty years.[8]

Yet time and technics speed ever on; long before the *Manning* and the *Gresham* had steamed their last mile, new needs and new technical possibilities had brought forth new cutter types. But in the salty memories of officers and men who drove them through the gales, and in the hearts of thousands of men and women whom they rescued from the storm, Shoemaker's fine ships won a never-dying glory that is inextricably woven through the legend of the United States Coast Guard.[9] Their first laurels were to be earned not for victories of peace, however, but in the field of war.

[8] See esp. Commander F. A. Hunnewell, U.S.C.G., "United States Coast Guard Cutters," in *Transactions, Society of Naval Constructors and Marine Engineers, 1938.*

[9] See esp. Felix Riesenberg, Jr., *Yankee Skippers to the Rescue* (Dodd, Mead, and Co., New York, 1941).

CHAPTER XII

Of War and Peace

THE SPANISH-AMERICAN WAR extended American commitments 7,000 miles across the blue Pacific and thereby forever ended all semblance of U.S. isolation. This momentous event held crucial significance for the subsequent history of the United States and of the world, and America's long delay in taking it into account as a prime political reality demanding radical reorientation of U.S. foreign policy simply magnified its fateful consequences.

Small profit can be gained from any attempt to focus on one person or one party as the scapegoat for such delay. A few men in public life (notably Theodore Roosevelt and the elder Henry Cabot Lodge) did recognize the political implications of the trans-Pacific movement at the time, but the decisive body of American political thought could not span in a single leap the chasm between local and global points of view. Chauvinistic writers and orators and professional isolationists interpreted the Spanish imbroglio to the American public in the narrowest of national terms. From rostrum and editor's sanctum they rationalized the war as many things—as a swift stroke in defense of national honor, as a blow of vengeance for the martyred *Maine,* as a crusade to eradicate Old World political stenches from a nearby neighbor's land. When they referred at all to the United States' Philippine enterprise, they were inclined to define it as essentially a cultural project, a pet charity: a matter of educating and medicating "our little brown brothers" lately liberated from the tyranny of Spain. But of the prime military and political realities arising from the war, in both the Atlantic and the Pacific communities, small word. Thus by smokescreens of misplaced emphasis, these purblind patriots preserved in the United States a spirit of isolationism long after the reality of isolation was dead—a political folly, priced in blood, payable in two World Wars.

And in the history of the Coast Guard, the war became likewise an important landmark: it revived public awareness to the Revenue-Marine's military function and thus prepared the way for an unequivocal statutory definition of the establishment's military status. This was an essential step in fixing the Coast Guard's precise position within the federal system.

Prior to the Spanish-American War, the military status of the service had been open to conflicting interpretations. The Act of March 2, 1799 had stated merely that the cutters should "cooperate with the Navy" whenever the President might so direct; it was loosely drawn and failed to close the primary question of whether the cutters formed *de jure* a civil or a military arm of government, although it imposed on them *de facto* the status of a naval reserve, organized, trained, and disciplined to naval standards and liable to naval service at all times. Further obfuscating the issue was the fact that although in war the cutters did become identified with the Navy, in the long periods between wars they engaged mainly in the pursuit of civil or quasi-civil duties under Treasury administration; thus, in the public mind, in peacetime they became to a great extent disassociated from the naval establishment, whose purely military tradition and single major function responded to few civil demands.

These circumstances led to confusion and partisanship on the floor of Congress whenever bills affecting the service were taken up. Because there was obvious nonsense in supporting two navies *per se,* some Congressmen held that since the Revenue-Marine could be defined basically as nothing more than a military force afloat—a small-bore counterpart of the Navy, so to speak—it should be incorporated with the Navy. This argument was often used to block appropriation bills for new and needed cutters and for modern equipment; in effect, it put a brake on technical cutter progress and operational efficiency. Other Congressmen on occasion contended that since the Revenue-Marine's duties were essentially civil ones, its personnel could be considered only as members of the civil service. Therefore, they argued, the application of the military services' old age and disability retirement privileges to cutter men would provide the entire civil list with an opening wedge to retirement legislation; against this nightmarish flirtation with "socialism," as some called it, they turned some of the most polished invective ever loosed in Congress. Their line of reasoning was used for many years to block general retirement legislation of the sort recommended by Captains Shepard and Shoemaker in their *Annual Reports,* with the unfortunate results which Shepard so carefully catalogued in the volume for 1891.

The war with Spain provided many cutters with an opportunity to gain recognition for military effectiveness at the very moment that the *Bear* and its Overland Expedition were earning the President's citation for their performance of civil duties in the Far North. The press—the "new journalism" of the late 1890's—broadcast news on the two forms of activity to all corners of the land. Inevitably, the public began to recognize the service as a military arm organized for the *dual* purpose of supporting maritime law and safety under all conditions of war and peace and of reinforcing the Navy on occasion as an efficient, trained reserve. The good sense of maintaining an agency so organized and so defined appeared confirmed in the headlines of the daily news.

By 1902, significantly, in debates on Senate No. 1025, *A Bill to Promote the Efficiency of the Revenue-Cutter Service* (by giving its officers rank, pay, and retirement on the basis of parity with Army and Navy officers), a minority based its opposition mainly on the stock arguments cited above, but the majority, voting for enactment, ranged itself with Representative William Sulzer of New York, who presented a common-sense view of the service's military status and dual function:

> Let me say, Mr. Chairman, that I am sincerely in favor of this bill . . . because in my judgment it is a just, a patriotic, and a meritorious measure. . . . Investigation proves beyond question that in its organization, general features, military character, naval discipline, and duties the Revenue-Cutter Service is now and always has been constantly regarded as a part of the military service of the government for both defensive and offensive operations. . . . The brave and gallant men of the Revenue-Cutter Service did heroic work in the Revolutionary war, in the war of 1812, in the Mexican war, in the Seminole war, in the Civil war, and in the war with Spain. How can anyone successfully contend, in the face of these facts, that the Revenue-Cutter Service is more civic than military? The record answers. The Revenue-Cutter Service is as much a part of the military arm . . . as the Marine Corps.
>
> The duties of revenue cutters in times of peace appeal to the public more forcibly than in times of war. These [cutter] men in time of peace do a great work saving lives, enforcing the law, and looking after wrecks and derelicts on the high seas. . . . They are always on deck, always on duty, always earning their pay, always in the service of their country. At the present time a cordon of cutters is cruising along our Atlantic coast. . . . Their work is never done. . . .
>
> The status of the Revenue-Cutter Service is therefore that of a *coast-guard* navy.
>
> . . . This bill passed the Senate without a dissenting vote. It ought to pass this House without division. . . . I hope, I believe, it will soon be law. (Applause.)[1]

By 1915, Sulzer's concept had become fairly well crystallized and generally accepted in Congress, and in that year the legislators cleared away a century and a quarter of confusion by declaring with simple finality that the service constitutes *"a part of the military forces of the United States."*[2]

For cutter men whose military exploits thus influenced the service's statutory background, the prelude to war commenced as far back as 1895. In that year, Cuba, last remnant of Bourbon empire in the New World, victim of four centuries of misrule and tyranny, flamed anew in insur-

[1] *Congressional Record* (57th Cong., 1st Sess.) Vol. 35, No. 86, April 2, 1902; p. 3813 *et seq.* (Italics ours.)

[2] Act of January 28, 1915, "Creating The Coast Guard."

rection. True to the pattern set by countless Spanish kings and regardless of its countless failures as a principle of government, the Bourbon monarch resorted to mass reprisals against the unarmed populace. Hoping by terrorism to quench patriot ardor, General Weyler ordered his king's men to round up the insurgents' families and hold them as hostages in concentration camps. In short order, starvation and disease laid hundreds of these imprisoned women and children low. The general effect of such strategy was to stiffen Cuban resistance to the limit of available money, munitions, men.

On the mainland, in Florida and in cities farther north, the Cuban underground purchased arms to smuggle out to the island forces, surreptitiously enlisted gentlemen adventurers and soldiers of fortune to go filibustering in support of insurrection. Regardless of popular pro-Cuban clamors, the United States was bound by international law to suppress such violations of its technical neutrality. Further, finding their profits dissolving in the smoke of rebellion, American sugar interests in Cuba urged vigorous protection of American neutrality (*i.e.:* suppression of filibustering and gun-running) as a means of denying fuel to the fire. And so President Cleveland in 1895 ordered certain cutters to establish a neutrality patrol. "The enforcement of the neutrality laws," said Captain Shoemaker in his *Annual Report* for 1897, "made necessary by many attempts to send illegal expeditions from our coast to Cuba in the interest of the insurgents, has compelled vigilant cruising by the Cutter Service."

Over the period 1895-1898, the *Boutwell, Colfax, Forward, McLane, Morrill,* and *Winona* maintained a patrol of the Straits of Florida and adjacent waters. They seized seven ships for violations of neutrality regulations, detained in port a dozen or so suspected violators, and broke up two organized filibustering expeditions. But war was brewing fast, and the destruction of U.S.S. *Maine* at Havana on February 15, 1898 marked the end of the neutrality era.

The conflict precipitated by the *Maine* incident was simple in strategy and swift in course.[3] By a famous dispatch dated February the 25th, Roosevelt, Assistant Secretary of the Navy, allotted Commodore Dewey's Asiatic squadron the task of preparing the way for American invasion and seizure of the Philippines:

Washington

Dewey, Hong Kong
Order the squadron, except the *Monocacy,* to Hong Kong. Keep full of coal. In the event of declaration of war Spain, your duty will be to see that

[3] Principal source consulted relative to the war's military pattern: Rear Admiral F. E. Chadwick, U.S.N., "The War with Spain" in *The Encyclopedia Americana* (Americana Corp., New York, 1940); Vol. 27, p. 439, *et seq.* Chadwick was Sampson's Chief of Staff in the North Atlantic Squadron.

the Spanish squadron does not leave the Asiatic coast, and then offensive operations in Philippine Islands. Keep *Olympia* until further order.

Roosevelt[4]

Establishment of a blockade preparatory to invasion of Cuba was a job assigned to Commodore Sampson's North Atlantic squadron. Operations incident to the fulfillment of these tasks were expected to break Spain's naval power and topple her colonial empire, and these results were in fact achieved by mid-summer. Seldom has victory been so swift, so cheap, or so complete.

But in the early days of '98, war enthusiasts in the U.S. could not escape the fact of American unpreparedness. The Army, minuscule and obsolete, mainly spread out in small garrisons through the West, bore no resemblance to the striking force actually required under the plan of operations. Although the Navy, well-trained and up-to-date, stood approximately equal to the Spanish fleet on a simple gun-for-gun basis, nevertheless it possessed too few ships to guarantee full coverage of commitments. Besides being charged with crushing the enemy in two oceans, the U.S. fleet was responsible for preventing that enemy from striking American seacoast towns and commerce—and no one knew where such blows might fall.

In the resultant feverish rearmament, scouting craft and dispatch boats thus received priority as American naval necessities; even before Spain's declaration of war, on April 24, the U.S. had begun combing foreign and domestic sources for such units, as well as for transports and auxiliaries for overseas landing operations. A headline in the San Francisco *Examiner* for March 9 told the story in three words:

MORE VESSELS WANTED

The item stated that a proposal to turn over revenue-cutters and certain of the better lighthouse tenders to the Navy for use as gunboats "received instant attention" in the Navy Department, which was then making "active preparations for hostilities." A few days later the same sheet declared:

REVENUE CUTTERS
TO BE PRESSED INTO SERVICE
OF THE NAVY

——— . ———

March 24.—The Navy Department today took steps towards utilizing ten of the seagoing revenue cutters. Captain Shoemaker, Chief of the Revenue Cutter Service, conferred with Assistant Secretary Roosevelt during the day on plans for turning over these cutters to the Navy. They will be first sent to Norfolk where additional guns will be mounted and then will proceed

[4] Walter F. McCaleb, *Theodore Roosevelt* (Albert and Charles Boni, New York, 1931); 77.

to Key West and become a part of the squadron there. Their main service will be as naval pickets, a fleet of these cutters being maintained outside the cruisers and battleships.

The Revenue Cutter Service now has ready for instant and active service 124 line officers, 74 engineering officers, 900 enlisted men, and 19 vessels, of which 14 are on the Atlantic Coast. Two others are in course of construction and with rush orders can be ready for service within three or four weeks. The *Manning,* the *Gresham,* the *Algonquin,* the *Onondaga,* and the *Windom* are all new, fast, and efficient vessels and can go anywhere and perform any service that any vessel of their class can perform.

Easterners and Navy officials were not alone in apprehensiveness of coastal forays by Spanish raiders. West Coast dwellers shared the same dark thought, and diversion of the Bering Sea Fleet (composed of cutters well-known in Pacific states) to their defense probably was calculated to meet the threat so far as possible and at the same time reinforce West Coast morale. This plan was reported in the *Examiner* for April 15:

REVENUE MARINE SERVICE
ABSORBED BY NAVY

Important Missions to the North
Have Been Abandoned

——— . ———

Officers of the Revenue Marine Service expect orders . . . placing them and their craft in the Navy. It is an open secret that the cutters *Rush, Corwin,* and *Grant,* now in port, will not go north this season. The cutters *Bear* and *Golden Gate* are also on the coast. The former is commanded by Captain Frank Tuttle, who has an excellent record. He is now hunting for the icebound whaling fleet in the Arctic. For years the *Corwin* and *Rush* have gone to the Bering Sea to guard the seal islands against poachers. The pelagic sealers and poachers should reap a harvest in the Sea this summer.

The *Rush, Corwin,* and *Grant* may patrol the Pacific coast. Either of the three could be armed so as to give good battle to ordinary privateers. For police work they could be sent out to sea to size up an approaching enemy. They could get to port with the news fast enough to give the alarm and have a force sent out to intercept the warships.

If the editor realized that three small cutters patrolling the entire West Coast against the approach of a raid presented a picture not entirely reassuring, or if in afterthought he awoke to the fact that there was no "force" available to send out as interceptor, he doubtless was relieved, next day, to be able to report:

CUTTER BEAR
TO BE
ARMORED

Revenue Vessel Will
Be Prepared To
Attack Spanish
Privateers

——— . ———

The U. S. Revenue Cutter *Bear,* now at St. Michael, . . . awaiting the return of Lieutenant Jarvis and Dr. Call, who started overland some months ago to relief of imprisoned whalers in Arctic waters . . . has been ordered back to Port Townsend and upon arriving on Puget Sound will be provided with defensive armor plate and sufficient guns to make it warm for Spanish privateers or in fact any of the smaller vessels of the Spanish Navy.

Some of these news forecasts came true and some did not. No Spanish privateer or raider struck at either coast, and the war, miraculously turned by Dewey, Sampson, and Schley into a naval victory parade, was over before the *Bear* could be armored or the *Gresham, Algonquin,* or *Onondaga* completed and sent to join the fleet. But the record shows that eight cutters sailed with Sampson on the Havana blockade, one was with Dewey at Manila Bay, four patrolled the West Coast against raiders, and seven others, working with the Army, patrolled harbor defense minefields guarding principal ports from Boston to the Mississippi Passes. Cutters that cooperated with the Navy were transferred to that Department by Executive Order dated April 9, 1898 and were returned to the Treasury shortly after cessation of hostilities.

One of the first offensive actions of the war involved a raid on enemy commerce by U.S.R.-C. *Winona,* Captain G. H. Gooding. The *Examiner* for April 25 reported:

REVENUE CUTTER WINONA
TAKES SPANISH STEAMER

Atlanta, Ga., April 24.—A special from Biloxi, Mississippi, says the revenue cutter *Winona* from Mobile captured the Spanish steamer *Saturnina* at Ship Island, Mississippi, at 1 o'clock today. . . .

For the newly-commissioned *McCulloch,* leisurely cruising on shakedown from her East Coast birthplace to her first station, San Francisco, via Suez and the Orient, preliminary war-orders waited in Singapore. Arriving at that port on April 8, two full weeks before war was declared, Captain D. B. Hodgsdon received from the American consul-general the following cablegram from Washington:

Direct commanding officer of the U.S.S. *McCulloch* on arrival proceed to Hongkong report his command duty Commodore Dewey Asiatic Station.
W. B. Howell
Assistant Secretary[5]

A few days later, *McCulloch* joined the squadron in Man-o'-War Anchorage, Hong Kong, where Hodgsdon reported to the Commodore as directed. "The vessel at once went under naval regime," stated the

[5] *The United States Revenue-Cutter Service in the War with Spain, 1898* (Govt. Printing Office, Washington, D.C., 1899); 13.

commanding officer's war diary, "and in the course of the next two days was coaled and painted 'war' color—a leaden gray—and received from the flagship copies of the naval signal books, sets of signal flags and night signals, copies of all existing squadron orders, and instructions regarding the cipher code and its key. Lieut. John Mel, USRCS, was assigned as signal officer."[6]

On April 24 the squadron shifted anchorage to Mirs Bay, China, where all ships stripped for action. On the 27th, at the Commodore's signal, the squadron weighed and stood out on its historic mission. Cruisers *Boston, Baltimore,* and *Raleigh,* and gunboats *Concord* and *Petrel* formed one column, led by *Olympia,* flag. To their right, *McCulloch* led her especial charges, the supply ships *Nanshan* and *Zafiro,* in a second column. Steaming toward Manila at 8 knots, the little armada made final preparations for battle. Loose gear was stowed, splinter mats rigged, and crews drilled at battle stations. Tension mounted as the miles slipped steadily astern. One afternoon, at the flagship's signal, the insolent proclamation of the Spanish Governor-General of the Philippines was read to the crews at muster:

> The North American people, constituted of all the social excrescences, have . . . provoked war with their perfidious machinations, with their acts of treachery, with their outrages against the Law of Nations. . . .
>
> A squadron manned by foreigners, possessing neither instruction nor discipline, is preparing to come to this archipelago with the ruffianly intention of robbing us of all that means life, honor, and liberty.
>
> The aggressors shall not profane the tombs of your fathers; they shall not gratify their lustful passions at the cost of your wives' and daughters' honor!

If any Yankee sailor had previously needed a spur to action, this was it. A naval officer present wrote: "The cheers which followed" the reading of the governor's polemic "could be heard from ship to ship throughout the squadron."[7]

Late on the afternoon of April 30, the squadron arrived off Subig Bay. Finding no enemy, it hove to in a flat calm sea while commanding officers attended a conference on board the flagship. The Commodore explained his plan of action and issued his instructions. By dusk the captains were back aboard their ships, and the squadron, now in single column with *Olympia* in the lead, steamed slowly down the coast towards Corregidor. Crews at battle stations lapsed into tense silence as night came on. "A first quarter moon revealed the ghostlike ships," wrote one of the *Baltimore's* officers, "and behind the shadowy outline of the

[6] *Ibid.*

[7] Principal sources consulted relative to the activities of Dewey's squadron include: *U.S.R.C.S. in The War with Spain, 1898, op. cit.,* 9-21; Capt. J. M. Ellicott, U.S.N. (Ret.), "Under a Gallant Captain at Manila in '98," in *U. S. Naval Institute Proceedings, January,* 1943; Rear Admiral Randolph Ridgely, Jr., U.S.C.G. (Ret.), "The Coast Guard Cutter *McCulloch* at Manila," in *U. S. Naval Institute Proceedings,* May, 1929.

mountainous coast there was an occasional flare of coppery lightning." As the *Olympia* entered Boca Grande, "the setting moon passed under a mat of cirrocumulus clouds spreading over nearly half the heavens, and everything was blotted out in darkness."

Stealthily the flagship led the column close over towards El Fraile Rock; the Commodore accepted risk of detection and fire from shore batteries rather than the blind gamble of ploughing through mid-channel minefields. By midnight, May 1, the flagship had passed in; successive ships, expectant and alert, followed in close order. At a quarter past twelve, just as *McCulloch* brought El Fraile abaft the starboard beam, the black stillness was broken: soot in the cutter's stack caught fire "and sent up a pillar of flame like a signal light." "Whether or not this was the first seen of our fleet by the Spanish gunners is not known," continues the ship's diary, "but immediately thereafter a shot was heard from a battery . . . on El Fraile . . . followed quickly by a second one, which passed whistling and tumbling over this vessel. The *Boston,* just ahead of the *McCulloch,* answered with a 6-inch gun, and the *McCulloch* fired three projectiles from her after starboard 6-pounder R.F. gun. A third shot came from the enemy's battery, and was replied to by an 8-inch shell from the *Boston,* after which firing ceased."—As well it might, for the enemy emplacement had been knocked out.

As the rock fell astern, Dewey reduced speed to four knots and steamed northward and eastward up the bay, so as to reach its head, where he hoped to find the Spanish fleet, in time to join action at daybreak. His order of battle required *McCulloch* to guard the precious storeships *Nanshan* and *Zafiro* from enemy gunboats and, as Randolph Ridgely, Jr., a lieutenant serving in the cutter, reported later, "to protect the ships in line of battle from surprise attack and in case of any ship becoming disabled, to tow her out of range and take her place in line."

At about 5:30 a.m., as Dewey maneuvered into position to loose his opening salvo, *McCulloch* herded her two charges into a safe position towards the center of the bay, then took up her own post, according to the ship's diary, "close in rear of our line of battle. Shells frequently struck around or passed over the *McCulloch,* and it is to be questioned, from the wild fire of the Spaniards, if the ship was not in as much danger in the position she occupied as if she had been in the actual fighting line."

Americans present on this day off Cavite long recalled, with utter satisfaction, that *McCulloch* found no need to tow any vessel out of the battle line: the great Commodore won a great victory between 5:40 a.m. and half past noon—with time out for breakfast—losing not a ship or a single sailorman.

Unconfirmed reports of Dewey's blow reached the U.S. via the Manila-

Hongkong cable almost immediately. The San Francisco *Examiner* on May 2 headlined:

WASHINGTON HAILS TIDINGS
OF VICTORY
——— . ———
News Meager

Then the Commodore cut the line (because the company refused to handle his official dispatches), and eager Americans focused on *McCulloch* as their source of hoped-for information. The *Examiner* believed it

> probable that immediately after the engagement today Admiral Dewey sent the revenue cutter *McCulloch* back to Hongkong with dispatches and that the first information from him will come from that point. It will take the *McCulloch* about two days to make the trip.

Dewey did so dispatch the cutter, but not until May 5; she anchored in Hongkong two days later, awaited by the world, and sent the flag lieutenant immediately ashore to cable home authoritative news of victory. A new pattern of power in the Pacific had been set.

Halfway around the globe, Sampson's squadron late in April established a blockade of Havana and the Cuban north coast; after Admiral Cervera took his Spanish fleet to cover in Santiago, the blockade was extended to that port to keep the Spaniards "bottled up." In a front-page item datelined April 23, reporting the southern movement of various blockading units, the *Examiner* for April 24 informed its readers that

> The *Morrill, Hudson,* and *Hamilton,* formerly revenue cutters and recently armed for service in the Mosquito Fleet, passed through Hampton Roads today and, after asking formal permission of the Commodore, proceeded to Key West. From that point they will join the Cuban blockading fleet.

The *Hudson,* it may be recalled, was a 96-foot tug; she carried a 5/8″ shield on her pilothouse and two 6-pounders on her deck. Had these been her sole accoutrements, her name probably would have been lost to history, but she had more—a secret weapon: the bold spirit of her crew.[8]

On joining the fleet, this bantam battleship was assigned to blockade the entrances of Matangas and Cardenas Bays and ordered to issue arms and ammuntion to rebel groups whenever possible. She soon discovered that three lightly-armed Spanish gunboats were holed up in Cardenas harbor; these embarrassed the tugboat's liaison with rebel bands. In vain

[8] Principal sources consulted relative to *Hudson's* war record include: *U.S.R.C.S. in The War with Spain, 1898, op. cit.,* 21-7; Captain T. G. Lewton, U.S.C.G. (Ret.), "Personal Recollections of The Cruise of The Revenue Cutter *Hudson* in The War With Spain in 1898," in *U. S. Coast Guard Academy Alumni Association Bulletin,* April, 1942; and "Hudson Memorial Medal," in *U.S.C.G.A. Alumni Association Bulletin,* June, 1943.

the *Hudson's* skipper, First Lieutenant Frank H. Newcomb, tried to lure them out to fight.—Newcomb was a veteran of the Civil War and, according to one of his officers, Third Lieutenant T. G. Lewton, "thought that when you went to war you were supposed to do a lot of firing."—Failing to trick the Spaniards into battle, he conceived a plan to carry a battle to them. The harbor's main entrance had been filled with debris, and Newcomb suspected the barrier concealed mines. But a short search disclosed a clear channel, very narrow, running close by several mango-covered islands to Cardenas' waterfront. This discovery suggested the feasibility of a raid, and Newcomb so reported to the naval commander at Key West upon the *Hudson's* next arrival at that place.

A few days later, the Navy dispatched its gunboats *Machias* and *Wilmington* and torpedoboat *Winslow* to join *Hudson* in a foray in the bay. They arrived off the entrance on May 11. *Machias,* too deep to clear the newly-discovered channel, remained outside and shelled the mango thickets as a discouragement to snipers, while the other ships ran through the tree-edged pass. Once inside, *Wilmington* steamed down the center of the bay, and *Winslow* and *Hudson* covered the south and north shores, respectively. The raid was on.

Only a few merchantmen, sunning themselves at anchor off Cardenas, were sighted until the attackers arrived directly in front of the town, when the hunted gunboats were discovered moored alongside some sugar wharves. Lewton says the *Winslow* immediately "shot in" towards them "like an arrow," evidently intent on blasting them at very close range. But before the Americans opened fire, Spanish shore batteries in the town began ranging on the *Winslow,* and within a few minutes a general engagement was in progress. *Hudson* closed towards *Winslow* at full speed, and the two steamed back and forth near the waterfront, probing with their guns for enemy emplacements. *Wilmington* remained farther out in the bay and supported their attack with 4" broadsides.

The Spanish batteries fired smokeless powder and thus could be located only by their intermittent flashes. Gunners on the American ships were hampered by smoke from their own black powder but nevertheless kept up a rapid and fairly accurate fire, blazing away at every flash on shore. The *Hudson* alone in 20 minutes threw 135 shells at the enemy; Savage, her negro steward, stripped and sweating and roaring *"There'll Be a Hot Time in the Old Town Tonight,"* passed up the ammunition in a steady stream.

The Spaniards' marksmanship was erratic, but they had the advantages of position, cover, and continuously visible targets. They were thus able to smother the raiders in a torrential fire, which poured down on the two little ships from five different directions. "Shells screamed overhead,"

Captain Leonard G. Shepard, U.S.R.-C.S.
First Officer to Serve as Commandant under
Statutory Authority
Commandant 1889-95
(Official C.G. photo.)

Captain Charles F. Shoemaker, U.S.R.-C.S.
Commandant 1895-1905
(Official C.G. photo.)

The Class of 1896, School of Instruction, U.S.R.-C.S.

1st row: Cadets Frederick C. Billard (Commandant, 1924-32, with rank of rear admiral); Benjamin C. Chiswell (later Assistant Commandant); L. E. Ashbaugh; Bernard H. Camden; Thomas L. Jenkins; James C. Hooker; and Captain Joseph Congdon, Superintendent of the School; Lieutenant Daniel P. Foley, Executive Officer; Lieutenant D. H. Jarvis, Instructor in Navigation.

2nd row: Cadets Harry G. Hamlet (Commandant, 1932-36, with rank of rear admiral); Randolph Ridgely, II (later Superintendent, Coast Guard Academy); Moses Goodrich; Leonard T. Cutter; Harry A. Pressey; Richard M. Sturtevant; and Dr. Strayer, U.S.P.H.S.

(Official C.G. photo.)

The *Algonquin, c.* 1898 (A *Manning*-class cutter)
(Official C.G. photo.)

Captain John C. Cantwell, U.S.R.-C.S
(Official C.G. photo, taken about 30 years after his Kowak River Expedition.)

Captain Frank H. Newcomb, U.S.R.-C.S.
(Official C.G. photo.)

The Cutter *Manning* Rendering Assistance
(From a painting by an unknown artist. Official C.G. photo.)

The *Hudson* at Cardenas Bay
(From a painting by J. Mullen. Official C.G. photo.)

says Lewton, who was spotting for the *Hudson,* "and lashed the water all around." Although solid shot rocked both vessels and shrapnel riddled their upperworks and stacks, Spanish gunnery dealt no crippling blow for nearly half an hour.

Then *Winslow's* luck ran out: two shells tore into her vitals and wrecked her steering engine and a boiler. Now helpless, she rode before the freshening breeze onto the shoals that reached the shore, into the jaws of the Spanish guns—her plain doom: to hit the beach and there disintegrate beneath a concentrated fire.

But the *Hudson's* people balked at letting *Winslow* make this voyage alone. Instantly the warrior tug stood shoreward into shallow water to take her friend in tow.

Deeper-hulled than the torpedoboat, the tug soon found herself practically aground, grooving the muddy bottom with her keel. Ten, fifteen, twenty minutes passed while *Hudson* backed and filled and ploughed her way along. Lewton says that during this time the Spanish fire was "very fierce." Lieutenant Bernadou, *Winslow's* commander, fell, wounded. Lieutenants Scott and Mead kept the tug's 6-pounders blazing; *Winslow's* guns flamed on, unfaltering in their rhythm.—More minutes wore away.

Slowly the tug drew into heaving-line distance of the other ship. Lieutenant Scott stood by the tugboat's rail, ready to cast a line to Ensign Worth Bagley, on the *Winslow's* deck. The next instant Bagley and three torpedoboatmen, cut down by a shell which exploded in their midst, lay dead. Other hands caught Scott's line, made fast, and *Hudson* pulled away. As she stood out, inching her bloodied partner to safety, the last shells in the engagement sailed overhead from *Wilmington* towards shore and silenced the Spanish guns. The sound, smoke, and smell of battle faded into the distance, into the past, leaving to Cardenas town the heat and humdrum of perpetual siesta and to the Coast Guard the memoried words "Cardenas Bay."

The action at Cardenas deserved small mention for its influence on the war; won, lost, or drawn, it would have been at best an insignificant affair from a strategist's point of vew. But this was not the viewpoint from which the nation saw it. Human values ranked by Americans among the highest had been displayed that day at Cardenas, and the entire press resounded with praise for the *Hudson's* act. Congress received news of the rescue from the President's own pen:

Executive Mansion
June 27, 1898

To The Congress of the United States:

On the 11th of May, 1898, there occurred a conflict in the Bay of Cardenas, Cuba, in which the naval torpedo boat *Winslow* was disabled, her commander wounded, and one of her officers and a part of her crew killed by the enemy's fire.

In the face of a most galling fire from the enemy's guns the revenue cutter *Hudson,* commanded by First Lieutenant Frank H. Newcomb, United States Revenue-Cutter Service, rescued the disabled *Winslow,* her wounded commander, and remaining crew. The commander of the *Hudson* kept his vessel in the very hottest fire of the action, although in constant danger of going ashore on account of the shallow water, until he finally got a line made fast to the *Winslow* and towed that vessel out of range of the enemy's guns, a deed of special gallantry.

I recommend that, in recognition of the signal act of heroism of First Lieutenant Frank H. Newcomb, United States Revenue-Cutter Service, above set forth, the thanks of Congress be extended to him and to his officers and men of the *Hudson;* and that a gold medal of honor be presented to Lieutenant Newcomb, a silver medal of honor to each of his officers, and a bronze medal of honor to each member of his crew who served with him at Cardenas.

WILLIAM MCKINLEY

By joint resolution, Congress carried these recommendations into effect.

Other cutters in the Cuban theater proved useful both in action and in the routine drudgery of war. More than a full share of the latter fell to *McLane,* which drew the monotonous task of guarding Sampson's main communication channel, the cable tying Key West Naval Station to the mainland. This cutter rode out the war in the vicinity of the Sanibel Island cable-crossing, encountered nothing more hostile than the mosquitoes she found infesting the place. Others had a better time of it. The old (1863) *Woodbury,* pinch-hitting as an auxiliary cruiser and mounting one 6-pounder, six 3-pounders, and one Colt automatic 6-millimeter gun, bolstered the Havana blockade from May until mid-August; she and the Navy's *San Francisco* on the final day of war drew the last shots fired from Morro's guns. *Morrill* and *Hamilton* saw action on the same blockade, worked effectively with naval units. And the *Windom,* Captain S. E. Maguire, matching the *Hudson's* combination of combat and lifesaving, won a sailor's accolade—a "well done" from the squadron commodore—for a minor engagement off Cienfuegos, 12 May, in which she covered the withdrawal of a Navy boat expedition crippled within range of the enemy on shore: at a critical juncture, *Windom* charged in close to the beach through heavy fire and with her 4" battery smashed the Spaniards' concentration, levelled their stone defenses, and bloodily harassed their disorganized retreat.

But of all cutters in Cuban waters, none set a higher mark for varied and sustained activity than did the *Manning,* under the command of Captain F. M. Munger; her diary records practically every type of combat service expected of a cutter *circa* 1898:

U.S.S. *Manning,*
Norfolk Navy-Yard, Va.,
August 22, 1898.

The Secretary of the Treasury,
Washington, D.C.

Sir:

I have the honor to report the arrival of my command at this yard today, after an absence on active war service of nearly four months' duration. During the period in question the *Manning* has been engaged in hostile action four times, and in one instance formed a unit in a fleet attack on shore works. The main and secondary batteries of the ship have fired in all about 600 rounds in hostile work, the main battery guns consisting, it should be stated, of 4-inch rapid-fire rifles.

Despite the exposed nature of her work the *Manning* has been remarkably fortunate in that not a casualty has occurred on board, nor has the vessel sustained in point of material or equipment any damage. There is no sickness on board, although both officers and men have been through a most trying and difficult period of work. There have been a number of malarial cases recorded, but all were well taken care of; except for the exhausting effects of tropical service, I may say that the general health of the command is excellent.

I took occasion to report to the Department the participation of the *Manning* in the engagements of May 12 and 13 last, at Cabanas and Mariel, Cuba, and I noted in my report of these operations the commendation of Commodore J. C. Watson, U.S.N., on the gunnery work of the *Manning* at Cabanas.

Following the convoy of the transport *Gussie* and the termination of that duty, the *Manning* was assigned to blockade patrol off the port of Matanzas. This work lasted until May 17, when the *Manning* was hurried off to the westward with orders to take station off Bahia Honda and watch for any intimation of the approach of Cervera's fleet. This duty was one of the most exacting of all which fell to the lot of my command during the entire summer. To understand its importance it must be known that the *Manning* stood between the Havana blockading fleet and the enemy. Our fleet off Havana depended wholly on the *Manning* for news of the approach of the enemy, and only the greatest vigilance on the part of those on the ship could insure a detection of the Spanish approach. This duty lasted until May 24, when news was received of the "bottling" of Cervera's fleet in Santiago de Cuba. Subsequent to the work just outlined the *Manning* aided in patrol duty before Havana, and on May 25, when the German warship *Geier* made a dash out of Havana without attempting to speak the blockading fleet the *Manning* was ordered to overhaul her. This was done in a smart run of a few miles, during which the ship made about 17 knots.

From May 24 to June 14 the *Manning* was employed on the patrol from Havana to Bahia Honda, but on the latter-named date this ship joined the naval convoy fleet charged with the protection of the Fifth Army Corps in its transportation to Santiago de Cuba. The convoy duty lasted from June 14 to June 22. The *Manning* did her share of the work equally with the other armed vessels of the fleet, alternating from steaming in column formation to scouting on the flanks and in the van and rear. On arriving before Santiago the *Manning* took charge of a division of the transports and held it together for a feint, as for landing, at a point about 15 miles to the westward of Santiago harbor.

On June 25 the detached squadron of transports was taken in by the *Manning* to the point of disembarkation at Siboney, and throughout that day and the one following dispatches were conveyed between army headquarters at Daiquiri and more advanced points occupied by the army. During this work the ship was under the immediate orders of Capt. C. T. Goodrich, U.S.N., commanding U.S.S. *St. Louis.*

On June 26 the *Manning* was ordered to take station at Daiquiri and guard the army base of supplies at that point from attack. This duty continued until July 14. On July 5 the *Manning* repelled an advance of the enemy on the base of supplies. The gunnery work of this day was exceptionally good, and the shots were placed in the enemy's position with precision and deliberation. I might mention at this point that in the internal arrangement for battle I was assisted on the bridge by First Lieut. C. H. McLellan, executive officer, and by Second Lieut. G. M. Daniel, navigating officer, while Second Lieut. G. L. Carden, ordnance officer, took immediate charge of the second division of guns, consisting of two 4-inch R.F.S. and two 6-pounders, and to Third Lieut. G. H. Mann was given charge of the 4-inch gun and two 6-pounders forward.

During the guard duty at Daiquiri a landing party of seaman infantry was organized in charge of Second Lieut. G. L. Carden, and was held in readiness for shore duty whenever occasion for the service should arise. The army guard force consisted of 100 men. At one time fever reduced the number of men on shore available for duty to 15. No surgeon being present with the army force, Dr. Mitchell took charge of the sick, and not one case was lost while in his care. On July 10, on the arrival of army reenforcements, Dr. Mitchell was relieved by Captain and Surgeon Ten Eyck of the Army. But for the presence of the *Manning* a considerably larger force from the Army would doubtless have been necessary for the protection of Daiquiri. All the supplies of the army of invasion, or the major portion of them, were in store at this point, and an attack was actually made when the small army guard was decimated by sickness.

On July 18 the *Manning* was assigned to duty with the squadron under Commander Todd of U.S.S. *Wilmington,* operating in the vicinity of Manzanillo. The cruising which followed was for the most part inside the cays stretching away between Cape Cruz and Quenos. As the *Manning* passed through the cay channel on July 18, and while off Neguerro, she was fired on by the shore batteries, but was not hit.

On July 20 Commander Todd's squadron, consisting of *Wilmington, Helena, Manning, Scorpion, Osceola,* and *Hist,* engaged the shore fortifications at Santa Cruz del Sur. The attack was in fleet formation, the *Manning's* place in the formation being number 3. On this occasion the *Manning* fired 102 shots, the range varying from 2,800 to 3,200 yards. Both the first and second [gun] divisions scored a number of excellent hits.

On July 21 and 22 the *Manning* assisted in dragging for telegraph cables off Jucaro and at a point about 25 miles to the westward of Jucaro.

Up to and including July 29 the *Manning* took station in the vicinity of Cape Cruz on blockade duty. My command was charged with the work of reducing the blockhouses before Neguerro, but on arriving off that place on July 25 the position was found abandoned by the enemy. The *Manning* was then worked up to a point a short distance to the westward, where a Spanish signal tower was shelled.

Following the duty off Cape Cruz the *Manning* was assigned to service on blockade off Cienfuegos, and she remained on this last-mentioned work until ordered to Key West on July 15 last. During the Cienfuegos blockade duty communication was had on two occasions with the insurgent camp, commanded by Alvarez, located about 13 miles to the westward of Cienfuegos.

Only July 14, when news was received of the signing of the protocol between the United States and Spain, I personally visited the insurgent camp, accompanied by Mr. Whitworth, and interviewed the insurgents, informing them of the general provisions of that treaty. On July 15, under orders from the senior officer present, Lieutenant-Commander Adams of the *Yankton,* I went in toward the entrance of Cienfuegos under flag of truce. The Spanish gun vessel *Alcedo* came out in response, and I sent Lieutenant Carden on board to acquaint the Spanish authorities with the orders we had received to raise the Cienfuegos blockade. On the return of that officer the *Manning* proceeded to Key West, where she arrived on July 17. On July 19 we left Key West under orders from Commodore Ramsey for this place, arriving off Cape Henry in sixty-eight hours' time.

I desire to commend my officers for having done to the best of their ability, and the men, one and all, gave the officers good and loyal support.

Respectfully yours,
Fred M. Munger,
Captain, R.C.S., Commanding *Manning.*[9]

When the war was over, Todd cited Captain Munger to the Navy Department, stating:

> I was associated with the *Manning* during the period of hostilities in the northern blockade, and the high opinion I then formed of the efficiency of the *Manning* has been more than borne out by her service on the south blockade, which I had the honor to direct. . . . I take great pleasure in calling attention . . . to the highly meritorious services of this officer.[10]

The American Navy demolished Cervera's squadron, soft core of Spanish power, early in July. Although the outcome of the war at sea had never been in doubt, the speed and total cost (16 killed, 68 wounded) of American victory in two oceans amazed the world. Men who sought a moral found one: superiority in matériel, training, and morale pay off. Stripped of seapower, Spain no longer could defend her far-flung empire. U.S. land forces in Cuba forced the surrender of Santiago on July 17, and on August 12 a protocol of peace was signed.

The order to cease firing signalled the cutters' return to peaceful duties and peacetime cruising stations but not to military limbo. On escort, blockade, and scouting duty, in landing operations and bombard-

[9] *U.S.R.-C.S. in The War With Spain, op. cit.*
[10] *Ibid.,* quoting *Wilmington* letter dated August 17, 1898.

ments far from U.S. shores, the service had renewed its reputation as a blue-water, fighting outfit, had played effectively on the Navy team and won the respect of Navy commodores. The statutory definition of military status which followed this demonstration of military utility strengthened the position of the cutter branch in the federal system and strengthened the nation's arms for the greater trials of force that lay ahead.

CHAPTER XIII

Pattern for a New Day

I

THE WORLD turned at the end of the Spanish-American War to face the dawn of a dynamic, streamlined age. Persistently, especially in the century past, scientists and engineers had pursued twin goals of accuracy in research and functionalism in design. They had placed their hands—however lightly—upon the controls of destiny, and at their touch vast technological and intellectual forces had been unleashed. By 1900, almost every factor of human existence had been caught up in the resultant current of mechanistic progress. Industry showed direct effects. Railroads and steamships, radically improved since 1860, had become the world's efficient carriers. The telegraph had woven its copper net around the globe, and the telephone, using a person-to-person mesh, had begun to weave another. Parallel advances had been made in the metallurgical and chemical industries, in agriculture, printing, the building trades, and in hundreds of other production fields.

Moreover, sensing the key to this success and driving ever onward towards complete control of nature, whole battalions of experimenters had continued hurling themselves against the crumbling bulwarks of impossibility. The first incandescent electric light had sent its rays from Edison's dingy Menlo Park laboratory in 1879 to banish darkness forever into interstellar space. Motorboats and motorcars by 1895 had chugged a few epoch-making miles. About the same time, Langley and the Wrights had commenced experiments that soon led to the installation of gas engines in gliders and thus, vindicating Icarus, to the achievement of sustained flight. The crowning miracle of the century, Marconi's establishment of wireless communication by electro-magnetic waves, had been performed by '98.

Startling new forms and applications of mechanistic power thus greeted the cataclysmic new century, but they were in no respect more revolutionary than the administrative techniques business men had designed for their exploitation. Utmost profit required that men, machines, and capital be brought together to produce a given product or service with a minimum of waste. Application of scientific principles in the business field promised to lead to this desired end. A business could be organized and managed scientifically at many levels; in the upper echelons, a whole industry might be streamlined, or rationalized, under a single directorate, thus at one swoop making possible the elimination of costly bottlenecks, the rectification of overlap or underlap in the functions of various segments, and the coordination of all units towards a common goal. Such procedures had become distinctive features of American economic life by the turn of the century; U.S. Steel, for instance, the world's first billion dollar corporation, in 1901 began its career of coordinating many components to the single purpose of making a profit out of making steel.

People invariably react to sweeping changes in technics and economic forms. The whole world had been compressed abruptly into one compact community by 19th century improvements in transportation and communication; human reactions to this new condition of life, by which every nation became in effect the close neighbor of every other, ranged within the next century from a potential for catastrophe, dimly visible through the flames of World War I and starkly clear in the glare of Hiroshima, to a potential for human progress beyond the bounds of imagination. Similarly, as modern capitalism in its search for profits revolutionized the socio-economic relationships of a major portion of the world's population, it evoked tremendous and widespread reactions. Married to modern industry, it was the most productive system the world had ever known and so was capable of great good. But, completely unfettered and with only a balance sheet for a conscience, it was also capable of great harm. As the public gradually became aware of the dangers in the system, it became also aware of the necessity for insuring the mass of men against them.

The public's acceptance of responsibility for such insurance was not entirely new. The trend had appeared in England as early as 1802, when, by the Health and Morals Act, Britons moved to protect children under nine years of age against barbaric conditions of labor then existing in their factories. Other British social insurance acts followed through the years in ever broadening scale and scope.

In the United States, one of the first attempts of Congress to regulate business in the interests of the public welfare had been the Act of 1838 (previously cited) establishing the Steamboat Inspection Service. Especially in its early days, steamboating had been a viciously competitive game, and shipowners, eager to pry loose the last penny of profit, sometimes had pared expenses for upkeep, equipment, and skilled labor far below the minimum required for safe operation. The Act referred to, together with subsequent supporting legislation, in general had aimed at coercing owners into relinquishing some part of their profits as necessary to insure proper upkeep and operation of their vessels and thus to contribute to the public safety. The main stream of federal regulatory legislation, however, commenced with the Interstate Commerce Act of

1887, an attempt by the public to protect shippers against discriminatory rates and certain other injurious practices of the railroads. From then on, the American people assumed more and more responsibility for insuring society against dangers and dislocations of the economic system. Anti-monopoly acts, investment banking laws, conservation laws, social security legislation, and legal recognition of the workingmen's right to organize and bargain collectively, outlined the trend between 1887 and World War II. And the social conscience that took satisfaction in such measures acted to strengthen humanitarian tendencies in numerous other directions; some of these which bore directly on the Coast Guard's early history have been mentioned in preceding chapters. After 1890, workmen's compensation laws, dangerous cargo acts, certain sections of the Seamen's Act, and many another piece of legislation were enacted in testimony of the willingness of Congress to safeguard the individual's health, life, and limb against a wide range of hazards that lurk in modern, mechanistic environments. The ideal of humanitarianism and social reform can be traced back to the far reaches of history, but the emergence of a sense of public responsibility to the individual strong enough to establish national laws such as those listed above is a modern phenomenon.

Federal agencies cannot exist *in vacuo;* they must live exposed to the winds of time. No exceptions to the rule, the Revenue-Cutter and related services felt the impact of many forces at the century's turn, and the measure of their response was the measure of their history in that period. For the Revenue-Cutter Service, lines of change were drawn by three successive Commandants: Captains Charles F. Shoemaker (cited previously), '95 to 1905; Worth G. Ross, 1905-11; and Ellsworth P. Bertholf, 1911 to the period's end.

II

Like industry, the cutter fleet rode the swelling current of technological progress and found itself swept forward to new gains in operational potential. The design of the *Manning* set the trend: it combined the best offerings of contemporary marine engineering and architecture in a cutter which proved more useful than any earlier type. In addition, construction and maintenance costs for the *Manning*-class were relatively low. The point of expense held special significance, for throughout the period the service was very short of funds. Recurrent depressions kept Congress acutely economy-minded, and, notwithstanding long-term upward trends of prices or gradual increases in the service work-load, both of which acted to raise cutter operating costs, the House seldom permitted annual appropriations for the cutter branch to top two million dollars, including all funds for new construction. So, needing more ships more than it needed radically better ones, the service refrained from extravagant experimentation. Quite a few new cutters were constructed, but all were *Manning*-like in general design except for power and speed. These characteristics suffered materially from limitations imposed mainly by rising costs. For example, in 1897 a *Manning* rated at 2,500 H.P., 17-18 knots, had cost only $175,000, but in 1911 a somewhat similar ship (*Miami*) capable of only 1,300 H.P., 12½ knots, cost $250,000. And a quarter of a million was about as much as Congress cared to pay. New units, therefore, ranged in length from about 165 to 200 feet, employed triple-expansion engines (single screws), and, except for *Mohawk* (1902), a sister of the *Manning*, averaged roughly the *Miami's* power and speed. Among them were the wood-hulled icebreaker *Androscoggin;* the *Seminole;* the *Seneca,* built as a derelict-destroyer on special order of Congress; the *Tahoma* and *Yamacraw,* 191 foot sister ships; *Tuscarora; Acushnet* and *Snohomish,* splendid seagoing tugs, 152 feet in length; *Miami* and *Unalga,* sister ships, 200 feet in length; and the *Tallapoosa* and *Ossipee,* a pair of 1,200 ton, 165 footers, built in 1915.

But within allowable limits of cost, service designers took full advantage of technological improvements and carried forward the development of the cutter as a distinctive type of ship. Experience dictated numerous architectural changes which the construction staff worked into later models; *e.g.,* the discard of the broken deckline characteristic of the *Manning*-class in favor of a clear, flush weather deck. The latter provided a more convenient working platform for assistance operations. Originally incorporated in plans for *Androscoggin* and *Seneca,* it subsequently became a distinctive cutter line. Other departures from the *Manning* model, such as the introduction of watertube boilers (*Pamlico,* 1907) and the shift to oil fuel (*Golden Gate,* 1910), reflected modern trends toward increased flexibility and efficiency in power plants. Still others, structural refinements, grew out of progressive improvements in materials and techniques used in American building yards.

When Captain Shoemaker launched his cutter modernization program in 1897, the cruising fleet consisted of eight so-called "first-class" units, small, underpowered, and old (average age: 19 years), together with about a dozen "second-class" units, even smaller and older. Considerable diversity existed, despite earlier attempts at standardization. The only completely up-to-date power plant in the entire service was in the *Hudson;* many of the first-class units, thumping along on single cylinder "mills," had been obsolete for twenty years or more. By 1915, practically all the ancients had been replaced. The fleet in 1915 was newer (average age: 14 years), larger (23 first-class cruising cutters), better designed, better built, technologically more advanced, and, consequently, far more capable of handling its job than the fleet which flew the cutter flag in 1897.

And by 1915, wireless telegraphy had multiplied the operational possibilities of this new fleet a thousand-fold. A search for historic "firsts" leads back to the first use of wireless aboard a service ship—in this case, a Lighthouse Service lightship. The following extract from the San Francisco *Call* for August 24, 1899, touches a romantic chord:

THE RETURN OF THE TROOPS
[via Transport *Sherman*]

Glad News Flashed by Wireless Telegraphy
From Behind an Ocean-Haze Curtain

"*Sherman* in sight." That was the message which came from the ocean yesterday to representatives of the *Call*. Inspired it seemed by some strange mystic power a telegraph instrument at the Cliff House ticked the welcome words and flashed to the watchers on the beach the glad tidings that California's heroes had ended their long journey from the wars and were approaching the Golden Gate. The news was sent into the city and in a few minutes the streets of the town were a bedlam. Cannon were booming, whistles were sounding their shrill blasts and thousands of men and women, given expression to excitement long suppressed, cheered in an ecstasy of honest gladness. The *Call* had scored a double triumph. It had the honor of announcing first to the people of San Francisco the arrival of its returning heroes and in doing so it demonstrated the absolute practicability of the latest of physical marvels—wireless telegraphy. It is a matter of unusual interest that the home-coming of the Californians was heralded in a test that is beyond question the most thorough and successful application of wireless telegraphy ever made in the United States.

The message came from out of the depths of the sea. For days the watchers of the *Call* had been waiting for it. Day and night men with keen eyes and ears stood by the telegraph instrument in the basement of the Cliff House. Now and again sounds created, as far as human senses could tell, by magic power would be heard. The instrument moved by the force of some subtle influence in the air. Messages were coming through the air from the sea. A new physical miracle was happening under the very eyes of those who watched.

As the time approached for the return of the troops the *Call* determined to send the news ahead of all other agencies into the city. There was but one possible means to accomplish this feat and that was wireless telegraphy. Six weeks ago experiments were made in telegraphing from the dome of the Claus Spreckles Building to Telegraph Hill, but with indifferent success. Local disturbances prevented accuracy and then the effort was made at the ocean beach. For five weeks expert electricians and telegraph operators labored on the strange problem and at last success was won.

Messages were sent and received at stations on the beach and then an attempt was made to telegraph over the water, to send words through the air to a determined point. Receiving instruments were placed on the yacht *Lurline* and the experiments began. They were in the highest degree successful. Messages were sent and received a distance of ten miles out at sea. In order that there might be no possibility of failure more sensitive instruments were secured and the watch for the *Sherman* began. Through the courtesy of Federal officials transmitting apparatus was placed on board the lightship number 70, which was anchored nine miles outside the Golden

Gate. Charles M. Fisher was placed in charge and Lewis McKisick and H. J. Wolters, expert telegraphers and electricians, superintended operations at the shore end of the strange line. The receiving instruments were placed in the basement of the Cliff House.

Day after day messages were sent and received. The wireless line was working perfectly. At noon yesterday there was no longer doubt of success. During the afternoon a heavy haze settled down over the ocean. Gradually it grew deeper and blacker and dropped down like a great curtain over the lightship. From the ocean beach the guardian ship was no longer visible, but the watchers at the Cliff House, alert, keen of ear and sharp of eye, sat at their instruments. Then, shortly after five o'clock, the instrument began to tick. Behind the haze curtain of the ocean the man on the lightship was sending the words, "*Sherman* in sight." Time and again the message came from the sea, thrilling those that heard it and spurring them to send it in all haste into the city. For the first time on the Pacific Coast and most successfully in the United States the *Call* had utilized wireless telegraphy.

Thereafter all the mystery of the message from the sea seems simple. In the sending station at the lightship was a Ruhmkorff coil, which transmitted the waves from the electric dynamos on the lightship. The Morse characters were made by the opening and closing of an ordinary telegraph key. This charged an aerial wire which was suspended 82 feet in a vertical direction from the top mast of the lightship. Electric waves were pulsated through the air and were received through a coherer from a similar wire suspended from the top of the Cliff House at the receiving station. This coherer actuated the Morse relay, which in turn worked the ink writing register, making the characters on the tape.

The experiment aboard Lightship 70 followed Marconi's first ship-to-shore transmission by a year and antedated the first successful spanning of the Atlantic by two. A little later, in 1904, the revenue-cutter *Grant*, Captain D. F. Tozier, cruising in the Straits of Juan de Fuca and Puget Sound, became the first U.S. ship to employ wireless for tactical purposes. Rear Admiral (Ret.) James F. Hottel, U.S.C.G., a lieutenant in the *Grant* at the time, describes the circumstances surrounding the cutter's historic innovation:

The smuggling situation was acute. Restrictive regulations and very high duty made the illicit traffic in opium to supply the heavy demand of the Oriental population concentrated in our West Coast cities very profitable. The successful landing of even a small quantity—a few tins of the prepared article or bladders of raw opium—netted a considerable sum. Running "Chinks" also offered attractive returns. Three to five hundred dollars a head was the going price. "Chinks" were not so easily hidden as the opium, and stories, very probably true, were going the rounds of runners who had knocked their paying passengers over the head and thrown them overboard when cornered (just as they did their dope) rather than be caught with the goods. The boats for the traffic were drawn from the large local fishing fleet which made every fisherman a suspect. Opium could be obtained from a number of merchants in Victoria without let or hindrance from the authorities and there always seemed to be a supply of Chinese who were ready and willing to take a chance, so business was never dull. The short distances involved and the numerous channels and landing places available made it an uphill fight for Captain Tozier with the *Grant* and the two 65-foot launches—the *Guard* at Friday Harbor on San Juan Island and the *Scout* at Port Townsend, each in charge of a commissioned officer.

Early in 1903 the Pacific Wireless Telegraph Company was organized for the purpose of extending telegraphic communication in the rapidly developing Northwest. The prospectus provided for a main station at wire end, Port Townsend, a substation at Victoria, B.C., and additional stations when and where conditions warranted. Captain Tozier saw at once the advantages of a hook-up with this outfit which would enable him to keep constantly in touch with his sources of information in Victoria and Port Townsend and to direct the movements of the two launches while the *Grant* was cruising. He contacted Mr. A. L. New, the General Manager of the Company who enthusiastically welcomed this unexpected Government business and support and agreed to the addition of a station to serve the San Juan Islands at Friday Harbor. Together they sold the plan to the Collector of Customs and as a result a proposal for service was drawn which provided for the location of the main station in the Custom House at Port Townsend, the installation of equipment and an operator on the *Grant* and schedules with Port Townsend, Victoria and Friday Harbor, the service to be extended to new stations as installed without additional cost. This proposal received the approval of the Treasury Department in August, 1903.

Most vessels of the service at that time were without electric plants and the *Grant* was no exception. To supply this deficiency a dynamo supplied by the company was mounted in the upper engine room, belt driven from the fly wheel of the circulating pump in the lower engine room through an opening cut in the deck for the purpose. The aerial was much the same as later became so general except that at the foremast head two coils three feet in diameter of several strands of heavy copper wire were mounted, one fore and aft, the other athwartships. A radio shack was built on deck abaft the foremast. The apparatus in the radio room was of the simplest: for sending, an adjustable spark gap with key and necessary appurtenances; for receiving, a box about the size and shape of the ordinary table radio fitted with plug-in for head phones, a push-pull switch or two and a turning knob and dial. Considerable mystery attached to this receiver. The cover of the box was fitted with a lock, the key to which was never out of the possession of the company's technician, and the box itself was kept under lock and key in the radio room when not in use. The "innards" were an unknown quantity to anyone on board. The operator, a Morse Code man from the local telegraph office, knew nothing of the mechanism.

The erection of the Port Townsend station and the installation of the apparatus on the *Grant* was accomplished without undue delay. As soon as these two were able to operate experimental work was started and many adjustments aboard ship and ashore during the next few months were found necessary before satisfactory results were obtained and reliable communication could be maintained. At first, on a still night, the spark could be seen and heard almost as far as the radio signal would carry; ultimately range to cover the usual cruising ground of the vessel, about a hundred miles, was obtained although moderately high land close to the vessel between it and the station would completely block traffic.

Hard luck and delay were encountered at Friday Harbor where the first masts were blown down in a gale. However, late in March the Company was in position to comply with the terms of its contract and regular paid service was started on April 1, 1904. While this date marks the start of regular scheduled traffic, practical use of the apparatus had been made on numerous occasions several months prior, messages of a confidential nature being handled in an improvised code.[1]

"No one at the time," according to Hottel, "realized the part they had played in the history of radio."—But it was soon clear that radio would play a major role in the history of the service. Within the next few years, cutters, together with the world's merchant and naval fleets, made radio their own. Significantly, the U. S. Navy erected its first shore radio station in 1905. The laws likewise began to indicate what was going on: first reference to radio in service law appeared in the Revenue-Cutter Service *Regulations* issued by Captain Ross in 1907 (Article 525 fixed responsibility for operation and upkeep of cutters' "wireless-telegraph system"); and an Act of Congress in 1910 (46 U.S.C. 484) prescribed the following rule for merchant ships:

It shall be unlawful for any steamer . . . navigating the ocean or the Great Lakes and . . . carrying fifty or more persons . . . to leave or attempt to leave any port of the United States unless . . . equipped with an efficient apparatus for radio communication in good working order, capable of receiving and transmitting messages over a distance of at least one hundred miles, day or night.

By 1910, seventeen cutters boasted wireless, and Acting Secretary of the Treasury Charles D. Hilles took pains to inform Congress that these installations had "proved a most important and potent factor . . . in relief and rescue work." To prove his point, he cited several early instances of the use of radio in assistance operations; one, involving a farflung hookup between cutters, merchant ships, and shore radio stations, reflected a relatively high development of radio's tactical possibilities. In this particular case, said Hilles, "four revenue-cutters started from distant parts of the coast for the sinking steamship . . . immediately upon receipt of her wireless call for help." One of them, the *Gresham,* picked up the distress call as a relay from a shore radio station; her report, as transcribed by Hilles, is quoted below. The year, 1909.

At 8.10 a.m. January 23 a message was received from the Wellfleet Marconi station addressed to the commanding officer of the *Gresham* and reading as follows: "Steamship *Republic* is sinking 26 miles southeast of Nantucket." Steam was immediately ordered and at 8.20 the *Gresham* got underway and started for the reported scene of disaster. A thick fog prevailed at the time and continued until 8 p.m. of that date. After rounding Cape Cod the *Gresham* was put at full speed, an engineer officer standing by for bells and two line officers stationed upon the bridge—this on account of the thick weather. The *Gresham* arrived in the vicinity of Nantucket

[1] *U.S.C.G.A. Alumni Assn. Bulletin,* Vol. III, No. 11, Jan., 1942.

light-ship early in the evening and cruised throughout the night in search of the *Republic.* Various wireless messages received and intercepted indicated that the position of the *Republic* was very uncertain, consequently the *Gresham* cruised in search of her until 10.25 a.m. on the 24th, when we spoke Nantucket light-ship and learned that the *Republic* was supposed to be 4 miles south of that position. At 11.10 a.m. the *Republic* was sighted and found to be in the position 9 miles S. ½ E. from Nantucket light-ship. Upon speaking her the master asked that the *Gresham* take his wire hawser, and it was agreed that an attempt would be made to tow the vessel into the nearest shoal water to the southward of Nantucket.

A 3-inch wire cable was then taken from the *Republic's* starboard bow, shackled to the port waist bitts of the *Gresham* and stopped to the corresponding quarter bitts, and at 12.33 the *Gresham* steamed ahead upon the tow. At this time the *Republic's* boiler room, engine room, and several other compartments were filled with water, which was rising, the ship drawing 40 feet aft, making her down badly by the stern, and her steering gear was disabled. She was found to be a very heavy tow. The British steamship *Furnessia,* which arrived at the scene shortly before the *Gresham,* dropped astern of the *Republic* and took a line from each quarter to assist in steering.

At 3.30 p.m. the crew of the *Republic,* except her commanding and second officers, left their vessel and took refuge on board the *Gresham,* by orders of their captain. The chief officer stated that it was believed that the steamer was in danger of sinking at any moment, and that Captain Sealby, of the *Republic,* requested that the commanding officer of the *Gresham* make arrangements to rescue him and his second officer should the *Republic* sink. Captain Sealby also, in response to an invitation by signal to come aboard the *Gresham,* stated that he would stand by his ship to the last and that his second officer refused to leave him. It was then arranged that, in case the steamer should sink after dark, a blue light would be shown from her bridge. In order that the *Gresham* might be able to free herself from the *Republic* in such an emergency, our 9-inch hawser was then bent to the eye of the wire towing cable, thoroughly protected from chafe, veered away to about 60 fathoms, and the *Gresham* resumed her towing, the ship's carpenter being stationed with an ax to cut away in case the *Republic* should founder. At 2.30 a wireless message from the U.S. revenue cutter *Seneca,* announcing that she was near to render assistance, was received, and a reply was sent that such assistance was badly needed.

During this time the wind and sea were increasing and continued to increase until the culmination of the events. At 4.30 p.m. the *Seneca* was sighted, and as that vessel came near, the executive officer of the *Gresham,* with our crew in the *Republic's* lifeboat, took a running line to her and her hawser was hauled aboard the *Gresham* and made fast to the starboard waist and forward bitts, after which she immediately proceeded ahead, towing and holding the *Gresham's* head up to the wind and sea, much better progress being immediately noticeable. At 7 p.m. the *Furnessia* parted her lines from the *Republic's* quarters and dropped off from the tow.

Night had now set in and the wind increased considerably, bringing on a choppy sea, with mist and rain. The *Republic* was faintly distinguishable owing to one small light on her bridge. At the time of his coming aboard, the chief officer of the *Republic* had requested the commanding officer of the *Gresham* to allow him the privilege of taking charge of the boat to rescue his captain and shipmate in case their vessel should sink, and that his crew be supplemented by some good men from our crew. The *Republic's* lifeboat had been secured to the lee side of the *Gresham,* properly provided, and held in readiness to drop off on the instant, four men of the *Republic's* crew and four of our crew being detailed to man this boat. At 8.10 p.m. a blue light flashed from the *Republic's* bridge, and it could be seen that she was rapidly going down. The lifeboat was promptly called away and the crew detailed sprang into her on the instant, and at the same time Gunner Johansson, of this vessel, leaped over the rail into the boat. As the chief officer of the *Republic* could not be discovered in the prevailing darkness and mist, word was passed to Gunner Johansson to shove off, and within one minute from the time the blue light flashed up the boat was off to the rescue. When the lifeboat shoved off much doubt was felt as to the prospect of her rescuing anyone and, owing to the state of weather, sea, and wreckage, the situation of the boat was at the least very grave. Immediately, as the boat got clear, the carpenter was ordered to cut away the hawser, and, this being done, the *Seneca's* tow line was cast off, and the *Gresham* was winded and lay to the leeward of the wreck. The searchlights of the *Seneca, Gresham,* and an unknown tug that had arrived after darkness and had held to leeward of the *Republic,* were kept playing over the scene, and at 8.45 p.m. the lifeboat returned, having rescued Captain Sealby and Second Officer Williams, the former having been taken from a floating hatch cover and the latter from some gratings. Both men were nearly exhausted and they were immediately taken below, rubbed down, provided with hot stimulants, and put to bed.

The *Gresham* shaped her course for a position off Gay Head and continued through the night, the *Seneca* in company. At 6.30 a.m. stopped off Vineyard Haven light-ship and after consulting with Captain Reynolds of the *Seneca* and Captain Sealby, it was decided that the company of the *Republic* should be transferred to the *Seneca* for passage to New York. This was accomplished by the boats of the *Seneca* and *Gresham.* The *Gresham* then proceeded to Woods Hole for fresh water.

During all of the above operations the wireless apparatus of the *Gresham* was in constant use, the operator rendering most exceptional, efficient, and arduous service. While interferences were encountered, dispatches of the most important character were sent and received, and after the rescue three messages were sent out for Captain Sealby, which not only assured those personally interested in himself and crew but gave information to the country at large in this important affair.[2]

Out of the *Republic* incident and many similar cases came early and ample proof of radio's great contribution to the cause of safety at sea and to cutters' operational effectiveness. By 1915 the entire cruising cutter fleet was "on the air," standing continuous guard on the radio distress frequency and thus bringing to the voyaging public a new measure of comfort and security.

Sentimentalized and stereotyped in this role by the nation's news-

[2] *H.R. Doc. 549, 61 Cong., 2nd Sess.,* 6, *et seq.*

The *McCulloch, c.* 1900
(From a painting by an unknown artist. Official C.G. photo.)

Early (1901) Motor Lifeboat
(Courtesy of Mr. A. H. Hansen.)

Officers of the Cutter *Thetis, c.* 1904

1st row: 1st Lieutenant Charles E. Johnston; Captain Oscar C. Hamlet, Commanding; 2nd Lieutenant of Engineers William E. Davis.

2nd row: 2nd Assistant Engineer William Maxwell; Surgeon Samuel Call; 3rd Lieutenant Hiram R. Searles; 2nd Lieutenant Francis R. Shoemaker.

(*Note:* The *Thetis* was an auxiliary bark, similar to the *Bear,* built in Scotland for Arctic cruising and transferred to the Revenue-Cutter Service from the Navy in 1899.)
(Official C.G. photo.)

The Practice Cutter *Chase, c.* 1906
(Official C.G. photo.)

Ship's Company, Practice Cutter *Chase,* 1906

1st row: 2nd Lieutenant P. H. Scott; 1st Lieutenant H. G. Hamlet; Captain W. E. Reynolds, Commanding; 2nd Lieutenant W. J. Wheeler; Dr. W. H. Frost, U.S.P.H.S. *2nd row:* Cadets P. H. Harrison; C. H. Jones; G. Bennett; J. R. Besse; C. F. Seiter; E. J. Donohue; F. A. Nichols; D. S. Combs; W. F. Towle; J. P. Gray; J. Pine; J. F. McGourty; M. J. Ryan; L. L. Bennett; R. R. Waesche; P. F. Roach; R. L. Jack; L. T. Chalker; T. A. Shanley; W. A. Benham. *3rd row: (Last six men to right):* Cadets S. V. Parker; J. J. Hutson; J. T. Drake; E. D. Jones; F. N. Gault; J. H. Cornell. *Others:* Unidentified enlisted men. [*Original caption lost.*] (*Note:* Reynolds and Hamlet served as Commandant in the periods 1919-24 and 1932-36, respectively. During World War II, Waesche served as Commandant, with the rank of admiral, and the following served with flag rank in various top Coast men, the cruising cutter became something of a symbol of America's humanitarian aspiration: it was, in common journalese, a "white-hulled mercy ship," pounding seaways, slashing gales, in answer to a whispered SOS. One sample, from a Sunday supplement (1915):

> When the red storm-flags are flying, cutters must be on the job at sea, with wireless keenly tuned. When the first call for help is heard, then stokers sweat below and officers brace themselves upon the bridge, as—no matter how wild the gale—the staunch cutter goes racing under forced draft, rolling and pitching and burying her nose in the ocean swell, to the endangered craft.[3]

Modernization of cutter matériel was paralleled in the Life-Saving Service by technological revolution: a shift from manpower to mechanical power for propelling boats. Life-savers had been unable to mechanize with steam; for one thing, 19th century steam engines had been too cumbersome and heavy for use in small life-saving boats. Development of internal combustion engines, however, radically changed the situation: these compact, lightweight, sealed-in motors promised to meet the surfmen's need. The problem was approached in 1899, when Lieutenant C. H. McLellan, revenue-cutter officer and experienced researcher in life-saving matériel, launched his first motor lifeboat. This event marked the beginning of a somewhat slow but continuing and remarkably successful process of adaptation.

The original motor lifeboat was no invention; it was an assembly. McLellan chose for his experiment a 2-cylinder, 12 H.P., Superior engine, driving twin, reversible-bladed propellers through rawhide gears, and he fitted it in the after air chamber of a standard 34-foot lifeboat. This boat's trials (conducted on Lake Michigan in September, 1899) encouraged the Department to establish a commission of experts, headed by Professor C. H. Peabody of Massachusetts Institute of Technology, to study the general subjects of lifeboat mechanization and design and to submit recommendations. The commission threw its weight in favor of power boats and offered invaluable technical advice.

By 1905, Sumner I. Kimball, General Superintendent of the life-saving branch, was ready to undertake a full-scale program of mechanization, which he placed under McLellan's charge. A dozen motor lifeboats were in service at the end of the first year. By 1913, lifesavers were operating approximately 70 motor lifeboats and 60 power surfboats and were continuing to "demand power craft to replace certain of the larger boats propelled by oars."[4] By 1915, they had 80 motor lifeboats and

[3] "The Work of the Seagoing Coast Guard," in *Virginian-Pilot* (Norfolk, Va.) May 2, 1915. Also *cf.* C. A. McAllister, "Saving Mankind at Sea," in *The Survey Magazine*, Vol. 33, No. 2, October 10, 1914.

[4] *U.S.L.-S.S. Annual Report;* 1913.

nearly 150 power surfboats distributed along the coasts. The lifeboats came in two sizes: 36-footers with 35 H.P. engines, and 34-foot, 25 H.P., rigs; all had self-bailing hull structures and heavy, self-righting keels. Of surfboats, the Beebe-McLellan model—a 26-foot, clinker-built self-bailer housing a 12 H.P. horizontal engine amidship—lent its design to the major group.

This motorized equipment, built to live and work in wild and broken waters, radically extended the area of life-saving operations and increased the surfmen's power against the fury of the storm.

Similarly, cutter officers lost little time in exploring the tactical possibilities of aircraft. Aviation's infancy extended from the year of Orville Wright's historic flight (1903) to the outbreak of the first World War. The existing body of aeronautical knowledge was very small; progress depended almost entirely on the genius and barehanded experimental work of Voisin, Farman, Blériot, Fokker, Sikorsky, and a few other pioneers of flight. Their achievements aroused interest in military high commands throughout the world. Orville Wright sold one plane to the U. S. Army in 1909. Glenn Curtiss produced a flying boat in 1912. About the same time, the U. S. Navy bought a plane or two and began training its first handful of pilots, at Pensacola, Florida. Other nations likewise brought forth embryonic flying corps. By the time the German Kaiser was ready to signal for the first movement of *"Deutschland über Alles,"* certain military circles held the belief that existent planes—with speeds of 60-70 miles per hour and ranges of 200 miles or so—might prove useful as scouts in support of combat forces on land and sea.

And if aircraft could be so used in war, reasoned Lieutenants Elmer F. Stone and Norman B. Hall, attached to the cutter *Onondaga* at Hampton Roads, they could be used with like advantage to support many cutter operations. Stone and Hall had search and rescue operations especially in mind. In that day, the wintry gales that sweep America's eastern sea approaches almost invariably brought trouble to the coastal schooner fleet. Dismastings and injuries to rudders accompanied most bad blows and lengthened the list of sailing vessels posted "overdue." Unequipped with radio, these ships could neither summon timely aid nor make their positions known, and rescue operations by *Onondaga* and other cutters were therefore often long-delayed by the necessity of extensive search. Such delays could only add to the misery and hazards borne by seamen in distress. Stone and Hall could see possibilities of expediting assistance by use of coordinated air/sea search, and with the approval of their commanding officer, Captain B. M. Chiswell, U.S.R.-C.S., they enlisted the cooperation of Captain Baldwin, a celebrated balloonist, then in charge of Curtiss Field. Baldwin lent them one plane, in which they flew scouting missions for the *Onondaga* through the summer of 1915.

Their simple plan—from which the considerable body of modern air/sea rescue tactics gradually evolved—soon proved its merit to the Commandant. Stone, together with five other officers and a dozen enlisted men, was sent to Pensacola for formal flight training; Hall was assigned to Curtiss Airplane and Motor Company to study aeronautical engineering and design. About the same time (1916), a Naval Appropriation Act authorized the Coast Guard to establish ten air stations along U.S. shores. But World War I abruptly interrupted these early plans for an air arm; the service's pilots and matériel were assigned to flight duty with the Navy and so served throughout the war. The next phase of Coast Guard aviation falls in the postwar period, and so this volume records only the introduction of aircraft as potential Coast Guard tools.

With new and improved equipment at its command, the service soon began establishing new records in the performance of historic duties. In one significant type of operation, namely, assistance to vessels in distress, the cutters' score rose from an annual average of 95 cases in 1898-1901 to 214 in 1914. And for practically every other class of cutter work, as well as for the Life-Saving Service's specialized function, annual returns showed similar operational gains.

III

While technological progress was thus increasing the service's effectiveness, other forces were enlarging the general scope of federal maritime activity and, correspondingly, the general scope of service operations. Mechanistic changes within the maritime industries, increases in tonnage and dollar value of American seaborne commerce, and a sharpening of the public's sense of responsibility for human welfare and safety—on the sea as on the land—served as major determinants of the trend.

In the field of law enforcement, every new Act of Congress dealing with maritime affairs brought added responsibility to the cutter fleet, either by the letter of the law or by executive action to implement it, and so the service retained its traditional role as general agent for the enforcement of federal law afloat. Some of the new laws carried federal authority into zones never previously occupied.

Their variety was notable. The method of prescribing and regulating anchorages in crowded harbors came under revision in 1915, when Congress abandoned its old legislative policy of framing anchorage rules by specific Acts for individual harbors in favor of a less cumbersome plan. Under the Act of March 4, 1915, Congress delegated to the Secretary of War general authority to make anchorage regulations for all U.S. harbors, and confirmed the cutter service as enforcement agency for these maritime safety measures.[5]

[5] 38 Stat. L., 1049, 1053.

Marking a distinct crack in the American tradition of permitting unrestricted (and sometimes extravagantly wasteful) exploitation of natural resources by private individuals and corporations, a handful of conservation laws was written into the federal code early in the century. One prohibited aliens from poaching in Alaskan territorial fishing preserves; it supported an earlier conservation Act (March 2, 1889) which had imposed certain rules upon the salmon industry. Another measure protected Alaskan wild life and furred animals, and another regulated the sponge industry in the Gulf of Mexico and Straits of Florida. An enforcement authority for each of these Acts was vested in the cutters.[6]

Continued U.S. efforts to prevent the extinction of Alaska's seal herd led finally to a noteworthy experiment in international cooperation and jurisprudence, as set forth in the Sealing Convention between the U.S., Russia, Great Britain, and Japan. Under this Convention, proclaimed by President Taft at Washington on December 14, 1911,

> The High Contracting Parties . . . [agreed] . . . that their citizens . . . be prohibited . . . from engaging in pelagic sealing in the waters of the North Pacific Ocean . . .[7]

Congress gave effect to the Convention by an Act requiring the President

> . . . to cause a guard or patrol to be maintained in the waters frequented by the seal herd or herds and sea otters, in the protection of which the United States is especially interested.[8]

The force—traditionally the Bering Sea Patrol Force cited in a previous chapter—designated by the President to maintain the seal patrol was now authorized, under the Convention and implementing statute, to seize any offending ship or person owing allegiance to any one of the High Contracting Parties and to deliver such offender into the custody of the government having jurisdiction in the case. For the purpose of the Convention, therefore, the cutters became *de facto* an *international* maritime police force, backed by the authority of four major powers cooperating towards peaceful ends.

Successfully upheld, the Convention brought an abrupt finale to pelagic sealing and gave the seals a new lease on life. By 1914, Commander, Bering Sea Patrol Force, could report the area entirely clear of marauding vessels throughout the season and, further, that the size of the Pribilof Islands herd had noticeably improved. Survival of a valuable asset and source of revenue to the cooperating nations was thus assured.

Passage of the Motorboat Act (so-called) of June 9, 1910 effected a

[6] *Aliens, fishing:* Act of June 14, 1906 (38 Stat. L., 263). *Salmon fisheries:* 25 Stat. L., 1009. *Wild Life:* Act of May 11, 1908 (35 Stat. L., 102). *Sponge fisheries:* Act of August 15, 1914 (38 Stat. L., 692).

[7] 37 Stat. L., 1542, 1547.

[8] Act of August 24, 1912 (37 Stat. L., 499, 501).

noteworthy extension of U.S. navigation law. This measure brought under federal supervision a class of vessels, namely motorboats 65 feet or less in length, not covered by the earlier steamboat inspection laws. It was a simple safety-at-sea measure, prescribing minimal safety requirements (lights, life-jackets, fire-extinguishers, *et cetera*) for motorboats.[9]

Such a law had been needed for some time. Better and better motorboats were being built, and after 1900 their popularity among sportsmen, fishermen, and other small craft users increased tremendously. The number of American motorboats in operation probably trebled between 1900 and 1910 and reached an estimated 110,000 by 1915. Their very numbers made them a prominent feature of the maritime scene. Many, improperly equipped (because of their owners' ignorance or carelessness) invited casualty; they were hazards to themselves and to everything else afloat. When, between 1904 and 1910, the rate of increase of motorboat casualties struck the alarming annual average of 45%, the time for federal police action had arrived. Regulations adopted by Congress under the Act of 1910 produced both an immediate and a gratifying effect; for 1911-'12-'13, the disaster rate dropped to 11% per year.

Executive policy (previously cited) vested in the cutter service a major share of responsibility for navigation law enforcement, and this traditional policy blanketed the Motorboat Law. Cutter officers enforced the latter by boarding boats and checking their equipment; as a valuable by-product, they gave expert advice to inexperienced boatmen. In general, they assumed a paternalistic rather than a legalistic attitude towards the smallboating fraternity: they tried to educate and assist the boatmen, not bombard them with assessments for trivial, unintentional violations. In this way they eventually secured a high degree of intelligent cooperation from thousands of American boat operators toward a common goal of safety on the sea.

Although specific data on the extent of motorboat boarding operations in the 1900-1915 period are not available, annual Revenue-Cutter Service reports show an inclusive category of "vessels boarded"; the increase from around 20,000 cases in this category in 1900 to 28,750 in 1914 is accounted for largely by operations in support of the Motorboat Act and gives a reasonable clue to the Act's fairly satisfactory long-range result. Of the latter—of the human life and blood and suffering spared—no adequate accounting ever can be made.

Maritime safety found further support in the Seamen's Act, although the latter was primarily a socio-economic measure—Zeis calls it "the most important law concerning the conditions of sea employment ever passed by Congress." Sponsored by Progressives and Wilsonian Democrats, the Act "embodied most of the objectives for which the Inter-

[9] 46 U.S.C. 511, 519.

national Seamen's Union had been fighting for many years"; it established legal safeguards for maritime labor against various forms of exploitation, abuse, and needless hazard. Certain sections—bearing directly on safety-at-sea—strengthened existing requirements for safety appliances aboard ship, instituted the 8-hour day for mariners (thus reducing hazards imposed by fatigue and overwork), and laid down a manning code calling for experienced seamen, lifeboatmen, and English-speaking persons in given ratios of the whole crew, on each American merchant vessel.[10]

In-port enforcement of most of these provisions normally was furnished by Steamboat Inspectors and Bureau of Navigation men; afloat enforcement fell within the scope of routine revenue-cutter boarding operations, where it added little to the service workload. However, the certification of lifeboatmen as required by the Act necessitated a practical test of each applicant's skill. Because cutters had the equipment and trained personnel to administer such tests, the work of certification became almost entirely an in-port cutter chore, involving thousands of examinations annually. The job at best was deadly dull, but it did provide an effective form of federal life-insurance for every individual who travelled by American ship.

The scope of the service's protective function likewise expanded during the 1900-1915 period. Besides quantitative increases in the cutters' traditional assistance work (previously cited and credited largely to the development of radio as a tactical tool), an important qualitative extension was effected in 1914 by a federal statute which provided the Revenue-Cutter Service with a regularized medical corps—and, thus, with the means for giving medical aid at sea. On the Commandant's recommendation, Congress authorized the Secretary of the Treasury to

> detail for duty on revenue cutters such surgeons and other persons of the Public Health Service as . . . necessary

and specifically directed the cutters to furnish medical and surgical aid to American deep-sea fishermen.[11] One cutter, the *Androscoggin,* was immediately fitted with a sick-bay and dispatched to the Newfoundland Grand Banks, where her doctor ministered to more than a hundred sick or injured fishermen between January and June, 1915. (On the same patrol, this ship assisted three distressed vessels valued at over half a million.)

Although the Act named only deep-sea fishermen as beneficiaries, in spirit it was entirely non-restrictive. By 1916, medical officers were serving

[10] Act of March 4, 1915 (38 Stat. L., 1164, 1182). Quotations are from Zeis, *op. cit.,* 70.

[11] Act of June 24, 1914 (38 Stat. L., 387). A few doctors had served on cutters prior to 1914 under various administrative arrangements. This Act regularized procurement and assignment procedures.

on ten cutters; under the sea's simple rules of courtesy, their skill was available to any and all seafarers within the cutters' range of action. A cutter doctor might see his patient fished aboard at the scene of some maritime disaster; he might be broken out in a gale-swept night to ride the cutter's whaleboat to a passing ship in answer to an urgent call for aid; or by an exchange of radio dispatches he might diagnose and treat a case a thousand miles away. But whether his patient was a fisherman with frozen fingers, a sailor with a broken back, a scalded engineer, or a yachtsman charred by flaming gasoline, the product of his service always was the same: seaborne aid to individuals in distress.

The federal statutes thus by 1915 defined a protective function embracing specifically the relief of ships and persons in distress at sea or on the coasts.[12] But emergencies not anticipated by the federal code occurred within the American littoral almost every day, and most of these presented urgent problems of on-the-spot relief. In such cases, human necessity—in its dictates as binding on the service as though chiselled in the statutes of the land—amply authorized ameliatory action. No federal law, for instance, specifically directed cutters to succor refugees from a volcano in eruption, and none required life-savers to transport their boats to the Mississippi and launch them there in aid of victims of the valley floods, but these and many other necessary things were done. Timely seaborne action in emergencies, especially in those beyond control by local agencies—in great fires along the waterfront, explosions, earthquakes, epidemics, floods, and airplane crack-ups in the bordering seas and bays: a whole list of disasters great and small, not specified in the public law—through the years wrote many a line in service logs and won the nation's approbation. Thus, in its logical, necessary extensions, the protective function by 1915 had become practically unlimited in scope, and the Revenue-Cutter Service, the implementing agency, had, as Bertholf phrased it, become "essentially an emergency service," specializing in the control of every sort of maritime disaster.[13]

And in the related field of disaster-prevention, a notable new responsibility was assumed by the federal government early in the century and added to the duties of the cutter fleet.

Like many another measure for insuring safety on the sea, this one

[12] *Assistance to vessels in distress at sea:* Act of December 22, 1837 (5 Stat. L., 208), *op. cit. Assistance to vessels in distress on Great Lakes:* Act of July 15, 1870 (16 Stat. L., 309). *Aid to vessels and persons, shipwrecked on the sea- and lakecoasts of the U.S.:* Act. of December 14, 1854 (10 Stat. L., 597), *op. cit.;* Act of April 20, 1871 (17 Stat. L., 5, 12), *op. cit.;* Act of June 20, 1874 (18 Stat. L., 125), *op. cit.;* Act of June 18, 1878 (20 Stat. L., 163, as amended August 3, 1894, 28 Stat. L., 225), *op. cit.;* Act of May 4, 1882 (22 Stat. L., 55). *Medical assistance:* Act of June 24, 1914 (38 Stat. L., 387), *op. cit.*

[13] *U.S.C.G. Annual Report, 1915;* 4, 43. Flood relief became a specific Coast Guard duty by the Act of August 29, 1916 (39 Stat. 601). Statutes covering assistance to vessels have been broadly interpreted to cover air as well as surface craft.

originated in a widespread reaction to preventable tragedy. The world was shocked by headlines in its press on April 15, 1912:

S.S. TITANIC STRIKES BERG, SINKS!—1,517 PERSONS LOST.

To millions of sea-minded people, this mightiest of ships had given hope of final victory against the elements: her very size (825 feet, 46,300

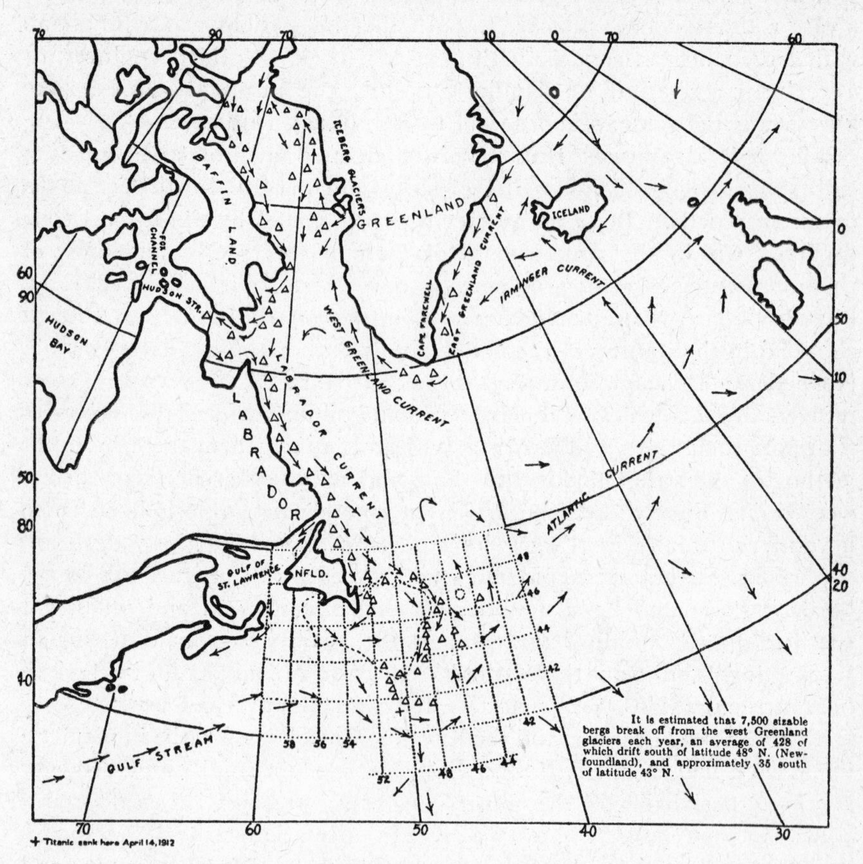

Drift of Icebergs From Their Source
Into the North Atlantic
(Official C. G. publication.)

gross tons) had seemed to guarantee security, and her speed (21 knots), proof of insuperable power. And yet, like many lesser ships cut down previously in random harvest, she could not stand against the Arctic ice. The evidence was in the headlines, black banners for the dead.

If even such a titan were thus vulnerable, could not some safe-conduct be devised?

Efforts to assess the problem stirred up universal interest in the subject of ice at sea. The public learned that the world's most-travelled

Worth G. Ross
Captain Commandant, U.S.R.-C.S., 1905-11
(Official C.G. photo.)

The Practice Cutter *Itasca,* 1907
(From "Tide Rips, '08.")

U.S.R.-C. *Androscoggin, c.* 1915
(Official C.G. photo.)

The Cutter *Seneca, c.* 1915
(Official C.G. photo.)

Ellsworth P. Bertholf

Captain Commandant, U. S. Revenue-Cutter Service, 1911-15
Captain Commandant, U. S. Coast Guard, 1915-19

(Official C.G. photo, taken about the time of The Overland Expedition to Point Barrow.)

The Cutter *Unalga, c.* 1915
(Official C.G. photo.)

Hazard to Navigation
(Official C.G. photo.)

Surfboat
(Official C.G. photo.)

The Cutter *Ossipee, c.* 1915
(Official C.G. photo.)

Rescue
(Official C.G. photo.)

ocean highways (the east- and westbound steamer lanes established by an international Transatlantic Track Conference in 1898) passed just south of Newfoundland's vast, fog-ridden, boisterous Grand Banks. Into this area from the fjords of Greenland, seasonally between April and late June, southward-flowing currents brought great glacial bergs. In their southward drift, these phantomic derelicts cut across the steamer lanes, where they menaced alike tramps and titanics, then passed on to their own destruction in the sweep of the warm Gulf Stream. In 1912 and earlier, shipmasters had no way of determining the shifting limits of the ice area or the exact positions of individual bergs upon the steamer tracks—they could only hold to established lanes, keep their lookouts bright, and hope for lucky passage.

While the world public faced these facts and mourned the lost *Titanic,* the U.S. government sent two Navy cruisers, *Chester* and *Birmingham,* to scout the danger area for the remainder of the season and broadcast berg-position warnings by radio to menaced ships.

Although this expedient filled an immediate need, it was beyond the normal scope of naval enterprise, and the following year found the Navy reluctant to assign vessels to the job. The shipping industry, therefore, seeking to insure the patrol, asked that responsibility for its maintenance be vested in the federal agency whose normal operations focussed upon the promotion of safety on the sea: the United States Revenue-Cutter Service. New York's potent Maritime Exchange voiced the industry's attitude in a letter dated 13 March, 1913:

> Hon. William G. McAdoo,
> Secretary of the Treasury,
> Washington, D.C.
>
> Sir:
>
> . . . the Maritime Association of the port of New York considers it of the utmost importance that a thorough and efficient patrol should be maintained each year during the season of danger, and in view of the expressed inability of the Navy Department to perform such service this season, this association believes that the United States Revenue-Cutter Service, to which our shipping interests are under great obligations for efficient aid at all times and for invaluable services rendered, is well equipped as regards ships and excellency of personnel to maintain such patrol, and therefore respectfully recommends to the honorable Secretary of the Treasury that, in order to provide every possible safeguard for trans-Atlantic shipping, he designate suitable vessel or vessels of the United States Revenue-Cutter Service to patrol the ice region during the coming season, and to report by wireless to all vessels navigating that region, and also to make regular reports by wireless to the nearest naval station from whence it may be transmitted to the United States Hydrographic Office, such service to continue as long as ice in dangerous quantities is reported. . . .
>
> Willard U. Taylor,
> President.[14]

[14] In *C. G. Archives.*

In response to such appeals, the government soon announced that:

For the purpose of safeguarding lives and property at sea, the *Seneca* and *Miami* have been detailed to proceed to the vicinity of the tail of the Grand Banks of Newfoundland and establish a patrol of the icefields and icebergs drifting down into those waters.

The object of the patrol is to locate the icebergs and field ice nearest to the trans-Atlantic steamship lane. It will be the duty of patrol vessels to determine the southerly, easterly, and westerly limits of the ice and to keep in touch with these fields as they move to the southward in order that radio messages may be sent out daily, giving the whereabouts of the ice, particularly the ice that may be in the vicinity of the regular trans-Atlantic steamer lane.

The patrol will begin in April and continue until the ice no longer constitutes a danger to navigation in the trans-Atlantic steamship lanes.[15]

Captains Charles E. Johnson and Aaron L. Gamble commanded *Seneca* and *Miami,* respectively, on this inaugural patrol; the ships based at Halifax, Nova Scotia, and alternated on duty in the danger area. Smothering fogs and frequent gales presented major operational difficulties, but the cutters nevertheless succeeded in keeping track of the bergs and warning shipping clear.

In addition, to gain clearer insight of the ice problem and thus to increase the effectiveness of patrol activities, Johnson and Gamble began a systematic study of oceanographic and meteorological phenomena in relation to the movement of ice within the patrol area. Their observations, published as *R.-C.S. Ice Patrol Bulletin No. 1,* constituted the first of a long and valuable series of documents produced by cutter officers in this field of scientific research.

Ice patrol, a rugged business, was from the first a successful enterprise, and it brought the service an immediate and new renown. Addressing the Secretary of the Treasury in a letter dated July 8, 1913, the President of the New York Maritime Exchange declared:

. . . The knowledge that the [*Seneca* and *Miami*] were alternately stationed on the ice fields, with facilities for furnishing to vessels on the trans-Atlantic route prompt and full information by wireless of ice, weather conditions, etc., not only created a feeling of security on the part of travellers, but was most reassuring to all interested . . . in trans-Atlantic traffic.

. . . That the United States Government had at its disposal two such serviceable vessels, officered by men especially fitted and qualified for this important duty, is a source of great gratification . . .

We believe the success of this patrol during the past season has been so marked as to justify its continuance each year, and we would therefore respectfully recommend that this special duty be made a permanent function of the Revenue-Cutter Service . . .[16]

[15] "Instructions to the Commanding Officers of Revenue Cutters on Ice Patrol, 1913," issued by the Secretary of the Treasury and dated 29 March, 1913. In *C. G. Archives.*
[16] In *C. G. Archives.*

The Maritime Exchange spoke for American interests; however, prevention of disaster on the trade routes concerned not the U.S. alone but the entire world. In a report to M. Jules Jusserand, French Ambassador to the United States, Commander Poncelet of the French Navy spoke for mariners of all nations:

> The value of the patrol conducted by Captains Johnson and Gamble, of the United States Revenue-Cutter Service, during the year 1913, is beyond appreciation. Their devotion, endurance, and intelligence probably saved many lives, and their observations will make it possible hereafter to adopt safer tracks than heretofore . . . One [of the cutters] . . . warned me long in advance of the presence of several icebergs directly on the international road of the sea. . . .[17]

Before the cutters sailed on their 1914 mission, formal recognition of the patrol's international character had been accorded and had made further unilateral action by the United States unnecessary. An international Convention for the Safety of Life at Sea, signed at London on January 20, 1914, provided for the establishment of an International Service of Ice Observation and Ice Patrol, directed by the United States but supported financially by the whole family of maritime nations concerned. Acting on this international mandate, the President on February 7, 1914 directed that the Revenue-Cutter Service undertake the task.

The first cruise as an international instrument for maritime safety was made by *Seneca;* this cutter sailed from New York on February 19, 1914 to make preliminary ice observations along the coast of Newfoundland. She was joined by *Miami* two months later when, the southward drift of the bergs having begun to threaten the steamship lanes, the ice patrol proper was begun.

At the end of the 1914 season, Ambassador Jusserand placed the stamp of world approval upon the Service of Ice Observation and Ice Patrol. Said he:

> . . . the services which the government of the United States intended to render . . . are fully as effective as expected and are such as to call for the sincere gratefulness of the mariners of all countries. . . .[18]

Subsequent operations through the years brought to the Coast Guard only confirmation of this international renown.

IV

While the 20th century was thus imposing an increasingly complex pattern of technics, tactics, and functions upon the cutter force, it was also imposing new conditions of service upon cutter personnel. For officers, the professional horizon expanded continuously. In their triple role as sea-

[17] Quoted in Jusserand letter to Secretary of State William J. Bryan, dated June 27, 1914. In *C. G. Archives.*
[18] *Ibid.*

going experts, specialists in maritime safety and law, and naval officers in reserve, these men found it necessary to keep abreast of a rapidly growing body of knowledge and skill. To insure that young officers be equipped with the fundamentals—the broad outlook, the basic skills, and the exact technical knowledge—requisite to success in so fast-moving a profession, demanded an almost continual revision and reorientation of the system used in selecting and training officer candidates.

One of the most far-reaching changes was effected in 1903, when Captain Shoemaker, then Commandant, persuaded Congress to extend the period of cadetship at the School of Instruction from two to three years.[19] (A fourth year was added later [1931].) This enabled the School to add certain (mainly, scientific) subjects to the curriculum and to extend others, so as to provide a broader and more advanced technical base to the cadet course.

Another important step forward was taken in 1906, when Congress, upon the recommendation of Shoemaker's successor, Captain Worth G. Ross, authorized the appointment of cadet engineers.[20] Up to that time, as noted previously, engineer officers had been commissioned direct from civilian life. Experience had proved this method seriously defective in its failure, among other things, to provide a probationary period wherein engineer aspirants might become indoctrinated and adjusted to service life and the service might spot and withhold commissions from those who proved unsuitable. The Act of 1906 provided a 6 months' period of cadetship for engineers; subsequent legislation extended this to a full year. (Much later (1926), the line and engineer corps were combined.) Competitive entrance examinations established for engineers were designed to admit only candidates with a background of advanced technical education. Cadet instruction for successful candidates included indoctrinational courses and such advanced engineering theory and practice as time allowed.

The same Act authorized the employment of two civilian instructors, and in 1906, under this provision, Professor Chester E. Dimick joined the staff. As Instructor in Mathematics, a post he held for forty years or more, Dimick's influence on the service was entirely beneficial. Ever an able teacher, wise counsellor, and friend to all cadets, he was, additionally, a vital force in shaping the methods and standards of the School to the demands of the 20th century.

Another section of the Act tightened control over cadet standards by granting the Secretary of the Treasury unequivocal authority to

> dismiss summarily . . . any cadet who . . . is found unsatisfactory in either studies or conduct or . . . not adapted for a career in the Service.

[19] Act of February 23, 1903 (32 Stat. L., 854, 859).
[20] Act of June 23, 1906 (34 Stat. L., 452).

Screening out unsuitable candidates for commissions thus became a statutory obligation for the School's academic staff.

The training cutter *Chase* trimmed her sails for the last time in 1907, when, passing in review before the fleets of the world (massed in Hampton Roads for the Jamestown Tercentennial), she rode gracefully to her retirement. A new ship, *Itasca,* steam with auxiliary sail, replaced her in the training system and provided the facilities for underway engineering practice that had been lacking in the *Chase.*

Since the commissioned corps at this time numbered few more than 200 officers, the cadet corps was correspondingly small; classes of 10 to 20 cadets were common. Even so, the physical facilities of the School at Arundel Cove were quite inadequate. The Arundel Cove development was essentially a boatyard and warehouse, not an academy, and its location, buildings, and general atmosphere were unsuited to academic purposes. Captain Ross, the first graduate of the School to reach the post of Commandant, sought to improve the institution's academic efficiency and prestige by giving it a functional unit of its own, with classrooms, laboratories, and other facilities especially adapted to cadet training ends. Unable at the time to secure funds for such a project, he prevailed on Congress to transfer Fort Trumbull, at New London, Connecticut, from the War Department to the Treasury.[21] To this historic site he moved the School (then under the supervision of Captain W. V. E. Jacobs) on September 15, 1910.

Although the Fort Trumbull establishment left much to be desired, it was a vast improvement over the original facility at Arundel Cove. (Two decades later, Congress authorized construction of a permanent and entirely suitable home for the Coast Guard Academy, a few miles up the Thames River from the old Fort Trumbull site.) Captain Jacob's relief as Superintendent at Fort Trumbull, Captain Frederick C. Billard, a later Commandant, continued to adjust the course of instruction to keep pace with current service needs and to raise cadet standards generally. By 1914 the Commandant was able to announce a change in name from "School of Instruction" to "Revenue-Cutter Academy," a term which he considered "much more in consonance with the standing of this institution for the education of cadets."[22]

By a series of statutes enacted between 1900 and 1916, Congress finally raised the commissioned corps to parity with those of the other military services in rank, precedence, and pay. One Act in 1902 applied the principle of equal pay for equivalent rank and granted general authority for retiring cutter officers on age (64 years) or physical disability. Another in 1915 authorized voluntary retirement on completion of 30 years of

[21] Act of February 15, 1911 (36 Stat. L., 906).
[22] *U.S.R.-C.S. Annual Report,* 1914; 93.

service. Still another in 1908 recognized the expanding scope of the service's position within the federal system by authorizing higher ranks for senior officers: the Chief of the Division of Revenue-Cutter Service was given the grade of captain commandant, to rank with captain in the Navy; the Engineer-in-Chief was raised in grade to rank with commander in the Navy; and a new line officer grade, senior captain, to rank with commander in the Navy, was established. The same measure abolished the titles by which engineers had long been known (*i.e.:* chief, first assistant, and second assistant engineer, ranking respectively with first, second, and third lieutenant of the line), and substituted the grades of captain, first, second, and third lieutenant of engineers; these carried the relative rank and pay of corresponding grades of the line. Finally, the precedence of cutter and naval officers was adjusted on the basis of complete inter-service parity by a measure (adopted in 1916) which provided that

> whenever . . . personnel of the Coast Guard . . . is operating with personnel of the Navy . . . precedence between commissioned officers of corresponding grades in the two services shall be determined by the date of commissions in those grades.[23]

The foregoing legislation not only rectified long-standing and indefensible inequalities between the services but also, by reducing age-levels and by making the profession more attractive to ambitious young Americans, acted as a continuing stimulus to further increases in the efficiency of the commissioned corps.

For enlisted men, likewise, professional progress entailed greater demands on individuals, brought greater satisfactions, than ever in times past. The increasing complexity of the ship-as-a-machine was working important changes. According to Brigadier General Dion Williams, U. S. Marine Corps, who served through the same era in the Navy and saw the old order pass:

> The days of sail were giving way to the days of steam and the day of electricity was dawning. . . . the improved machinery constantly being added to the ships required a new kind of personnel to meet the requirements of the new mechanical age. . . . In the old days . . . control over personnel was a "discipline of fear," but conditions were shaping this into a "discipline of reason," . . . later . . . a "discipline of pride."[24]

Aboard ship, as in industry ashore, mechanization and good adminis-

[23] Act of August 29, 1916 (39 Stat. L., 556, 582, 600), quoted. Other Acts mentioned in this paragraph include: Act of April 12, 1902 (32 Stat. L., 100); Act of January 28, 1915 (38 Stat. L., 800); Act of April 16, 1908 (35 Stat. L., 61). Additional grades both for line officers and engineers were authorized by legislation enacted subsequent to 1916. Military ranks prescribed for the Navy were prescribed for the Coast Guard by the Act of June 5, 1920 and subsequent enactments.

[24] "A Higher Standard," in *U. S. Naval Institute Proceedings,* February, 1934.

trative practice fostered division of labor. Even in sailing days, differentiation of cutter men by special skills had been necessary: in 1790, ships and crews were small, and a rough distinction (based on age and "saltiness") between "men" and "boys" had quite sufficed; later, as somewhat larger cutters came into use, traditional sailing-ship rates (boatswain, gunner, carpenter, cook) had been added to the crews. A considerable increase in the shipboard need for specialists had arisen with the introduction of steam propulsion, around mid-century. By 1894, division of labor on cutters was well-defined; *Regulations* issued in that year authorized petty officer ratings in nearly a dozen specialties, including "oiler" (enlisted engineer). Within the next few years, engineering progress—marked especially by the introduction of shipboard electrical appliances and by the adoption of relatively high steam pressures for main propulsion plants —forced further specialization of engineering personnel. Two petty officer ratings, "electrician" and "watertender" (boiler expert), were created to give distinction and pay to qualified technicians. These, together with "ship's writer" (yeoman), were authorized in the 1907 edition of the *Regulations*. Altogether, the latter listed some 14 technical specialties open to enlisted men; six years later the list included several more.

Increased prestige, security, and pay accompanied these distinctions of ability (although parity with naval pay scales was not attained for a year or two after the first World War).[25] A Civil War statute (Act of February 4, 1863) raising the pay of petty officers and crews of cutters to the level of "average wages paid for like services . . . in the merchant service" was upset by the Act of April 16, 1908, which gave a flat 20% pay boost to all enlisted men, authorized additional increases for longevity and provided for retirement on three-quarters pay after 30 years of service. Further security was added by the Act of January 28, 1915, which extended to enlisted men the same provision for retirement on age or disability that had been granted to officers in 1902.

One of the greatest single encouragements for men to look upon the service as an honorable career offering a just reward to capable technicians was given under a *General Order* issued in 1898.[26] This Order definitely fixed the status of the so-called "forward officers" (master technicians in certain specialties) as a grade above enlisted and below commissioned personnel. For a century or more, boatswains, gunners, and carpenters had been known variously as "forward officers," "petty officers," "warrant officers," and (in the *Regulations*, 1894, and others) as "petty officers of the first class." Under established custom, they had held their

[25] On pay parity, see Act of May 18, 1920 (41 Stat. L., 601, 603, 604).
[26] *Division of Revenue-Cutter Service General Order No. 35,* dated August 2, 1898, as supported by *General Order No. 36* (same date) and clarified by *General Order No. 45,* dated December 31, 1898. On the early status of forward officers, see also Smith, *op. cit.*, *passim,* and sundry volumes of early *Registers* and *Regulations.*

positions on recommendation of their several commanding officers and by appointment ("warrant") of the Secretary of the Treasury. Their legal status, however, had remained that of enlisted personnel and they had been so classified in 19th century *Regulations* generally. The new *Order* set them, together with chief oilers (machinists) in a class apart. (Other specialists were added later.) It officially raised their status from enlisted "petty officer of the first class" to "forward officer," directed officers and men alike to address them as "mister" (traditional seagoing title of respect reserved for junior officers), and prescribed a distinctive forward officers' uniform, similar to commissioned officers' (though less ornate) with a distinguishing touch of gold. They were recognized as "warrant officers" in the statutes by the Act of May 26, 1906 and were granted increased pay, together with age, disability, and 30-year retirements, under the several pay Acts cited previously. And the Act of April 16, 1908, by requiring a qualifying examination for promotion to the grade, insured a uniform standard of proficiency within the warrant corps.

Thus, obviously, technological changes within the service were establishing new norms for personnel. Whereas once the emphasis had been on brawn, it was turning now towards brain, and, to attract suitable men into the service, Congress was finding it necessary to offer material benefits comparable to those offered industrial technicians ashore. But intelligent volunteers, free citizens all, could not be induced to reenlist for service under arbitrary or brutal rules; such men could be led, but they would not long be driven. To give all revenue-cutter ranks and rates a single, simple code of law, Congress in 1906 enacted a measure "to regulate enlistments and punishments in the United States Revenue-Cutter Service."[27]

In general, this Act clarified the legal relationship between cutter personnel and the United States and established a system of military law to deal with infractions of the code. Jurisdiction over specified offenses against service discipline was reserved to commanding officers and Revenue-Cutter Service courts, while jurisdiction over offenses against other laws of the U.S. was reserved to civil courts. Further, the Act set limits of punishment for offenses within the service's disciplinary jurisdiction. Authorized punishments included: dismissal (officers), dishonorable discharge (all others), imprisonment, and fine. Generally higher limits of punishment were set for officers than for other personnel. Although severe, the code was clear and unequivocal. By defining offenses and limiting punishments, it adequately defended the government's interest while safeguarding personnel from arbitrary and unusual disciplinary measures.

[27] Act of May 26, 1906 (34 Stat. L., 200).

A system involving clearly defined rules and penalties amounted to a "discipline of reason"; to avoid penalties, a reasonable man might be expected to obey the rules. But in complex modern ships, a discipline based solely on some Benthamitish doctrine of pleasures and pains—on simple self-interest—left something to be desired. Such a discipline might insure order—ever a shipboard necessity—but nothing guaranteed that a merely orderly crew would operate its ship efficiently. And under the new technology, captains could no longer check personally on every detail of 'boardship activity. Technicians necessarily stood important watches, performed important special functions (many involving the safety and effectiveness of the ship), with little or no immediate, move-by-move supervision from any officer. In the complicated ship-mechanism, each man had his place; efficient operation resulted when every job was faithfully performed and coordinated with all the rest.

Under such conditions, the crew became in fact a team, a group whose effectiveness rested not only upon the intelligent self-interest of its members but also upon each individual's psychologic drive towards co-operative effort. To supply the latter, the needed human motive power, the service undertook the development of a conscious leader-psychology in its officers. At the Academy, cadets who lacked potentiality as leaders found it impossible to make the grade. Moreover, the 1907 *Regulations* dug up an ancient precept on the basic subject, *"Discipline, how maintained,"* and applied it to the field with new significance:

> *Art. 717:* Discipline depends in a large degree upon the example set . . . by officers.

This article is important historically as a gauge of attitude. It underlined a complete awareness to the value of leadership, and it cleared a way for the 20th century concept of the ship-as-a-team. The latter, gaining rapid acceptance throughout the service, carried to every man a motivation for mass effort towards making his ship the best in all the fleet, an inclination to look upon his officers as coordinators, coaches of the team. Here were rules under which intelligent, self-respecting Americans could always play.

And so cutter men met the new era under a "discipline of pride."

V

Thus buffeted from all directions by new developments and trends, the archaic organizational system with which the cutter branch entered the 20th century could not long withstand extensive change. The modifications necessary to adapt it to its new environment were few, but they were vital. Most had been forecast by Captain Shepard, somewhat earlier. In brief, they provided a stronger and more adequate Headquarters echelon; they rationalized the service cadre, cleared its channels of command, gave it a rudimentary shore establishment, improved its operational flexibility and control, and tended to clarify the definition of its place within the contemporary scene. Accomplished, more or less, by 1915, these changes served not only their immediate purpose of furnishing the cutter branch with an operational and administrative system capable of functioning effectively in an electronic age, but they served also to condition the Revenue-Cutter Service for its role as nucleus for an inclusive agency for maritime law enforcement and marine safety.

Specifically, in Washington, rapidly increasing complexities of service administration soon forced a full acceptance of military staff principles and procedures, and the Headquarters organization, which in Shepard's time had been embryonic and entirely undifferentiated except for Naval Engineering and Construction, by 1911 was divided functionally into Operations, Personnel, Engineering, Construction, Ordnance, Supply, and Law and included officers to advise and assist the Commandant in these specialties.

In the field, operational and administrative control finally was stripped from collectors of customs and vested in service officers. As though significant of the change, and because collectors for years had exercised a questionable prerogative in flying the cutters' distinguishing flag from their customshouses, President Taft on June 7, 1910 ordered that

> the distinguishing flag now used by vessels of the Revenue-Cutter Service be marked by *the distinctive emblem of that service* [*i.e.*: crossed anchors mounting the seal of the Treasury, marked with the name, motto, and year of origin of the cutter branch].[28]

A more practical measure was taken the next year, when two Revenue-Cutter "districts", so-called, were established on the West Coast. Senior Captain John F. Wild, Commanding Southern District, made his headquarters in San Francisco, and Senior Captain Francis M. Dunwoody, Commanding Northern District, made his in Port Townsend. These officers originally acted as inspectors of cutters in their respective districts and performed certain additional administrative functions; gradually they acquired an operational authority over all cutters within their district boundaries. Somewhat similar functions were performed in the region of New York City by Senior Captain Oscar C. Hamlet, Supervisor of Anchorages at that port. By 1913, this type of field organization had proved its effectiveness, and *General Order #22,* issued in that year, formally established the Northern Division (Pacific Coast, north of Cape Blanco), Southern Division (Pacific Coast, south of Cape Blanco), Eastern Division (Atlantic Coast, Maine to Block Island), and New York

[28] In *C. G. Archives.* (Italics ours.)

Division (Atlantic Coast, Gay Head to Delaware Breakwater). Division headquarters were set up in Port Townsend, San Francisco, Boston, and New York, respectively.

As field commanders subordinate to the Commandant, division commanders were given general operational and administrative authority within their division areas and were charged with certain phases of logistic support for units under their command. Cutters assigned at ports beyond established division areas were made independent commands directly responsible to the Commandant.

This reorganization linked all elements of the service in an unbroken chain of military command and thus provided a unity wherein responsible leadership might be freely exercised. From the standpoint of operations, the new system, implemented by radio, proved revolutionary: it permitted close control of operational units in coordinated effort—the ideal condition for efficiency.

Moreover, by removing Customs men from the chain of command, it placed relations between cutters and Customs on the same plane as those between cutters and all other federal agencies. It thus assured complete operational discretion to the Revenue-Cutter Service in covering commitments to all federal agencies that depended on the cutters for aid.

Further, in acquiring division offices the cutter service acquired a shore organization of its own, rooted in the nation's major centers of maritime activity. As noted previously, the primary purpose of division offices was to provide better operational control and more adequate administrative support of floating units. Shore depots for the cutters' logistic support were added also in this period. The Arundel Cove project was expanded to include a supply facility for ships on the East Coast, and a similar unit was set up at San Francisco to supply those on the West. This supply system, soon coordinated with the Navy's far more extensive one, served to standardize items of outfits and insured the economy of quantity purchasing.

The shore establishment as originally laid out proved basically sound and strengthened the service internally. Moreover, indirectly, it produced important external effects. Simply by being, it met, to a fair degree, several major conditions (*e.g.:* office accommodations, regional controls) to the amalgamation of shore-going maritime safety and law enforcement agencies, such as the Steamboat Inspection Service, with the cutter branch in a unified agency.[29] And by providing fixed points of contact between the service and the governmental agencies and general public served, it helped the latter to a better knowledge and understanding of the cutters' place in the government. Division commanders (later known as "district commanders") became *ex officio* the Revenue-Cutter Service's

[29] *Supra;* Chapters III and X.

regional representatives with federal, state, and local authorities and furnished the close liaison with those officials that federal involvement in maritime affairs was beginning to demand. Liaison with the general public was similarly assured: *General Order # 22* required division commanders "to keep in close touch with maritime interests on shore." This injunction, broadly interpreted, furnished (and doubtless always will define) the central *motif* of Coast Guard public relations policy: to insure maximum utilization of service facilities by keeping shipping interests, fishermen's associations, yachtsmen, press, radio, and the general public continuously aware of the agency's existence, purpose, and availability. Regional activity by division commanders and their staffs in support of this policy increased the tax-payers' per-dollar return on the cutter force and, in addition, helped crystallize in the public mind a concept of the service as the nation's principal agency for safety and security afloat.

In the Lighthouse Service, no less than in the cutter branch, a trend towards a stronger central administrative authority existed at this time. By the Act of June 17, 1910 (36 Stat. L., 534), the cumbersome Lighthouse Board was abolished in favor of a Bureau of Lighthouses headed by a single commissioner. Mr. George R. Putnam was the first Commissioner appointed under this authority.

VI

On the national stage, the 1900-15 period moved with a surface quiet long recalled with nostalgic overtones in native song and lore. For a great many Americans whose day it was, harsher realities were obscured by the satisfactions and security of life in a bounteous and mighty land and by obvious and abundant evidences of God's pleasure at the ingenuity of men. But harsher realities there were, and they were not long to be denied. America's spectacular industrial growth, so largely responsible for rife optimism at the century's beginning, had been unattended by comparable progress towards political maturity. Men who faced the fact could see its consequences in political and economic abuses which spewed corruption and misery on the land. One realist, Mr. William Howard Taft, distinguished, selfless, and conservative, described the situation as he saw it:

> For thirty years, we had an enormous material expansion in this country, in which we all forgot ourselves in the enthusiasm of expanding our material resources and in making ourselves the richest nation on earth. We did this through the use of *the principle of organization and combination,* and through the development of our national resources. In the encouragement of the investment of capital, we nearly transferred complete political power to those who controlled corporate wealth and we were in danger of a plutocracy.[30]

[30] Quoted in A. M. Schlesinger, *Political and Social Growth of the American People, 1865-1940* (The Macmillan Co., New York, 1941); 296. (Italics ours.)

Drummed up by muckraking journalists, whose *exposées* of frauds and skullduggeries in high places aroused the nation from political lethargy, and led through its initial stages by Rough Rider Roosevelt, President from 1901 to 1909, the revolt against "plutocracy" soon became an all-out battle for general reform, as progressives in both political parties brought a crusading spirit to bear against iniquities of many kinds.

In economics, the "new liberals" sought to avoid the extremes of *laissez faire* individualism and of paternalistic socialism by a middle course of intelligent control designed to eliminate the abuses yet retain the advantages of large-scale private enterprises. Anti-trust legislation and railway regulation marked their progress on this front. Politically, they sought to democratize the government, to eliminate "plutocratic" influences, and to make the legislature more responsive to popular demands. The movement for women's suffrage, the 17th Amendment (providing for election of senators by popular vote), and a law passed in 1907 forbidding corporations to contribute campaign funds in federal elections, were substantial gains along this line. And in social fields, progressives won historic victories, especially in the state legislatures. There many social security laws were passed—laws governing child labor, workmen's compensation, minimum wages, hours of work, and related insurances. In all, the American people strove by constitutional means to strengthen their institutions against the pressures and strains of the new century and thus to contain the forces of materialism and direct them towards the welfare of mankind.

In the midst of this welter of reform, the machinery of government, no less than the aims, came in for overhaul. There was no doubt in most men's minds that Taft's "principle of organization and combination" together with up-to-date methods, so profitable in the world of business, could be applied in the field of government to similar advantage. An editorial in the Washington, D.C., *Evening Star* for April 5, 1912 defined the problem in simple terms:

> The government's departments and bureaus have developed *without the guidance of any central principle* during many years. There is no established type, and the assignments of duties have been governed by immediate circumstances rather than any definite policy. The consequence is a scattering of duties, a multiplication of offices, and a resultant waste of time and effort and money. [Italics ours.]

The editor proposed that "the way of true economy" (as he titled his column) must be based upon

> a most careful and scientific investigation of the conditions in the executive branch of the government and look to the establishment of a more consistent and businesslike plan of operation.

Certainly, among the agencies performing federal maritime safety and law enforcement functions there existed both multiplicity and dispersion.

The Revenue-Cutter, Life-Saving, and Customs Services had remained in the Treasury, but in 1903 the Lighthouse Establishment, Steamboat Inspection Service, and Bureau of Navigation had been transferred from their original location (Treasury) to Commerce and Labor. (The three last-named were assigned to the Commerce Department in 1913, when Commerce and Labor split.) Responsibility for sundry special maritime functions, notably regulation of movements of vessels in the St. Mary's River, regulation of anchorages, and the boarding of vessels in the enforcement of navigation laws generally, which originally had been vested in the Secretary of the Treasury, was now vested in the Secretary of Commerce and Labor (later, in the Secretary of Commerce), although a major enforcement responsibility remained in the Revenue-Cutter Service.[31] But although each of these maritime agencies had specific duties of its own, there were numerous points—as the Secretary of Commerce and Labor carefully explained in his first *Annual Report*—at which the work of one agency coincided more or less with that of another. Further, several of them maintained similar operational and administrative establishments, often side by side. For instance: Life-saving stations and lighthouses in many instances were located in proximity with each other; the administrative organizations and procedures of these two branches were quite similar; and cutters and lighthouse tenders cruised over much the same territory in the prosecution of their respective jobs. For such reasons, the existence of numerous maritime agencies dispersed under various departments presented a somewhat confused and irrational organizational pattern.

And all of these agencies except the Revenue-Cutter Service were essentially unifunctional, that is, specialized, more or less, in one specific type of police operation. Thus, the lighthouse branch maintained aids to navigation–highway markers, in a sense; the Steamboat Inspectors examined ships and officers to insure that they met the standards specified by law; and the Bureau of Navigation issued licenses to vessels and performed other incidental administrative duties. Only the Revenue-Cutter Service spread its operations across the entire spectrum of federal maritime safety and law enforcement activity. One way or another, besides performing its own specific duties, it aided each of the maritime bureaus (as well as certain other federal agencies, *e.g.*, Department of Justice), mainly by operational support afloat. It was thus, *de facto*, in an operational sense, the one inclusive federal maritime safety and law enforcement agency. Under this "central principle," beginning in 1915, this sector of the federal government was integrated and rationalized.

A first approach to such reorganization was made by President Taft,

[31] The function of prescribing anchorage regulations was transferred to the Secretary of War in 1915; *supra*, Chapter XIII (III).

proponent of "organization and combination" and up-to-the-minute business practices in government. Under the Acts of June 25, 1910 and March 3, 1911, Taft obtained Congressional authority to appoint a commission to inquire into the methods of transacting the public business and to advise as to ways and means for improving economy and efficiency in the government service. This Commission aimed a broadaxe at the cutter branch, for its advice relative to reorganization was based on the assumption that multi-functionalism in federal agencies is necessarily uneconomic and it failed to distinguish a legitimate, generalized federal function of maritime law enforcement and safety in the work performed by the cutter force. Nonetheless, indirectly and ultimately, its report exerted a constructive influence on the development of the Coast Guard.

Headed by the Honorable F. A. Cleveland, the Commission undertook a detailed examination of the federal machinery and of the business policies and techniques used in the several departments. From its researches, the Cleveland Commission brought forth many concrete proposals which Taft indorsed and which Congress and the executive branch used over a period of many years as guides to effective action. Its recommendations, diverse and in some details controversial, ranged from an attack on remnants of the Spoils System in the appointment of civil officials, to an indorsement of the merit system of promotion in the civil service, to a reshuffling of bureaus, to an unsnarling of the confused pattern of laws governing travel allowances for government employees, to an espousal of the window envelope and the dictaphone—all as means towards cutting costs and increasing production in the federal service.[32] Some of these recommendations acted with immediate effect as a cool breeze down Washington's musty corridors; others in circuitous by-passes lost their force for good or ill. But in evaluating the general effect of the Commission's work, it is perhaps less important to prove its specific conclusions right or wrong or to add up the algebraic sum of their beneficial and non-beneficial results than to stress the precedent which the Commission established merely in being: it was an honest attempt at non-partisan, objective investigation of the federal machinery. As such, it deserves a wholly creditable page in history.

In bringing its light to bear on the maritime bureaus, the Commission soon found organizational parallels and functional overlaps galore. Especially in the latter, it ran into a persistent problem of structure: unifunctionalism *versus* multifunctionalism in governmental agencies, and, apparently feeling forced to render an unequivocal decision between the two, it gave its full weight to the former. Perceiving a least common

[32] *H.R. Doc. No. 670, 62 Cong., 2 Sess., "Economy and Efficiency in the Government Service"* (being a "Message of the President of the United States transmitting Reports of the Commission on Economy and Efficiency"); (Govt. Printing Office, Wash., D.C., 1912).

denominator—*protection*—in the single functions of the Lighthouse Service and Life-Saving Service, it recommended that these two agencies be merged in a maritime protection bureau under the Department of Commerce and Labor. Applying its unifunctional theory to the Revenue-Cutter Service, it recommended an apportionment of cutter components among (1) the Navy, for deep-sea "marine-police" duties, as the Commission labelled offshore distress work, derelict destruction, and one or two other non-military functions, and (2) the several civil maritime agencies, for their respective unifunctional purposes.

From this point, the Commission's report became involved in *a priori* arguments designed to prove the economy of its plan. These failed to take many important factors into account, and so were discounted easily. The Captain Commandant of the Revenue-Cutter Service, Ellsworth P. Bertholf, presented a strong counter-argument:

> There would be no economy in the proposed distribution of duties and equipment. On the contrary, there would be . . . a decided increase in cost. . . .
>
> As the country grew and developed, the maritime functions and obligations of the Government increased . . . [but] there was an insufficient amount of such maritime work in each of the several departments to warrant the maintenance of a separate service by each. Quite logically, therefore, these duties were successively added to the Revenue-Cutter Service, until today its functions relate to maritime matters in almost all of the departments. . . .
>
> While none of these [mainly police matters] individually requires constant attention, all of them are of such a coordinate nature as to permit them to be accomplished satisfactorily by one organization. [This] constitutes a legitimate and logical field of activity and permits centralization, specialization, and coordination—the elementary principles of economy and efficiency.
>
> The Revenue-Cutter Service today . . . exists as a compact organization representing a concentration of governmental maritime functions, administered economically and efficiently. [To reshuffle] its duties and equipment . . . would inevitably result in the establishment of several services, each under a separate organization and administration. . . . Each of these services would require as many vessels as the Revenue-Cutter Service now periodically uses for that particular class of duty, if the same results are to be obtained. As none of these [unifunctional] services could use the vessels or do the work of another service (otherwise the object sought in the proposed redistribution would be lost) this would necessitate a far greater number of vessels in the several services than is now needed by the [multifunctional] Revenue-Cutter Service for the accomplishment of all. . . . This would result in confusion . . . lack of coordination . . . duplication of equipment and administration . . . inefficiency.[33]

In arguing their case, the Commissioners glossed over numerous other points wherein their plan was open to question. Three or four are

[33] *Ibid.*, 396-7.

sufficient for citation here. First, the Commission's assumption that increased economy without decreased efficiency would result from having each civil maritime agency do its own work afloat using cutter service equipment manned by civilian crews, was based on incomplete evidence. The Commission cited only the fact that payrolls would be less for civil than for military crews. In this it was, at the time, correct. However, the fact that these civilian crews, unlike Revenue-Cutter Service crews, would be ineligible, untrained, and unavailable for instant military duty in time of national emergency, went unmentioned. Thus, for the small payroll saving anticipated by the Commission plan, the Navy stood to lose a trained reserve which through the years had proved a valuable arm in the national defense.

And in this same regard, it was questionable that low-priced civilian crews could or would perform the civil functions at stake with the same efficiency that somewhat higher-priced, professional cutter men performed them. By discounting the cash value of experience, specialization, *esprit de corps,* and high morale—traditional earmarks of the professionals—the Commission erred.

Moreover, in its proposal to transfer certain non-military functions to the Navy, the Commission compromised the unifunctional theory it seemed intent upon supporting. Arguments favoring this inconsistency on the grounds of economy and efficiency were weak, for it was obvious that the proposed transfer would reduce assistance to distressed vessels from a primary cutter function to a secondary naval concern; no one was ready to argue that any civil function given the Navy should have priority over the Navy's readiness for war. On the other hand, saddling the Navy with extraneous functions for its fleet might compromise the national defense. On this point, the Secretary of the Navy was outspoken:

> [While] the chief functions of the Revenue-Cutter Service can be performed by the Navy . . . this cannot be done as stated in the Cleveland report in the regular performance of their military duties. All duties which interfere with the training of the [Navy's] personnel for war are irregular and in a degree detrimental to the efficiency of the fleet.[34]

Finally, the basic issue of unifunctionalism *vs.* multifunctionalism has and probably never will be categorically solved. As pointed out above, the Cleveland plan itself fell short of a truly unqualified solution. Satisfactory enough as an abstraction in aid of theorizing on governmental structure, unifunctionalism frequently falls short in practical application. In the growth of government after the Cleveland Commission's day, multifunctionalism in federal agencies became accepted as a not necessarily evil form, and investigators turned towards application of pragmatic, rather

[34] *Ibid.,* 381.

than of dialectic, tests. One distinguished analyst, Mr. Lewis Meriam, Chairman of the Brookings Institute for Governmental Research, stated the later view:

> Successful organization appears to consist of . . . developing an organization which works reasonably well under actual conditions. In practice, most successful organizations are developed or evolved. . . . Many of our existing agencies [were] not created for a single purpose: they have several different objectives and one would have great difficulty in stating their major objective. If they were classified on the basis of one objective that was called major they would overlap other agencies with respect to objectives classified as minor. . . . [In a well run multifunctional agency], *the inevitable overlappings are taken care of by cooperation, a matter not of organization but of management.*[35]

The Cleveland Commission sent its plan to the President with no claim to infallibility or suggestion of finality but with the declared intention simply of "raising an important issue in definite form." Had the Commission's specific proposals been adopted, the course of Coast Guard history doubtless would have changed, although there are reasonable grounds for speculating that a coast guard eventually would have been created even so, possibly in the Navy as a separate corps similar in status to the Marines—a sea police force to match the soldiers of the sea. However, the Commission's plan was not adopted. The cutter organization, product of experience and evolution, had worked well in the past. Neither the sharp historical break nor the doubtful theoretical gains of the Commission's plan recommended themselves to the Congress. Other ways of achieving the same end ("organization and combination") remained to be explored. But to this process the Commission's work was nonetheless significant, for in raising the issue of rationalizing federal arrangements for the performance of maritime functions it acted as an effective catalytic to a vital phase of the Coast Guard's historical development.

If the Cleveland Commission could generalize a "marine-police" function of only three or four component duties, the Secretary of Commerce and Labor apparently could distinguish a much broader one. And this official, the Honorable Charles Nagel, seemed to hold no special brief either for or against multifunctionalism in a federal agency so long as the resultant organization worked reasonably well. In suggesting a substitute for the Commission's plan, therefore, the pragmatic Nagel in effect called for creation of a federal maritime safety and law enforcement agency much like the Coast Guard which in fact eventually did evolve, having (1) *protective,* (2) *preventive,* and (3) *law enforcement* functions covering practically the entire zone of federal maritime involvement. Recom-

[35] Lewis Meriam, *Reorganization of the National Government* (The Brookings Institution, Washington, D.C., 1939); Chapter III, *passim.* (Italics ours.)

mendations made to the President by Nagel in letters dated 10 January and 8 February, 1912 would have resulted in an experimental merger of Lighthouse, Life-Saving, and Revenue-Cutter Service components under the general administrative direction of Nagel's department. Had his suggestion been as concrete in its implementing details as his approach to the problem was logical, quite possibly it would have received immediate acceptance.

As it was, a somewhat less ambitious plan put forth by the Honorable Franklin MacVeagh, Taft's Secretary of the Treasury, won Congressional support and approbation. In a long and spirited letter addressed to the President and dated February 28, 1912, MacVeagh took issue with the Commission both as to the basic issue (multifunctionalism) and as to the Commission's specific proposals for dividing up the Revenue-Cutter Service. On the former, he declared:

> A tendency to think a service is misplaced if it does not exclusively act for a single department is evident in this recommendation. . . . I came to Washington with [the same] notion, and it has taken three years to modify it. . . . No department can or should be complete within itself nor even homogeneous. . . . Nor is it possible or desirable that no two departments . . . do the same sort of work under any circumstances. . . . It isn't possible to have the departments homogeneous [unifunctional] unless you largely multiply the number of departments.

On the latter, he took the view that the Revenue-Cutter Service had stood the test of time:

> Its efficiency and discipline and esprit de corps are at their best today, and the service is at the highest point of its 120 years. . . . Disintegration . . . of a service with such a record and such present significance would be unprecedented . . . and its division among various departments would [result in] scattered administration . . . almost necessarily more expensive than concentrated and centrally organized administration. . . . Nothing could be gained.

Further, on the reception given by the press and public to the Commission's plan, the Secretary stated that:

> No newspaper, no commercial organization, and no individual in Washington or throughout the country, so far as I am advised, has approved the suggestion.

Then the Secretary advanced a counter-plan which was simple, concise, easy to implement, and oriented down the main stream of historical development. Wrote he:

> [The Commission's plan] to add further separation between these two great services [Revenue-Cutter and Life-Saving] would be the greatest mistake in the world. . . . [The Treasury Department has] been working to secure a closer relationship between the two . . . *and that is the line of progress* . . .

> *of development.* It might be very well *to make the Life-Saving Service a part of the Revenue-Cutter Service,* and I believe that will be done.

MacVeagh immediately undertook the task of translating his plan to the realm of reality by bringing together the Captain Commandant, Bertholf, and the Superintendent of the Life-Saving Service, the aged Kimball, to draft a bill of merger for Treasury sponsorship.[36]

While this spade-work was going on in Washington, a distress incident occurred on Long Island and, receiving wide publicity, gave the public a fresh demonstration of the simple logic in the plan MacVeagh proposed. As reported in the influential New York *Times,* the case showed clearly the inseparable bond between cutter men and life-savers in the great work of providing an effective force for safety and security afloat. Commencing in the issue for April 9, 1912 under a headline

ONTARIO ASHORE NEAR
MONTAUK POINT

a series of articles in the *Times* reported how the *Ontario,* found hopelessly ablaze off Long Island by the cutters *Mohawk* and *Achushnet,* had been escorted by them towards Montauk Point, where her captain had run her aground in a forlorn hope; told how her crew and life-savers from nearby Ditch Plain Station had battled flames until, the ship's sides red-hot, the captain gave the order to abandon ship; and how then the station crew with breeches buoy and the cutters with their boats had removed the gallant merchant sailors from the flaming steamer in a coordinated rescue that called forth national applause.

Editorial reaction to the Cleveland Commission's plan in general strengthened the Secretary's hand. Opposition was widespread. Some editors, like *Outlook's,* offered constructive criticism; this particular one not only opposed splitting up the cutter branch but suggested that, instead, the Revenue-Cutter Service be utilized as the nucleus for a large-scale merger of all the nation's civil maritime agencies into an inclusive, military, "coast guard service."[37]

And at the same time, the *Titanic* disaster broke into headlines as front-page news and froze public attention on the general subject of safety and security afloat. Sections of the American public that previously had never heard of a cutter now discovered the existence of a flexible cutter force ready without ado to accept the Ice Patrol responsibility and found therein a source of national pride and international satisfaction.

The Republicans went out of office before MacVeagh's bill of merger could be enacted into law, but the plan drew strong bi-partisan support

[36] Nagel's letters are contained in *H.R. Doc. No. 670, op. cit.,* 378-81; MacVeagh's, 382-9. (Italics ours.) See also *Congressional Record,* Vol. II, Part 2; 63 Cong., 3 Sess.; 1968.

[37] "A 'Little Navy' That Does Big Work," in *The Outlook,* Vol. 100, No. 6; 10 February, 1912; 296.

and the new administration placed it high on its legislative list. As Senate #2337, the bill passed the upper chamber in March 1914. The following December, President Wilson addressed a note to the House Democratic leader, as follows:

White House
Washington
December 19, 1914

Hon. Oscar W. Underwood
House of Representatives

Dear Mr. Underwood: I hope that you will not think I am unduly burdening you if I write to express my very great interest in the bill which has been passed by the Senate and is pending in the House which provides for the consolidation of the Revenue-Cutter and Life-Saving Services. It is of the highest consequence for the efficiency of both services that this bill should pass, and I hope that some chink may be found for it even in the rush hours of the House Calendar.

With warmest regards,
Faithfully yours,
Woodrow Wilson[38]

With the great Virginian's indorsement, the bill was worked into the House calendar. Representative William C. Adamson, of Georgia, who steered it through the House, asked passage principally on the score that the bill would (1) reorganize the two services on a logical basis and result in increased efficiency, (2) improve the status of the life-savers and thus facilitate the recruitment of desirable men, and (3) "create a naval reserve . . . without any additional cost to the Government as such . . . ready at a moment's notice to operate under the Navy Department whenever the President directs." With World War I already aflame, Mr. Adamson suggested to the Congress that:

While the question of national defense now more than ever before is brought into prominence, it is well to consider the advantages of the coast guard from a strictly military standpoint. . . . The very nature of [the corps'] emergent duties in peacetime will make [its members] quick of action, resourceful, and disciplined, all of which, it must be admitted, are absolutely essential to success in modern sea fighting. . . . Simply by a stroke of the pen, the President can transfer this highly efficient corps of men, armed, trained, and disciplined, into the regular Naval Establishment at any time. . . . This asset of military preparedness must therefore not be overlooked when appraising the value of the coast guard to the Government.[39]

In an easy passage, the Act to Create the Coast Guard was approved by the House on 20 January, 1915. The record vote showed 212 for, 79 against, with the "yeas" spread fairly evenly between both major parties.

[38] *Cong. Rec.*, Vol. II, Part 2; 63 Cong., 3 Sess.; 1964.
[39] *Ibid.;* 1950-1.

The President signed the Act on the twenty-eighth. Pertinent sections follow:

AN ACT TO CREATE THE
COAST GUARD

There shall be established in lieu of the existing Revenue-Cutter Service and the Life-Saving Service, to be composed of those two organizations, the Coast Guard, which shall constitute a part of the military forces of the United States and which shall operate under the Treasury Department in time of peace and operate as a part of the Navy, subject to the orders of the Secretary of the Navy, in time of war or when the President shall so direct. . . .

All duties now performed by the Revenue-Cutter Service and Life-Saving Service shall continue to be performed by the Coast Guard, and all such duties, together with all duties that may hereafter be imposed upon the Coast Guard, shall be administered by the captain commandant, under the direction of the Secretary of the Treasury.

Immediately upon passage of the organic Act, a board of cutter officers met with representatives of the Navy Department to lay plans for Navy-Coast Guard collaboration. Another board, made up of cutter officers and former Life-Saving Service district superintendents, met to arrange the details of the merger; this it accomplished by drafting the initial *Regulations, U. S. Coast Guard,* which set the organizational, operational, and administrative pattern for the new service.

The merger itself was consummated two days after the President signed the Act. On the day of its creation, the Coast Guard comprised approximately 255 officers (13 of whom were former Life-Saving Service district superintendents; the balance, former revenue-cutter officers) and 3,900 warrant officers and enlisted men, manning a headquarters in Washington, 17 regional commands, 4 depots, an academy, 25 cruising cutters, 20 harbor cutters, and 280 lifeboat stations. The New York *Times* for January 31, 1915 reported the event as follows:

REVENUE-CUTTERS NOW
COAST GUARD

Our Famous Force of Little Ships
Merged with the Life-Saving Service
New Law Puts This Highly Trained
Body of Sea Police
in the Military Establishment

In Navy in Time of War

With the flashing of wireless messages from every Government station along the Atlantic and Pacific coasts yesterday, the United States Revenue-Cutter Service ceased to exist as a unit, and men and vessels became a part of the United States Coast Guard, [under] the provisions of the law recently passed by Congress and signed by President Wilson on Thursday. . . . The Revenue-Cutter Service has played an important part in the affairs of this country, both in times of peace as well as war. . . . Its duties were manifold . . . its cutters policed the coast. Now known as Coast Guard cutters, [they will] continue [their] same duties. . . .

All life-saving stations will be controlled by the Coast Guard, and all life-saving crews will be made up of regularly enlisted men detailed from the new organization. Here-to-fore the Life-Saving Service has been carried on the civil lists. . . .

The Coast Guard comes into being with 4300 officers and men, combining highly educated officers and trained seamen from the revenue-cutters and the best surfmen in the country from the lifesavers.

The training and development of the new body will devolve upon the former revenue-cutter officers, and its active management will be directed by a captain-commandant. . .

[Under] this law, the service becomes a part of the regular military establishment of the United States.

The *Act to Create the Coast Guard* began the process of applying President Taft's "principle of organization and combination" to the several agencies dealing with maritime law and safety. This organic Act integrated the federal government's *protective* maritime services in the Coast Guard and confirmed the latter in responsibility for the sundry *preventive* and *law enforcement* functions which had been vested in the parent agencies. No other federal service held so broad a responsibility for maritime law enforcement and marine safety, and thus, on the day of its creation, the Coast Guard became *de facto* the principal agency in this field of federal enterprise.

Postscript: 1915-1950

SUBSEQUENT developments in federal law and practice confirmed by observance the definition whose evolution has been traced in the preceding chapters. Major determinants of the trend up to the period immediately following World War II are listed chronologically below:

1917) — As a part of the Navy in World War I, the service was called upon
1918) primarily to provide men and ships for combat (mainly ocean escort) work, and secondarily to intensify some of its normal (peacetime) operations to meet the requirements of war. It experienced no great expansion either in size or scope.

1936 — In one of the most sweeping grants of police authority ever written into U. S. law, Congress designated the Coast Guard as the federal arm for the *enforcement of U. S. laws generally* on the high seas and navigable waters of the United States. (Act of 22 June.)

1939 — Under Congressional authority to reorganize the executive branch of the government, President Franklin D. Roosevelt amalgamated the Lighthouse Service with the Coast Guard and thus began the integration of federal services primarily concerned with the *prevention* of marine disasters.

1941 — By the Act of July 11 (14 U.S.C. 1), Congress reconfirmed the Coast Guard's military status, stating: "The Coast Guard shall be a military service and constitute a branch of the land and naval forces of the United States *at all times* and shall operate under the Treasury Department in time of peace and operate as a part of the Navy, subject to the orders of the Secretary of the Navy, in time of war or when the President shall so direct." [Italics ours.]

1941) — In World War II, to an even greater extent than in any previous
1945) conflict, the military significance of maritime law enforcement and marine safety work was clearly recognized. The Coast Guard, acting as a part of the Navy, furnished trained forces for combat operations in all theaters of war; nonetheless, the main functional demand made upon it was for an extension and intensification of normal (peacetime) operations, especially in the categories of aids to navigation, search and rescue, beach patrol, port security, and enforcement of marine safety laws and regulations. Because of the importance of this latter category to the war effort, the President in 1942 temporarily consolidated the Bureau of Marine Inspection and Navigation (comprising the earlier Steamboat Inspection Service and Bureau of Navigation) with the Coast Guard. To perform all these varied duties under conditions of total war, the Coast Guard expanded to nearly 200,000 officers and men.

1946 – The consolidation of the Bureau of Marine Inspection and Navigation with the Coast Guard was confirmed as a permanent measure of reorganization of the executive branch; this was an important step in the integration of federal agencies primarily concerned with the *prevention* of marine disasters.

1946 – President Harry S. Truman's Air Coordinating Committee formally designated the Coast Guard as the federal coordinating agency with primary responsibility for furnishing search and rescue facilities and services to meet United States obligations to the International Civil Aviation Organization ("ICAO") for the *protection* of international civil aviation over water areas.

1948 – By Public Law No. 738, Congress extended the Coast Guard's functions both of *prevention* and *protection;* this law authorized the service to operate ships on ocean stations for the purpose of carrying out weather reporting, plane guard, communications, and assistance operations along transoceanic air routes as a special U. S. obligation to ICAO.

1948 – By Public Law No. 786, the same Congress further extended the scope of the Coast Guard's disaster-*prevention* function by authorizing the service to continue the work (begun as a war measure) of providing aids to navigation for military and naval bases beyond continental U.S. and of operating the LORAN (*i.e.:* "LOng-RAnge-Navigation") chain of electronic aids to navigation.

1949 – By Public Law No. 207, approved on August 4th, the 81st Congress revised, codified, and enacted into law Title 14 of the United States Code, entitled "Coast Guard." This Act redefined the service as a branch of the Armed Forces of the United States, confirmed it in its general functions of marine safety, maritime law enforcement, and military readiness to operate as a service in the Navy upon declaration of war or when the President directs, and reiterated and clarified its specific duties, responsibilities, and authority.

1950 – By the Act of May 5, 1950 (64 Stat. 107), Congress unified, revised, and codified the Articles of War, the Articles for the Government of the Navy, and the disciplinary laws of the Coast Guard and thereby established a *"Uniform Code of Military Justice,"* for the "government of the armed forces of the United States."

1950 – With sharp increases in the temperature of the "cold war" against Communist aggression, Congress recognized the need for prompt and positive measures for insuring the safety of U.S. ports, especially against sabotage. Action was hastened on the Magnusson Bill (amending the Espionage Act of 1917) so as to permit the President to institute port security measures without declaring a national emergency. Shortly after "police action" by United Nations forces against North Korea commenced, Congress enacted the Bill, which the President signed on August 9, 1950. Under this Act (Public Law No. 679, 81st Congress, 2nd Session), the President issued Executive Order 10173, dated October 18, 1950, granting the Coast Guard

> broad powers for safeguarding ports, harbors, vessels, and waterfront facilities within the jurisdiction of the United States, and directed the Coast Guard to initiate a limited port security program designed to meet immediate dangers. The Executive Order in effect reconfirmed the Coast Guard as the principal federal agency for the security of the ports, the funnels of United States military might.

Thus, in the period following World War II, the Coast Guard's military status rested firmly on precedent, law, and proved utility. Its responsibility covered practically the entire zone of federal activity in the field of maritime law enforcement and marine safety. Its duties, scaled to current needs, were being carried out by some 28,000 officers and men with up-to-date equipment and techniques. The definition, the philosophy of coast guarding, which seemed to describe the curve of the service's development from the time of Hamilton and Washington to the dawn of the atomic age seemed likewise a valid central principle to guide its development and useful employment in the years ahead.

Index

Ships' names: In many cases, two or more cutters have borne the same name; those indexed below may be differentiated by reference to the text for period, building data, etc.

Persons' names: Naval titles used below without other identification indicate Revenue-Marine (Revenue-Cutter Service) personnel.